Facilitating Group Learning

Facilitating Group Learning

Strategies for Success with Diverse Adult Learners

George Lakey

JOSSEY-BASS
A Wiley Imprint
www.josseybass.com

Published by Jossey-Bass
A Wiley Imprint
989 Market Street, San Francisco, CA 94103-1741—www.josseybass.com

Jossey-Bass books and products are available through most bookstores. To contact Jossey-Bass directly call our Customer Care Department within the U.S. at 800-956-7739, outside the U.S. at 317-572-3986, or fax 317-572-4002.

Jossey-Bass also publishes its books in a variety of electronic formats. Some content that appears in print may not be available in electronic books.

Library of Congress Cataloging-in-Publication Data

Lakey, George.
  Facilitating group learning : strategies for success with adult learners /
George Lakey.—1st ed,
    p. cm.—(The Jossey-Bass Higher and adult education series)
  Includes bibliographical references and index.
  ISBN 978-0-470-76863-1 (hardback)
  1. Adult learning. 2. Group work in education. 3. Learning strategies. 4. Continuing education. 5. Adult education. I. Title.
  LC5225.L42.L35 2010
  374'.22—dc22

FIRST EDITION
HB Printing   10 9 8 7 6 5 4 3 2 1

The Jossey-Bass
Higher and Adult Education Series

Contents

Part III
Designing Learning Experiences

Part IV
Facilitation

Resources

Acknowledgments

As a working class boy, I'm proud to acknowledge how much this book is a collective product. Kathi Bentall and the Rivendell Retreat in British Columbia invited me to be their first writer-in-residence, kindly affording me the space and time to write the first draft of this book. The board of Training for Change (TfC) excused me from some training and administrative work so that I could write. Daniel Hunter, Judith C. Jones, other co-facilitators, and the staff of many client organizations helped me to learn from my mistakes and successes. They helped me to see that we really were evolving something worth sharing. Some TfC trainers wrote specific contributions to this book—Betsy Raasch-Gilman, Erika Thorne, Matt Guynn, Skylar Fein—and I'm grateful to them for sharing their experience.

The leadership, staff, and worker educators of the Canadian Union of Postal Workers were courageous in making their union a laboratory for many of these ideas. Denis Lemelin, the current CUPW president, was key in introducing the union to direct education, along with David Bleakney and Lynn Bue. Johnny Lapham, Viki Laura List, Carolyn McCoy, Frances and Howard Kellogg, Ann Yasuhara, and many other generous individuals shared not only their purses but also their hearts to keep TfC's training on the growing edge.

The Eugene M. Lang Center for Civic and Social Responsibility at Swarthmore College supported the book project, including my research assistant Markus Schlotterbeck. For a decade and a half Central Philadelphia Monthly Meeting of Friends (Quakers) supported my ministry for nonviolent training; without that support neither Training for Change nor the book would have happened.

A network of friends and friendly teachers read early drafts and gave me helpful feedback, including Antje Mattheus and Nancy Brigham. I'm lucky to have them as well as all the teachers from whom I've learned so much, especially Niela Miller, Rod Napier, and Arnold Mindell. I've been helped by the participants in my workshops and classes who took the time to give me feedback.

I dedicate this book to the memory of George and Lillian Willoughby, who passed away during the book's last year of preparation; they were mentors for me my entire adult life and continued to support education for change well into their nineties. In this same year a new life began: my granddaughter Ella Sophia Goldman. Some of my deepest learnings and greatest joys have come from my family, and I dedicate this book to its members, especially the newest ones: Ella and great-grandsons Christopher Smalls Jr., Yasin Ali, and Zaine Thomas. May they grow up to a world of justice, peace, and environmental harmony.

About the Author

George Lakey is Visiting Professor and Research Fellow, Lang Center for Civic and Social Responsibility, Swarthmore College. He has led over 1,500 workshops on five continents and authored eight books. He co-founded Training for Change and directed it for fifteen years, which included consulting with labor unions and other adult education programs. While teaching at the University of Pennsylvania, he innovated in a gender-sensitive leadership development curriculum and has wide experience in other anti-oppression work, including with grassroots activists.

1

Introduction

Direct Education for Adult Learning Groups

This book is for everyone who assists groups to learn, whether formally or informally, through workshops or courses, as facilitator or teacher or trainer. I wrote it to share a lifetime of confronting mysteries in how individuals learn in groups.

I was twenty when I was first paid to lead learning groups of adults. At first the job was a bit intimidating for me; each Friday in the late afternoon I met fifteen or twenty strangers and led them through a volunteer weekend at a psychiatric hospital so they could be helpful to patients and learn about the mental health system.

I admired the content of the weekend. The volunteers let go of stereotypes, learned skills for relating to mental health consumers as human beings, and got the latest theories on mental illness and treatment from occasional meetings with staff psychiatrists. As a facilitator I found out that the sequence of material and experience mattered a lot to how much the volunteers could learn.

By working with the same setting and same core curriculum but with ever-changing groups, I learned that each group had a personality of its own. I observed how the atmosphere of a group influenced how much and how fast the volunteers learned. I saw that different groups needed differing amounts of help in making their diversity work for them.

The volunteers came from markedly different settings. Most came from the colleges of the region, ranging from state to elite schools. Some participants were out of college and in workplaces, establishing themselves as adults building a life. These subgroups meant a lot in the beginning of each weekend, but then shifts could occur, with new subgroups and new dynamics among them that affected the learning the volunteers were doing.

I found that by accident I had signed onto a laboratory in adult learning, and I was hugely stimulated. I found that learning in groups is not at all straightforward. I had more and more fun wading into the complexity, intuitively experimenting with different approaches and interventions. Even though we had no rigorous evaluation process in place, I could see that the group dynamics very much influenced the learning curve of the volunteers and how much they were willing to risk to achieve their goals.

Thanks to the Quakers who ran this program, I was well-launched on a lifetime quest to evolve a pedagogical approach that could optimize learning in diverse groups. My quest included leading over fifteen hundred courses and workshops for adults, mostly in the United States but including countries on five continents. My journey included teaching in colleges, universities, and graduate schools. The main points of what I've learned so far are in this book. I call the approach "direct education."

Making Our Peace with the Complexity of It All

Luckily, the supervisors in my early teaching and facilitation jobs didn't tell me at the outset how complex a learning group is! The layered reality dawned on me gradually, at a pace at which I could stay excited about it.

I came to believe that individuals in the learning group learn in different ways from each other: some learn chiefly through their ears (auditory), others through their eyes (visual), some learn mainly through their bodies in motion (kinesthetic), and others learn by making a gut-level connection with the information and the group (emotional). Of course, some tune into a combination of these. I learned that the very concept of "intelligence" has also been re-evaluated, with recognition that broad diversity shows up even in that dimension (Gardner, 1983).

The communication styles and life experiences of different racial and ethnic groups strongly influence how they learn, including what they learn from the same presentation. Gender matters. Class background makes a strong difference; public education levels the playing field only in our dreams.

At one point while teaching at the University of Pennsylvania, I grew tired of how the students were writing papers, so I substituted journals to see what would happen. After some coaching, most of the thirty-five students wrote deeply personal reflections on their encounters with the course. Our agreement was that they could keep confidential whatever they wanted to, as long as they would share with me four pages a week from their larger journal. As the semester went on and trust grew, more and more divergence of experience was revealed, and by the end I realized that instead of teaching one course, in the experience of the students I was teaching thirty-five courses!

I've made my peace with the reality that participants in a learning group pursue their own agendas, whatever my intentions are. At the end of one training of trainers workshop, a young man came to me. "Thank you for the breakthrough I had this weekend in my relationship with my dad," he said. Surprised, I asked him how he managed that, since nothing of that work had been visible to me.

"Well," he said, "you reminded me of him from the moment I walked in, and of some of the ways he drives me crazy, and so I used the workshop to confront my issues with him." He smiled. "I was up half the night with my journal, and I had a breakthrough. So thanks."

"You're very welcome," I smiled back, shaking my head at how much goes on under the surface.

Not only is the facilitator or teacher facing many kinds of diversity—the learners' agendas, culture and class background, and learning styles are just a few—but there's another level of influence operating powerfully in most groups: the characteristics of the group itself. Since my first job, this principle has been reinforced through the years to the point that it is one of the things that keeps me from burning out: I can't get bored in teaching, because the next group will be a new adventure.

Letting Go of the Old Paradigm of Education

Thomas S. Kuhn (1962) argued that when a paradigm is wearing out, people increasingly notice exceptions to the rule. "Yes, the earth is flat, but it's also true that Columbus made it back to Spain." "Yes, only violence is capable of overthrowing a dictatorship, but in 1989 some East European dictatorships were overthrown nonviolently."

The old paradigm of education is also wearing out, and parts of the new paradigm have been emerging in my lifetime. John Dewey (1966) famously insisted that "we learn by doing." During World War II the U.S. government's effort to educate families to eat foods formerly wasted discovered that homemakers were far more likely to change through discussion groups than through lectures. Brazilian educator Paolo Freire (1972, 1994) found that peasants learned to read more effectively when he used participatory methods that supported their power; his work flowered into popular education. The activist intellectual Ella Baker gained influence in the U.S. civil rights movement through her brilliant organizing skills and coached the young activists of the Student Nonviolent Coordinating Committee to use her version of popular education to empower Southern African Americans to stand up to the Ku Klux Klan (Ransby, 2005).

Some founders of the Movement for a New Society (MNS) were active in the civil rights movement and then in the early 1970s began a training program that became international in scope.

Drawing on activist experience, on Freire, and on early insights from mediation training and encounter groups, MNS trained trainers for a variety of groups and published the widely read adult educators' guide *Resource Manual for a Living Revolution* (Coover, Deacon, Esser, and Moore, 1977).

Experiential trainers like those who started Outward Bound got life-changing results through group challenges and adventure-based learning. Religious educators made their work come alive through hands-on and participatory methods, which now permeate adult education.

I was lucky to be taught at a young age by a couple of innovators who had begun to tune into the new paradigm of education. They planted seeds that later sprouted; they gave me early personal experience with a model more complicated than that of traditional educators.

Ruth Frederick had a sharp eye and a commanding presence. We fifth graders thought it really was possible that she could see every one of us and at the same time write on the blackboard with her back turned. Unlike some of the dowdy-looking teachers in our school, she wore colorful dresses that fit her snugly, and her brown hair shone as it fell in a wave to her shoulders. Maybe being daughter of the mayor of my town, Bangor, Pennsylvania, added to her air of authority.

Ms. Frederick was full of surprises. She gave each of us a German pen pal—this not long after World War II—and we were soon puzzling about what we could possibly write back to these youngsters with their fractured English and postcards showing strange-looking towns. Another day she took me aside and told me that, instead of reading each of the stories in the fifth-grade reader and completing workbook exercises, I was to choose a few of them and turn them into plays. English class shifted immediately from a chore to a thrill. Finally, she astounded us all one morning when we arrived to find all our desks had been re-organized into a giant circle. "It's time you look at each other when you speak," she said. "We need to have real discussions. You're growing up, you know."

In eleventh grade I again had one of those rare teachers who had a more complex view of education than the mainstream paradigm. Carmela Finelli, I now realize, looked at us and saw thirty adolescents with scant attention for the names and dates of great American authors. We hungered for knowledge, but not names and dates. We most of all wanted to learn to know ourselves, obscured as we were by awkwardness, anxiety, and competition.

"Finelli," as we referred to her, had grown up in the Italian town next door to mine. Roseto, Pennsylvania, later became famous among epidemiologists because of its low incidence of stroke and heart disease despite a diet of rich food. A study of Roseto concluded that the closely-knit Italian community itself was one protection against the stress that promotes heart trouble (Bruhn and Wolf, 1979).

Finelli acted as if she knew how to heal our teenage heart trouble, because from the first day she built community in her English classes. Her method sent the message of affirmation. She used small groups for sharing our essays about the authors. She patiently taught the talkative students that our quiet class members had important things to say. She used debate and dialogue to engage us in the great themes in literature: integrity, relationship, individuality, and courage. The class became a learning community of trust and growing self-respect. Of course, Thoreau mattered, and Emerson, and Hawthorne, and Whitman! How had we coped up till now without them?

Lucky me. I did have some teachers who even in the conformist 1940s and '50s glimpsed the complexity, the multidimensionality of the learning process. Now even Ruth Frederick and Carmela Finelli might be boggled by what pioneers have learned about learning, but I like to think that they would be pioneers today, too, handling in their graceful way the risks and challenges of a learning group.

What Is Direct About Direct Education?

Direct education cuts through the fluff and pretense that distances learners from the subject. It drops unreal expectations—for
example, that kinesthetic learners will somehow learn from Power-
Point presentations—and unreal assumptions—for example, that
a group is simply the sum of the individuals. I call this kind of education *direct* because it brings focus to the encounter of teacher and
group; it replaces scatter—of teacher preoccupied with curriculum
and participants preoccupied with distractions—with gathered
attention. *Direct education takes the most direct path to the learner in
the here and now.*

Because this approach builds so strongly on the achievements
of popular education, the reader might wonder if there really is
a difference. In 2005 I became the chief consultant to a million-
dollar leadership education course of the Canadian Postal Workers
Union. The course was based on popular education, and it had
produced good results in its first dozen years. The union aimed to
make it even better. I spent many hours in the back of the room,
observing popular education applied to their content, and that
woke me up to the distance that direct education has evolved from
popular education.

Direct education is highly experiential, using a variety of methods to move participants out of their comfort zones into encounters
with new possibilities. Although exercises are structured, they
stimulate spontaneous responses rather than demonstrations or
rehearsal of previous thinking: facilitators choose interventions
that go for the "here and now."

Direct education is multicultural and integrates perspectives
developed by movements against sexism, racism, and the other
forms of oppression. As you'll see in this book, direct education
doesn't compartmentalize "diversity work" but instead merges
anti-oppression work into its method, into the very framing of the
learning group itself.

Direct education works the four major learning channels as naturally as a circus works its three rings. Unlike both traditional education and popular education, direct education highly values the kinesthetic and emotional learning channels. Content is not organized according to linear logic but instead according to how people actually learn. Direct education understands how natural it is for people to resist learning, even in settings favored by popular educators, and it provides strategies for working with resistance.

The natural rhythms and cycles of groups are used to accelerate learning rather than being ignored or subjected to efforts of control. Conflict is frequently encouraged as a promoter of learning. Direct education integrates lessons from humanistic psychology and group dynamics. Design for courses includes the use of the group as a laboratory in which to try new behaviors and apply new insights.

Working with so many variables swirling around in the learning group opens some participants to a deeper adventure than adding skills and knowledge. Some of them (and sometimes even whole groups) want to unlearn the attitudes that slow them down. Sometimes they want to let go of their emotionally held limiting beliefs! When that door opens, the advanced practitioner of direct education gets to do transformational work. The arena of limiting beliefs is one place where most people hold back their own power. The tools we use for transformational work go to a new level of empowerment.

Direct education was evolved by the trainers associated with Training for Change, a nonprofit organization that works with grassroots and nonprofit groups in the United States, Canada, and over a dozen other countries. Training for Change (http://www .TrainingforChange.org) teaches educators how to invent their own tools and adapt them to their own cultures.

The Method of This Book

Because direct education is a way of handling complexity in a learning group, this book relies partly on stories to show its strategies for success. Stories include more details than expository writing and therefore reveal more nuances and layers of the facilitation process. Narratives include but go beyond articulating principles because they show the unfolding—what really happens when facilitation works.

Stories have been central to my pedagogy since my earliest teaching, and I'm pleased to see that they are achieving greater theoretical legitimacy. In a recent "state of the art" volume, *Transformative Learning in Practice*, Jo A. Tyler (2009) describes how and why stories work in terms of Jack Mezirow's adult learning theory.

I do take the precaution of changing many of the names in my stories and sometimes disguising the situations, because of the expectation of confidentiality that usually accompanies this work. I hope that the stories in this book illuminate a twin possibility: admitting the complexity of teaching *and* shaping the complexity into a journey of discovery which includes fun, struggle, lightness, connection—and joy.

In four main sections the book explores key concepts and tools that make direct education work:

> *Part I*. Traditional education pretends that a class is simply a collection of individuals, even though every aware teacher knows that's far from true. Part I offers a useful way to understand the relation between the individual and the group, and how to generate synergy. Groups are mysterious; they have secret lives. There are very specific ways that facilitators can influence, and benefit from, the secret life of the group.

Part II. Participants in a learning group are amazingly different from each other, even if they believe they are homogeneous. How is our handling of difference influenced by social class? How is difference acknowledged, supported, or confronted? How can conflicts aid learning? How do we assist emotional expression to support the process?

Part III. Whether the content of the workshop or course is learned depends hugely on the design. Design in traditional education was controlled by logic, and most people forgot the content fairly soon after the end of the course. What are the principles of design that actually work?

Part IV. Good facilitation is more than mechanically implementing a design; it's more like stalking the teachable moment. How do we make the interventions that heighten the design, experiencing the joy of fine-tuning to stay very close to the developmental life of the group? How does cross-cultural training achieve its goals, when it does? And how do advanced practitioners of direct education do transformational work when participants are stuck and their learning curve is in decline?

Additionally, the book offers four resource appendices. Appendix A addresses educator burnout: how can we thrive in the long run? Appendix B addresses the idealist inside the facilitator and teacher: how do we keep green the vision that motivates us while getting satisfaction from the day-to-day work? Appendix C addresses the teacher as lifelong learner and provides suggestions for further reading to engage the intellectual context of this book, formed as it is by several fields: educational theory, group dynamics, humanistic psychology, and social activism. Appendix D addresses the technician: where to get the detailed instructions for using direct education tools, those that are included in this book and those that aren't, and what to keep in mind as you apply them.

Part I

The Learning Group and the Individual

2

The Role of the Individual and the Group in Direct Education

"Who am I in this group?" is the participant's preoccupying question as any learning group convenes, and there's limited capacity for learning anything else until this question is answered. I learned this fundamental principle in my first job, facilitating adult volunteers at a psychiatric hospital. I started out eager to begin the orientation on Friday evening over supper, since there was a lot to cover. I supposed that they would be eager to start and to ask their questions about this strange new adventure. To my surprise, I would have barely launched into the material when I would see some people's eyes glazing over and others shifting restlessly in their seats. This happened week after week.

As an experiment, one weekend I tried not starting the orientation over dessert. I just watched the group dawdle over their cake, then over the cleanup, and I finally gathered them in the workshop space. By that time they were bursting with curiosity, and we had a clean and efficient orientation, finishing early!

I continued with this new approach and paid more attention to the content of the participants' interactions over supper and cleanup. Maybe I could learn what was so important about their informal banter and what I was interfering with when I tried to impose what I thought was more important. What I first thought was random conversation among the participants turned out to be very serious indeed: they were establishing a status hierarchy among themselves, and they needed time to do it! Once they'd done that, they could relax and attend to the service learning they'd come to do.

In order to learn, people need to feel safe. In a course or workshop or service learning project, they find safety by creating a social order of some kind. When I moved on to other courses, I noticed that the order some groups created was more effective in supporting the learning than others, and so I began to intervene proactively to shape a supportive atmosphere.

What Makes a Pro-learning Social Order?

When I began to make theory out of this, I realized that in the old paradigm of education, participants in learning groups are left to their own devices to create their informal social order. The traditional teacher may imagine that her or his order is the only one that exists in the classroom, or the only one that counts. What I found, though, was that the order that counts for active learning is the less visible one, consisting in subtle signals among the participants. The participants' own order can distract from—or even sabotage—the formal learning task.

And so we are forced back to assumptions. I assume that to learn, people need to risk: to revise their conceptual framework, try a new skill, unlearn an old prejudice, admit there's something they don't know. To risk, people need safety. To be safe, they need a group and/or a teacher that supports them.

I call the kind of social order that supports safety a "container." The metaphor of *container* suggests that it might be thin or thick, weak or robust. A strong container has walls thick enough to hold a group doing even turbulent work, with individuals willing to be vulnerable in order to learn.

I believe that at some level, perhaps unconscious, most participants want to be safe so they can be themselves. Their own deeper learning goals can't be reached from a place of pretense. They need a strong container to do their best work, to feel proud of themselves, and to experience their power.

Whose Responsibility Is the Container?

In the beginning of every group, the teacher or facilitator gets the job. Even in encounter groups, where the facilitator may sit silent for the first five minutes of the session while the group squirms and begins its journey, the facilitator's presence is, in effect, holding the container.

In direct education, teachers are proactive. They set up exercises for introductions, do icebreakers to lighten the atmosphere, set up buddy pairs or small support groups. The sooner the group begins to share the job of building and strengthening the container, the better. It's better for the group; if their work becomes conscious, participants learn how to influence group dynamics. It's better for the facilitator, because holding the container is only one of her many tasks.

Participants hold and strengthen the container in dozens of ways: non-put-down humor, authentic conversation over breaks, keeping the site cleaned up, admitting confusion, going to a participant who looked puzzled or upset and doing active listening, acknowledging someone's courage, acknowledging someone's difference from most people in the group, praying, sharing vulnerably.

To help them to get into the swing of it, positive reinforcement from the facilitator means a lot. For example, during break I might say, "I saw you listening to Kai over lunch—looked like you were giving her something she needed." "I notice you love to tell jokes, Juan, and your sense of humor doesn't depend on putting anyone down."

What's the point of positive reinforcement? People grow as a result—even on the level of skills! Social psychologist Howard Kirschenbaum set up an experiment at a bowling camp by creating two teams with the same gear and same amount of practice (Cooperrider, Sorensen, Yaeger, and Whitney, 2001). Team 1 spent the day practicing and in the evening viewed videos of their performance, edited to include only things they did well. Team 2 also did daytime practice, but in the evening they were told they were going to learn from their errors of the day by watching videos of their mistakes. Over the week of the experiment both teams were measured for performance. Both teams improved. Team 1 improved 100 percent over Team 2—Team 1 learned 100 percent faster with positive images! Teams were also compared with each other along another dimension. They were rated by how much they did or didn't affirm the efforts of the less skilled players. Less skilled players performed far better when they were part of a team that cheered them on rather than criticized or corrected them.

My experience even in highly competitive university environments has been that students can sometimes set aside the behaviors that reflect their insecurities and, by halfway through the semester, take some responsibility for holding the container. They are then amazed to find how much they look forward to the class—and how rapidly they learn.

On a good day, participants can use your learning group to discover one of life's basic truths: we co-create the world we live in.

"There's No *Time* for Container Building!"

This claim comes from people teaching a forty-five-minute class or leading a one-hour workshop, but my experience is that skipping container building wastes time. The first five to ten minutes are often wasted while members of the group are thinking about the phone call they made before coming in, or the pressing item on their to-do list that didn't get done, or why this is their second bad hair day of the week, or how they can make a favorable impression on that attractive person sitting over there. The mere physical presence of a collection of bodies in the room is no indication that someone is learning something.

Instead of wasting time pretending to teach while waiting for minds to arrive, I prefer engaging participants in activities that assist their minds to show up. For some groups the activities may be quite brief. A few questions that are responded to with raised hands (and, if appropriate, a humorous remark) can be enough: "How many of you wish you'd gotten more sleep last night?" "Who here knows more than two other people in the group?" "Who's wondering how yet another workshop on diversity could possibly make the world a better place?"

Even when I'm asked to give a lecture to a large assembly of people, I find it makes a difference if I ask the crowd to turn to each other in their seats and share, for example, (a) how they heard about the meeting, and (b) something they're looking to get out of it. After a few minutes of that, the crowd laughs more easily and is more responsive to my lecture. Before turning to the question-and-answer period, again audience members turn to each other to reflect, and sharpen their questions and comments. The buzzing is always intense, with short bursts of laughter and animation on most faces. The Q and A period is then lively and exciting. Even a large crowd of strangers—as mob psychologists have found—can create a container with its own norms and attitudes. The question for the facilitator or teacher is, Are we willing to build a container that supports learning, or simply leave it to the group to go its own way?

I found in teaching college and university courses that building the container was as important for them as for other forms of adult education. For example, at the start of the semester I shared the technique of what I called co-learning. Students paired up randomly. Time was divided equally (in the beginning, we started with ten minutes: five minutes each). Each student pair decided who would talk first, and who would listen. I might offer a suggestion for what to talk about, but usually not. The listener's job was to pay attention in a focused and affirming way, without asking questions or commenting. The talker's job was to share whatever he or she wanted to, including feelings if that felt safe. These pairs remained stable over the semester, and I gave co-learning time at least once in each class, often in or near the beginning. I was available to assist if a pair had difficulty settling in. Most pairs grew their trust level rapidly, and some met outside class to use this method for longer periods. As they progressed, the whole group container grew stronger.

One reason a stronger container brings more learning is that participants feel safer in expressing their questions and confusions. Some teachers may believe that when they ask for questions and receive none, they have been amazingly lucid. More likely, the container is simply not strong enough to support the questions participants want to ask. Any learning group, when it is awake, has questions (and *not* from the same two or three people!). The issue is, Will the container support those questions being voiced?

Let Them Know About the "Comfort Zone"

A concept that directly supports individual learning and the strength of the container is the "comfort zone." I generally teach this concept very early, in almost every workshop I do.

Each of us has a comfort zone that consists of those habits, beliefs, relationships, feelings, thoughts, and actions that for us are comfortable or familiar. While the comfort zone is reassuring, it can also get stuffy and boring. Humans often leave their comfort zones, for the stimulation and excitement. We may raft on white water, drive too fast, ride a roller coaster, date someone very different from ourselves, or see a scary movie. Some people will pay a great deal of money to become uncomfortable and climb a distant mountain or enter an exotic race.

When leaving their comfort zone, many people check to make sure they'll be safe: the bungee cord won't break, the date will happen in a public place. People intuitively know that *safety is a different issue from discomfort*, but they might forget the difference when they are uncomfortable in a course. I wish I had a dollar for every time I have heard a participant say, "I don't feel safe," when what was really meant was "I don't feel comfortable."

I use a graphic that puts the "self" in the middle of a large circle, labeling the space inside the circle as the "comfort zone." The space outside the circle I label "learning zone" in order to emphasize that learning can happen when people venture out, take risks, entertain new thoughts, and do things that feel scary. I stress that my ideal as a teacher is to see participants uncomfortable for most of the course. That usually gets a laugh and discussion, and I return to the point as soon as possible afterward. Then, when a participant complains about feeling uncomfortable, I hasten to congratulate him, point to the comfort zone graphic, and congratulate him again for entering the zone of learning.

Container Building Is Acknowledging Reality

Whether the initial period of container-building takes a short or long time, the common element is acknowledgment: "Some of you may be eager for this course and others wish you were elsewhere ... I want to welcome you all."

Most of the activities invite disclosure from the participants themselves: "How many of you ...?" "Turn to your neighbor and tell what motivated you to come here tonight." "In this mingle, move around the room and see how many people you can meet and share with."

Container-building is an invitation to be real. It proceeds step by step, through acknowledgment and mutual disclosure. Participants pretend and hide out in the beginning of classes and workshops because they are afraid to be real. By taking small steps, they gain mutual trust and realize they are safe, at least a little bit accepted for who they are and what they think.

When participants are still busy putting energy into pretense—"the good student," "the avid listener" "the know-it-all"—they have less attention for actual learning. As the container strengthens, they can relax and pay attention to the content of the workshop or class. Learning happens.

3

Harnessing the Power
of Intention

Goal setting is the activity of a powerful person. Or, to be more accurate, I should say, "Intentional, explicit goal-setting is the activity of a powerful person." Human beings set short-term goals all the time, and these unconscious goals are often about avoiding pain and seeking pleasure rather than going after their own growth or making a difference.

What accelerates and deepens learning for adults is for goals to become explicit, because the explicitness forces them to choose. What are my personal or professional priorities? In this course, shall I commit to learning this, or that, and how much of what? What is my *intention*?

Participants cannot become powerful learners while coasting on the objectives set out in the curriculum. Each participant needs to state what it is she or he wants to learn, concretely and realistically. I rarely believe it important for me to know what each person's goals are, but it *is* important that someone in the group—a learning buddy or members of a support group—know what each person's goals are. Witnesses often empower us to be our best.

The very act of creating learning goals reminds participants of their power. In Los Angeles I once spent *three* hours assisting participants to set realistic and passionate learning goals for themselves. The workshop had tapped into a "go with the flow" crowd, and the participants were languishing in wimpishness, unable to exert force except when angry. For them it was a wonderful contradiction to their culture of resignation to set some goals for themselves, and the hours spent in the beginning paid off in powerful learning.

Taking responsibility is an act of power. Therefore, many who have an investment in their own powerlessness avoid it. They may have been beaten, physically or emotionally, and decided victimhood is their lot. They may be part of an oppressed group and learned to blame the oppressors for all that they lack. They may be activists and believe that power is a zero-sum game and that it is righteous not to have any power. They may have experienced educational abuse and been forced to sit in endless days of boredom by pedants who themselves believed they couldn't change anything important.

Compassionate teachers and facilitators know that no matter how invested in powerlessness someone is, there's a reason she got that way and she would love to find a way out. Aren't we all moved by the story of deaf and blind Helen Keller, a furious child until she discovers that she, too, has the power to learn? Her tutor Anne Sullivan was too compassionate to be gentle with that little girl caught in her victimhood. Sullivan's toughness enabled Keller to start on a journey that made a difference to the social movements of the day (Keller, 2003),

In a course or a moderately long workshop, midpoint goal checking is important so participants can affirm their progress, modify their goals, or change their strategy to make sure they achieve them. Designing a course to help them revisit their goals helps them to resist getting sucked into a vortex of group-think and to remain on track with their clearest thinking about how, as individuals, they want to grow.

An exercise we frequently use at Training for Change is Maximize/Minimize the Value of a Learning Experience. The facilitator asks participants to recall ways that they have personally found work well when they make full use of a learning opportunity. These aren't advice to the facilitator; they are methods that diverse individuals have found pay off for themselves, like asking questions, taking notes, or talking about the content at break time. These are listed on newsprint. The facilitator then asks for ways in which they have *minimized* the value of a learning experience. After a moment of seeming amnesia during which the facilitator says something like, "Come on, it's honesty time," participants admit to a variety of methods: telling themselves they know the content already, distracting themselves with a things-to-do list, judging the facilitator, judging other participants, and so on. Of course the facilitator relaxes and elicits this information nonjudgmentally. As participants cop to their methods for reducing the value, smiles of recognition appear frequently and the room loosens up. The facilitator usually asks participants what works to pull themselves back into the "maximizing" mode, and participants are happy to share with each other their secrets for effective learning, which are also listed.

The exercise invites participants to clarify their intention for the course: Do they want to go through the motions, or do they want to learn? It invites them to become accountable to the most important person in their lives, themselves.

Teachers' Expectations When Working with Disadvantaged Groups

Our own expectations, sometimes unconscious, influence the learners' attitudes toward themselves. It can be hard for us to ground our expectations in reality when the participants are from oppressed or disadvantaged groups. Some teachers get off center by leaning toward one of two opposite images: Bootstraps Hero and Poor Victim.

Facilitators who hold the Bootstraps Hero image acknowledge that there are institutions and forces that hurt people, but they insist that all individuals, one by one, have within themselves the power to change their lives fundamentally, without participation in collective action. Consider the heroic individuals who have climbed out of desperate poverty and dysfunctional families to change their lives dramatically, they say. In this view, oppressed individuals are largely trapped in illusion. They're in a blame game that evades personal responsibility for their plight. Iconic figures who have "made it" are held up by the teacher as role models for us all.

I also meet trainers who seem unconsciously to operate from the other extreme, the Poor Victim narrative: People are ground down by centuries or millennia of oppression. Diminished as they are, most can't do much on their own, but with allies they can become stronger in naming oppression when it's happening and confront it. At the right historic moment confrontations can become mass upheavals that open the possibility of a better society. The children of that society will less strongly bear the marks of oppression, and so there is a contribution from today's victims.

I don't want to look at participants in my learning groups as either Poor Victims or Bootstraps Heroes. If I see people as Poor Victims, I'm likely to collude in their discouraged view of themselves and not challenge them to take responsibility for being the change they want to see in the world. If I see them as bootstrap heroes, I'll minimize the reality of their context and justifiably lose my credibility with them.

On a good day I remember the perspective I first encountered when I studied Mohandas K. Gandhi and discovered how tough he could be (Gandhi, 1940). "The British are only here," Gandhi said, in words to this effect, "because we allow them to be. As soon as we decide to give up our fear of them, they will be out the next day." Gandhi was completely unwilling to regard his people as victims at the mercy of the perpetrators. He had no illusions about the British; he expected them to pursue profit at Indian expense until the Indians forced them out. He was confident that Indians using nonviolent struggle were more powerful than the British, and that the British would be forced against their will to leave. The missing piece, he told his suffering people, was their accepting their responsibility and stepping into their power. No bleeding heart, Gandhi!

In the stories we make up about our participants, the Poor Victim and Bootstraps Hero are mirror images of each other, equally distorted. Those sympathizing with the Poor Victim omit the strength of the inner life. Those extolling the Bootstraps Hero omit the strength of the outer life. One denies psychology; the other, sociology. Although some proponents of the Bootstraps Hero call themselves holistic, their view is as narrow and one-dimensional as that of the sympathizers of the Poor Victim. The Poor Victim view may be especially attractive to teachers who stem from oppressed groups. The Bootstraps Hero view seems to be more attractive to teachers who are privileged. Each is projecting, and their projections keep them in their comfort zones.

In my experience the facilitators who buy the Poor Victim and those who buy the Bootstraps Hero are both at risk for burnout. I've seen Poor Victim trainers collude with the oppressed participants in their workshops and get little change as a result. It's tough to keep giving workshops when one sees little change! On the other hand, I've seen Bootstraps Hero trainers fade out when they get strong resistance to their attitude; the trainers just can't create rapport with people who see them as clueless about the realities that participants face in their own context.

I'm grounded by the view of three perspectives on power suggested by Starhawk (1988): power-over (oppressing people and holding them down), power-with (the influence one has in a group of equals—and I would add facilitating collaboration), and power-from-within (the hope, courage, and compassion needed for the long run). When I invite participants to tap power-with and power-from-within, I notice that I'm centered.

Framing the Experience as an Act of Self-Responsibility

I find it helpful in the beginning of courses or workshops that might be stressful for some participants—especially those which are a weekend or longer—to post on the wall a few guidelines.

These are guidelines that more deeply challenge participants to take responsibility for their learning.

->• *Use everything for your advancement.* I explain that the workshop might have ups and downs for them individually, and the way to get the most learning from the downs as well as the ups is to follow this guideline. If they find themselves unable to sleep one night after a compelling evening, rather than lapse into resentment or discouragement, they could use the sleepless hours for their own advancement. Maybe the breakthrough they're meant to have in this workshop will be at 3 a.m. instead of 3 p.m.

->• *Take care of yourself so you can take care of others.* Some participants avoid the harder lessons in life by busying themselves taking care of others. I explain that in this workshop everyone is expected to take care of himself or herself first, as when the flight attendant on the air-plane says we should first put on our own oxygen mask before assisting the child sitting next to us.

->• *Complete the training.* In most workshops there are a couple of participants who come with a private con-tract they've made with themselves: if the workshop becomes (a) boring, (b) repetitive of prior learning, (c) stressful, (d) weird, (e) full of participants who are jerks, or (f) all of the above, they will bail out. This is true even though in advance publicity I always state that the workshop is an experiential package and participants must take all of it or none.

By raising this third guideline in the beginning, I encourage participants to change their internal contract and make a new one, with the group and me. (The group has an investment in this, since it is destructive to the learning group if a participant or two is sitting with their eye on the door.) Occasionally a participant will acknowledge difficulty with this guideline, and conversation in front of the group will clarify whether it's best for the person to stay with a new commitment or simply to leave right away.

Push Them to Deal with Their Ambivalence

In some workshops, especially short ones, it's not appropriate to work with the guidelines or individual learning goals, and yet you notice when you step into the room that participants have serious ambivalence about the workshop. You might sense when people are unwilling to take responsibility for learning, for example, if informal conversation while people gather is marked by gossip and complaining. Or you might suspect that a number of the participants are there mainly because it is the "correct" thing to do, like learning conflict resolution skills or reducing their carbon footprint or making the most of diversity.

Ambivalence is the enemy of learning unless the teacher acknowledges the ambivalence in some way and assists it to get resolved. I often use what we call the "ambivalence chart"; here's how it worked at an evening workshop of students and community people in Hanover, New Hampshire.

The auditorium at Dartmouth College was full. The workshop title was "Diversity," and it must have been a hot topic that year. I wondered if people were there because it was fashionable, so I decided to test how much the participants really wanted to learn. In the process, we might build a strong enough container to do some risky work.

After people turned to each other in pairs to share why they'd come and what they hoped to get out of the evening, I explained that "diversity" is a concept like most concepts: it has an up side and a down side. I suggested we take a few minutes to explore what the up side and down side of diversity might be. On newsprint, I put

"DIVERSITY" in the center top and on one side a plus sign and a minus on the other.

The pluses came abundantly, if not with much originality. The "plus" list became longer and longer, and finally someone said, "Having people around with differences can make me shy and awkward." I wrote it down under "minus." More pluses were volunteered, and then someone said, "Differences usually bring conflict." Ahhh, I thought, at last the minuses will come. And so they did, until we ended up with a roughly balanced list of pluses and minuses.

"Well," said I, "it looks like we have a lot of down side to the topic of diversity, so I don't know if it really makes sense to pursue it." I read out some of the more compelling minuses. "Do we really want to spend the evening on this? There's probably time to still get to a good movie, and I'm always behind on my movies," I said with a relaxed smile.

The group got into an intense discussion reflecting their ambivalence about difference, then reached a working consensus that they wanted to go ahead with the workshop.

I remember that the intense workshop that followed had the "feel" that usually comes from a group of twenty or thirty at work, even though they were 150. I saw individuals risking a lot to pursue their goal of learning to counter oppression. The high degree of unity and purpose that allowed hard and vulnerable work to be done came from the twenty minutes we spent at the beginning resolving the ambivalence of the participants.

How is it that individuals can be so affected by a group process as to make themselves vulnerable and get in touch with the power of their own intention? Every reader has seen this happen, but to make it happen in a predictable way, it helps to learn more about the optimum relationship between the individual and the group in adult learning.

The Individual Versus the Group

Carmela Finelli, my eleventh-grade English teacher who brought her Italian working class roots into our classroom, asked us over and over again: "Which is more important, class, the individual or the group?" I wanted to believe it was the individual. A teenager tired of his small town, eager to break free of the bonds of church and family, I wanted to put myself first. Later, in college, I read Henrik Ibsen's play *An Enemy of the People* and raced to the end. I was so excited by the last line in the play that I paced the campus, unable to sleep. Thorvald says, "The strongest man in the world is he who stands most alone."

And yet I was unwilling to walk my talk. In high school I had joined committees and choirs, the newspaper, and the yearbook staff. I had written scripts and directed plays. In college it was the same story, as well as walking picket lines. In my daily life I proved over and over that my life was unthinkable without groups.

Finelli's question didn't go away, though. I experienced the tension between claims of group and individual, and times of hard choices. In graduate school, especially, the climate of competitive individualism increased the pull of one side, while the content of the sociology I was studying increased the pull of the other.

Dr. Martin Luther King Jr. helped me to clarify the issue by linking it to world-historical ideologies. He wrote, "Truth is found neither in traditional capitalism nor in classical Communism. Each represents a partial truth. Capitalism fails to see the truth in collectivism. Communism fails to see the truth in individualism. Capitalism fails to realize that life is social. Communism fails to realize that life is personal. The good and just society is neither the thesis of capitalism nor the antithesis of Communism, but a socially conscious democracy which reconciles the truths of individualism and collectivism" (King, 1967, p. 187).

Anthropologist Ruth Benedict then opened a window for me, a very big window. At Columbia University and in her fieldwork she made cross-cultural comparisons while asking Finelli's question: Which is most important, the individual or the group? What Benedict found was that *cultures vary according to how big that question is for their members* (Goble, 1970).

Some cultures are designed in a way that makes it a harsh choice: Shall I choose my interest or that of the group? But other cultures, Benedict discovered, are organized so that it is hardly a choice at all, because the individual's interest and the interest of the group are in alignment. She called the latter kind of culture *synergistic*.

So Finelli's question is itself a social construction! It only gets asked when, in societies like mine, social design forces a choice. Not all societies are constructed the way mine is. "Get the government off my back!" is not a phrase one would hear in a high-synergistic society, nor President Kennedy's "Ask not what your country can do for you but what you can do for your country."

The creation of the tension is itself a product of the system. It's possible to design social arrangements where the individual's well-being is in alignment with society's well-being.

Benedict gave me optimism on two counts. First, synergy or lack of it is a result of social construction, not of human nature. What is constructed can, in principle, be reconstructed. Second, some human societies have been designed for synergy. It can be done.

What does that mean for teachers and facilitators?

Workshops and Courses Are Social Constructions

A course or a workshop is, of course, an invention, intended to nurture the learning and growth of participants. We teachers/inventors get to express our values in the way we set things up. If we go with the flow of typical high school and university design, we'll continue with the implicit structure of competitive individualism in our workshops and courses. If we want to prioritize the group, we'll put all our eggs in the basket of collectivity. I've done both, and I know from experience that both these alternatives heighten the tension between the individual and the group.

Direct education is a third way, an attempt to construct Dr. King's "higher synthesis" for the limited time of a course or workshop. We emphasize the strength of the individual through self-responsibility and the strength of community through container building (discussed in Chapter 2). What puts these two forces in alignment, creating synergy, is in the rest of this book.

Direct education is not about *balancing* the competing claims of individual and group. It's about dropping the competition. It's about supporting both, in such a way that the whole experience becomes greater than the sum of its parts. The learning breakthrough available to the participants is a product both of their own motivation and responsibility *and* of the considerable support of their group. It's the combination that makes it possible.

Having offered practical ways to strengthen the individual side in this chapter, it's important to move on to explain how to strengthen the container to support a still more synergistic relationship between the individual and the group.

4

Strengthening the Container
Subgroups Join the Mix

Every learning group consists not only of individuals but also subgroups. Subgroups influence the amount of learning that individuals can do. Sometimes a subgroup accelerates the learning of individuals, whom Canadians call "keeners." Sometimes a subgroup holds them back. Sometimes unaddressed jostling of subgroups creates so much static in the group that it distracts seriously from the learning task.

I acknowledge the pioneering work of psychologists Arnold Mindell and Amy Mindell and their associates in providing a manageable way of facilitating our way through the complicated web of relationships that exist in a group (Mindell, 1992, 1997). Their theory of mainstream and margins has supported and illuminated my own discoveries in tapping the power of the group to accelerate and deepen learning.

Every group has a mainstream and one or more margins, the Mindells explain. Every course and workshop, like other groups, has a mainstream: those qualities, behaviors, and values supported by the group. Other qualities and behaviors are put out of the center, to the periphery.

No matter how homogeneous the group believes itself to be, a careful look shows that some characteristics are marginalized. A group known for vigorous and noisy debates has some quiet members. A solemn and highly disciplined group includes a few who, out of sight during break, love to crack jokes and be rowdy.

Margins in a group might be defined by gender, class, color, or by religion or lack of it, or political opinion, or by physical ability or age, or even recreational preference. Groups are ingenious in seizing upon differences to define mainstream/margin dynamics.

A mainstream is not defined by numbers. The Republic of South Africa was world-famous for its mainstream being white although a racial minority. The mainstream, in a country or a workshop, sets the tone, sets the communication style, and gets to have its own preferences more or less accepted by the margin.

Sometimes a teacher can observe subtle ways in which a mainstream pushes individuals or subgroups into a marginal position. Sometimes it seems a subgroup or individual chooses to be on the margin. Whatever the reason why some participants find themselves on the margin, facilitators need to figure out how to relate to the peripheral people in a way that supports their power and safety, and therefore their ability to learn well.

How Can We Acknowledge Margins?

Building a strong container requires acknowledging margins somehow or another. The individual participants in a group are wondering not only how they fit in regarding their unique characteristics but also whether the group has space for their group identities. Will this be a typical mixed-gender group in which men talk 80 percent of the time, the women ask themselves. Will this be a typical mixed–sexual orientation group in which all the references to relationship are heterosexual, the sexual minorities ask themselves.

These questions being silently asked around the room matter hugely for a facilitator or teacher, because, in general, the more "at home" the margins feel, the more they can learn. The less they experience the group as a safe place for them, the less they can learn.

There are many options for facilitators to use in acknowledging margins. For one thing, we can sprinkle our speech with these kinds of comments:

> "This generalization may fit many of you, but I imagine some of you have a different experience."

> "A lot of people want to do it this way, and I realize some of you don't. In this case, I think we'll go ahead with the way we're doing it now."

We can launch our courses and workshops with a structured acknowledgment of mainstreams and margins. The Mindells' Process Oriented Psychology has created a ritual, and I find it works every time in strengthening the container. I call it a Diversity Welcome. My version goes like this:

> I want to welcome you to this workshop. I'd like to welcome those of you who came from a distance to be here, and also welcome those who live nearby. Welcome to the youngest participants here—what, are you teens? Welcome! And welcome also to those of you in your twenties, and in your thirties, and your forties, and fifties, and sixties, and seventies! Welcome if this is your first workshop of this kind, and welcome if you've done this kind of thing before.
>
> Welcome if you are 100 percent enthusiastic and glad to be here, and welcome if you feel a pull not to be here because of other things on you right now. I'd like to welcome you if you are a Native American or African American, and if you're Asian Pacific American, and also if you're from a Latin background, and also if you're European American—all of you are welcome here. Welcome to those of you who are female, and the males, and welcome to you if the usual gender categories don't

work for you. Welcome if you have a lot of schooling in your background, and welcome if you haven't done much with school—everyone belongs here. Welcome to the lesbians here, and the gay men, and bisexuals and queers, and those whose sexuality doesn't label easily, and welcome also to heterosexuals.

I'd like to welcome those with hidden disabilities as well as those whose disabilities are apparent. There's a lot of diversity here, and I'd like to welcome those parts of ourselves which might show up in this workshop: the sad parts, the cheerful parts, the anger and despair, the hopefulness, the silliness and the solemn parts—we can be ourselves here. Are there aspects of our diversity that I've left out? [Include what's suggested from participants.]

Yes, and finally I'd like to welcome the ancestors who lived in this land where we are just now. The indigenous people whose homeland we're sitting in just now; I'd like to acknowledge them and welcome their spirits to this place. Thank you.

Margins Emerge in the Course

For courses and workshops that are two days or longer, strengthening the container pays off in accelerated learning. Usually at least one margin presents itself for attention as the course unfolds.

An interfaith activist group in Boston asked me to facilitate a weekend retreat where the members could learn tools that would increase their effectiveness. The leadership was proud that youth outreach had been strong, and they expected that teens and young adults would be strongly represented.

As it turned out, although the group of forty was one-third youth, the young people spoke much less than one-third of the time, even in small group work. From the start I worked to establish rapport with them, and about halfway through the weekend suggested that they could do an exercise that would support their playing a stronger role in the retreat. They agreed to try it.

I gathered the young people in the front of the room and explained to the adults that this would be an important chance for them to learn about intergenerational dynamics. I asked the young people to talk spontaneously about what they liked about being the age they are. The initiative of the bolder ones soon stimulated quieter youths to talk, and I noticed the body language: standing taller and with more animation, as well as humor.

I then asked the young people what was hard about being the age they are. As they responded, the sharing became more vulnerable and even included painful ageist incidents that had happened during the retreat.

When they were finished, I pointed out that some of the adults in the room might be interested in becoming allies to the youths. I asked them what specific advice they had for older allies. Again the young people responded from the heart and, judging from the faces of the adults as I looked around, the young people were heard.

More importantly, in terms of the goal of supporting the margin, I saw the young people step up their participation markedly in the rest of the retreat, and the entire group moved more quickly through the curriculum I'd designed for the weekend.

How Ground Rules and Group Agreements Can Build the Container

When the teacher or trainer presents clear norms for individual behavior, I call them ground rules. If a group is rowdy and potentially violent, ground rules offer reassuring structure. If the culture of the participants has taught them to respect rules, and they have little experience consciously creating their own norms, ground rules can be just what they need to experience enough safety to learn at the beginning of the learning group's life.

Alternatively, a group can create its own norms through a process of agreement, facilitated by the trainer or teacher. If it's a fairly small group, I simply ask for proposals, write them on newsprint, and then ask for questions and discussion. The discussion may eliminate a few proposals. I then go down the list formally asking for agreement, usually signified by raised hands (for the kinesthetic learners). When we reach the end of the list, I often ask people to stand if they are in agreement, as a way of underlining their personal responsibility. Sometimes someone fails to stand, and we get to work with the proposed agreement they're having trouble with, perhaps eliminating or rephrasing it.

If it's a larger group, I find it needlessly tedious to stay on the whole-group level. I form small groups and ask them each to propose three possible agreements that their small group members can agree with. We then harvest the results, and follow the procedure I use in smaller groups.

When I'm smelling contentiousness in the room or I'm in a group that seems fairly unconscious, I add another criterion to the small group work. I ask them to propose agreements that they believe will be agreeable to everyone in the whole group. This pushes them to increased awareness of who is present in the large group and also pushes them into the attitude of consensus building.

The process of agreeing on a set of norms can itself be container building, especially if the norms are elicited from the group. As the members propose various options and negotiate with each other, they are getting to know each other and developing unstated "rules behind the rules," or meta-norms. On rare occasions power struggles emerge in the group and take substantial time to resolve; in the process I've seen the container's walls grow dramatically.

Ground rules also provide a convenient opportunity for facil-itator interventions later in the workshop if it seems that the container is weakening. They provide an opportunity to check in: "How are we doing on ground rules? Are the rules working as you'd hoped?" Facilitators can use the process to reflect back to the group dynamics they are noticing, which builds the group's awareness.

Beyond Ground Rules and Group Agreements

I use ground rules and group agreements much less often than I used to. I find participants using group norms to hide behind, becoming less authentic than would serve their own learning. Some groups use ground rules to legislate against "misbehavior," when the group would learn far more if the behavior actually showed up. For example, in a workshop on communication it might be far better for a man to interrupt a woman and use his louder voice to get the floor. At that point the group could intervene and practice handling the problem, with the support of the facilitator. Far more might be learned about dynamics of gender and power, for application in the real world, than if the group agreements result in polite correctness and head-nodding proprieties.

I now take a hard look at the politics of legislating correct behaviors, by asking who is empowered in the process. The group legislates, initially, through negotiation and agreement. The exec-utive function is implicitly left to the facilitator; participants typically project on us the duty of enforcing the rules. Where is the initiative of the individual participant in this scenario? Where does she learn to stand up for herself or stand up as an ally? In a learning group (in contrast with meetings and other kinds of groups), the ground rule approach might actually diminish learning.

Another liability of group agreements is that they are rarely the preference of the whole group. The norms selected are almost always those of the mainstream of the group. Take, for example,

"No interruptions," a frequent ground rule. This rule privileges one communication style over another; it enforces, for example, the style of Northern European middle classes over Southern European working classes. (Of course this difference shows up between other cultures as well.) In hundreds of workshops where I have seen this rule proposed, I have never seen it objected to by someone whose communication style will be discounted by it, even though I know such people are in the room. Subtly, the mainstream has its way.

This poses a personal dilemma for me as facilitator. I was myself brought up working class and I know from personal experience what grand, truth-seeking, and passionate discussions I've been part of which were full of interruptions *and* were also full of learning from each other. A no-interruption rule would have been absurd to us, an intrusion that drained the juice from the dialogue. Knowing that, do I want to be in the role of enforcer of a group agreement called "No interruptions" which privileges many middle class people? I'm open to doing so, but the reasons need to be very clear, for *this* group at *this* time to further a particular learning goal.

Who's the Enforcer of Group Norms?

I am. It goes with the facilitator job, at least in the beginning when a lot of the container holding falls to the teacher. Cultures vary regarding how much the group members may participate in enforcement. But note: participants have not entered a contract of mutual enforcement simply by agreeing to the ground rules. Their agreement is to live by the norms personally, not to enforce normative behavior on others.

Maybe some of them not only think of the norm-setting as a personal promise to comply, but also see themselves as legislators who together have created a set of laws. Fine. It's nevertheless true that in many societies the legislative function is separate from the executive function: members of Congress don't go out and arrest people who break the law. Enforcement is a separate function.

Of course facilitators have a variety of styles when it comes to enforcement: storm trooper, charmer, martyr, comedian, neutral commentator. What matters is that we do enforce the agreements. If we don't, morale sags, the container weakens, we get bored, resentments accumulate, and participants pass up chances to risk and learn.

Functions of the Container

Intelligence, it is said, lies in the ability to make connections. The wide-awake learner is busy making connections between the content of the curriculum and her or his own previous experience and cognitive map. Supporting this bottom-line task is the strength of the connections already made in the room. Because human beings are social creatures, we make connections best when we are already connected.

Readers who like lists will be happy to notice that we have another list! The container

- breeds collaborative spirit, so participants learn from each other;

- encourages participants to be real rather than pretend to be "the good student," so authentic curiosity can emerge;

- creates safety for taking risks;

- creates an affirmative environment (in the bowling camp people learned more in an affirming group);

- reduces the distractibility of the group and therefore saves time for more content; and

- assists people to make connections in the content of the curriculum—connected people make more connections.

How People Teach Themselves When the Container Is Strong

When participants in a workshop know their goals—and the container is strong—they can thrive with their initiative in teaching themselves. I had an experience of that in Decatur, Illinois, when I led a two-day course in nonviolent civil disobedience for three unions that were on strike.

By the end of the first day of training, the container was strong. I was invited to the union meeting that evening and stood to one side of the crowded union hall, watching the proceedings with a cup of coffee in my hand. A woman came up to me. "Have you seen the posters around the building announcing support groups for women?" she asked.

Getting a "yes," she went on. "Well, those are for the wives and mothers of male workers, not for women workers like me in the union. What do you think? Should we female workers have support groups, or would that be divisive?"

"Well . . ." I took a sip of coffee, looking her in the eye. "What do you think?"

"I think we need them!" she said vehemently. "I come from several generations of women who worked in factories, and we deserve a place where we can be together. What do you think?"

"That's an interesting idea," I said. "What do you think?"

"We *do* deserve our own space!" she said. "It won't be divisive at all. I'm putting up posters announcing a meeting tomorrow. Thanks," she said with a smile as she walked off.

Hardly fifteen minutes went by before an African American man came over to me, and we repeated virtually the same conversation, replacing *blacks* for *women*. He also thanked me as he left, and I smiled while thinking that facilitation is sometimes the easiest job in the world.

Every group has a mainstream and one or more margins. The margins, like the European American woman and African American man in this story, usually go along with the mainstream—unity is important, especially to a labor union on strike. Because direct education methods affirm the voices of all, participants with marginal identities are empowered to connect the dots on their cognitive maps and take their next steps.

The facilitator can honor them by refraining from telling them what to do. Our job is different—to mobilize their confidence, to share tools, and to challenge them to think for themselves. The rest of the book explains how.

The Secret Life of Groups

By *secret life* I mean the interactions and dynamics in the group that take place outside or below the surface of the classroom or training room. These can be vivid, challenging, uplifting, painful, and closely related to the content of the workshop or the course. I remember my peace studies class at Haverford College in which small groups initially set up for inside-the-room support undertook social action and research projects outside the college with blithe disregard for credit.

The secret life of groups can support participants' pursuit of their learning goals or undermine them. The informal dynamics can support and give added vigor to what goes on in the formal, public space, or they can detract from and even sabotage what happens in the training room. Groups sometimes hold back on showing their brilliance because of the dynamics of their secret life.

I like to take a training as a participant from time to time to remind myself of how much the group life matters, especially in a group of peers, and how layered that life can become. Even inside the training room, undercurrents exist: sexual attractions, power struggles, projections of many kinds including projections on the facilitator. The undercurrents inside the training room are amplified, however, in the resonating drum of the group's culture expressed outside the room.

The good news is that facilitators and teachers can relate to the secret life of groups and often influence it in a way that serves the learning goals of the participants.

How Can the Secret Life of Groups Accelerate Learning?

No curriculum or teacher can take account of everything going on in a learning group: the diversity of learning channels; the variety of kinds of intelligence; the participants' differing degrees of experience and background in the content matter; the complex realities of rank, class, and ethnicity that influence participation; the projections being made on the teacher or facilitator; the degree of participants' self-confidence and/or assertiveness; the relation between the mainstream of the group and its margins; and the multiplicity of individual learning goals.

But a self-organizing group can, given some time, operate with this degree of complexity! It can create a system in which an amazing number of needs can be met. I can illustrate this point with how a group dealt with my white racism.

Over three hundred people were gathered from dozens of countries in a hill town near Mumbai, India, for a Worldwork seminar. On the third day the floor was opened for a leadership initiative from small support groups. To my surprise Satish, one of my group members, took the floor and called for the rest of us to follow. I enthusiastically jumped in, motioning to the others who reluctantly followed.

We sat cross-legged on the floor, looking expectantly at Satish to launch into something. Satish's winning smile turned uncertain as he searched for something to do. "If you don't have something, give up the floor and give others a chance," someone called, and murmurs of agreement came from around the circle.

A Worldwork facilitator took the microphone and said, "It's time to let these folks go, but before we do, let's find out what's just been going on. I'm curious."

Satish spoke first, confessing that he leapt into the center with absolutely no idea in mind. "George," the facilitator asked, "what prompted you to lead the rest of your gang into the center?"

"I wanted to give a vote of confidence in Satish," I said. "We're in his country, after all, and he's such a bright and articulate young man. I wanted him to lead."

Another support group moved into the center to lead as our gang rejoined the audience. On the way to my seat, a participant said, "Hey, George, you might want to think some about what you just said."

Later, during the break, two different participants came up to me, independently suggesting the same thing: reflect on what I said in response to the facilitator's question. I drew a blank, just as I did when the first participant offered the suggestion.

Later that night, as I was preparing for bed, my roommate said, "By the way, George, that was interesting what you said in the center about your reasons for mobilizing around Satish. I hope you'll think more about that."

He turned out the light.

At four in the morning I was suddenly awake, completely alert and ready for inner work. What was that thing about Satish really about? It hit me. How many years has it been that white colonialists have come to India and other countries and selected leaders? How perfect that I used the tip-off word *articulate*. How confidently, and unconsciously, I stepped into the role of designator of "native leaders," I with my higher rank and cluelessness about what was really going on inside Satish at that moment.

I spent the rest of the night confronting this layer of racism within me, venting my sadness and despair that I've been conditioned so deeply and praying for the strength to learn to be a better ally. In the morning when the seminar reconvened, I asked for a brief moment at the microphone to share what I'd learned and to thank the participants — all of them white — who got on my case so thoughtfully.

The encounters with other participants, out of public view, brought me to my epiphany. For me the workshop continued in the middle of the night, thanks to the secret life of the group.

Good News for the Facilitator

It's certainly true that a facilitator could have worked with me on my racism publicly in the training room the previous evening. That would be a reasonable facilitator choice. My teachable moment was relevant to others as well.

On a good day, however, hundreds of such teachable moments occur in a seminar, teachable moments that are part of the seminar design. There's no way that more than a small fraction of them can be processed publicly. A far higher proportion can be worked with privately, however, thanks to the informal life of the group.

Knowing this gives the teacher or facilitator a source of hope and relief. The hope is that participants can gain far more during a course or workshop than that which is happening under our facilitator noses. The relief is that it's not all on us to make sure the learning is happening—we are indeed engaged in co-creation and the participants are mainly responsible for what they learn, using the assistance of us and the group.

Knowing about the secret life also offers a strategy for intervention. We can choose to get the ball rolling and then let go, having some confidence that others, perhaps a buddy or support group, will continue to work for a breakthrough. That's what the Worldwork facilitator did with me.

Time and again participants report to me that brief questions or nudges from me in public get follow-up from other participants that enables them to gain a new understanding. When I encounter resistance from a participant, I can detach if I choose to. I can practice letting go, as the Buddhists advise, realizing that there is far more resource in the room than my immediate attention.

Creating Bridges to the Secret Life of the Group

When I'm working with a group, I'm relieved to hear that the group's secret life is a vital place full of learning and growth. Sometimes, however, I learn that it's not.

Because covert activities can undermine learning, I want to invent bridges between the group's private life on one shore and me and the group's public life on the other shore. When bridges exist, I'll hear about dysfunctionalities in the group's secret life. On a good day, I'll be able to give the group a hand.

Some of the support tools that strengthen the container are useful also in providing a bridge to the informal life of the group. I often use a "buddy system"—randomly selected pairs whose job is to listen to and challenge each other to achieve their learning goals. Sometimes I use small support groups instead, especially if the workshop content is related to leadership, conflict, team dynamics, or personal growth. The support groups provide a here-and-now context in which participants can experiment with new behaviors. Both kinds of support—buddy pairs and support groups—often become a resource to participants outside the training room and help them negotiate the group culture that forms there.

Hanging out with participants in the informal times—breaks, mealtimes, after the session is over for the day—also provides a bridge. Personality styles differ, from the teacher who enjoys being "life of the party" to the one who chats one-on-one or quietly rearranges the books and flipcharts. The key is accessibility. Participants who know you are there will find you!

The listening committee is another bridge. This is a representative group of participants who agree to meet with the teacher or facilitator and share concerns and observations about how the training is going. In a long course or workshop, the membership often rotates after a period of time. Other participants know they can go to members of the listening committee to share observations and feedback, and some do. The listening committee is also a venue in which a facilitator or teacher can try out ideas and plans for feedback. The listening committee is not a planning instrument; it has no decision-making power. It's an information channel, highly useful in the complex system of a long workshop or course.

While working in Russia, I learned a bridge that's popular among adult educators there. "We will now have a weather report," announced Ivan Timofeev, one of the Moscow-based group of trainers known as Golubka.

I was startled. It had been snowing for a week with no sign of change. Why a weather report?

"When it's your turn," Ivan continued, "please tell us how your internal weather is, and you can finish by giving a number from one to ten to indicate how pleased you are—or not—with your condition."

Ahhhh—it's a metaphor! Surely I should know Russian culture well enough to know that metaphors are like music to them!

"I will start," said Ivan. "It's an uncomfortably hot day with a stiff breeze and dark clouds moving in; I suspect a storm is on its way. I will say 8." The weather report is another means through which the informal life of the group can show up in the training room.

Inviting participants to accept a discipline during the entire workshop creates a wide bridge between inside and outside the room. I sometimes ask participants not to drink alcohol, for example. I explain that alcohol erodes the container and reduces participants' access to their full awareness. Nicotine and recreational drugs are put aside for the duration of some workshops. Horace Godwin, Jonathan Snipes, and I used to lead weekend workshops for gay and bisexual men and allies in which we would seek the men's agreement not to have sex during the weekend; the men reported in evaluations that the discipline increased the value of the workshop on several levels. The agreement to a common discipline that operates around the clock dramatically increases the flow between what happens inside and outside the training room.

The marathon provides another possible bridge, especially if put early in the design. I participated in a workshop led by Rod Napier and his colleagues in which we worked continuously all day, all night, and all the next day. Not only did this style move us forward on our individual learning goals (to learn to facilitate a group under stressful circumstances) but the marathon also bridged the "off stage" and "on stage" spaces of the group. By working together while deeply fatigued, we relaxed our inhibitions and "let our shit show." When the workshop shifted to a more usual working day, the wall some groups have between "on" and "off" was for us only a thin membrane.

Pretense is the enemy of learning. Adults have many years of experience pretending to be students, going through the motions, eyes on the lecturer while the mind is a million miles away. Real learning happens when people decide to be real. Although it may be anxiety-producing for teachers who enjoy the appearance of "the good student," our full power as teachers is only available when participants drop their pretense.

I risk another generalization: the more the classroom or training room is a place of pretense, the more vivid and undermining will be the secret life of the group. If ambivalence toward the facilitator cannot be expressed in the room, it *must* be expressed outside the room—and amplified. If unhappiness with "obnoxious" participants cannot be expressed in the room, it must be expressed outside the room—and amplified. The same with racism and other dynamics that undermine learning. I've worked in settings where a high proportion of the participants came to us traumatized by violence. We didn't give them a chance to work on that in the room, so they drank heavily each night during their secret life, and their brains were too addled to learn much during the day.

Although a marathon may be the most efficient way to dissolve pretense safely, some facilitators find it is beyond their stamina even when working as a team with short nap breaks. A variation that I've found highly effective is to design the workshop around twelve- to sixteen-hour days. This design approach dramatically reduces pretense, reveals to participants sources of energy they didn't know they had, and increases the availability of resources for pursuing learning goals.

When the Group Wants to Become a High-Performance Team

Sometimes a dynamic in the group is so secret that the group even in its private life doesn't see it coming. I'm referring to the "storm," a phenomenon that shows up in public but isn't explicitly linked to the curriculum. I'll describe a personal facilitation case in story form, the better to encourage the reader to notice layers and complexities in the experience the group and I shared. This is from a national student workshop in building organizational skills, held in Philadelphia.

The young man was big enough to be a player in the National Football League. He was headed for the door, anger pulsing from his body. I got to the door first, blocking it.

"You look really frustrated ... " I began, but was cut off. "Damn right I'm frustrated, and mad as hell, and I'm gettin' out of here!"

"You're mad, and look at the other participants — frustrated as can be."

"Right! Anybody would be. Nothing is happening here and you're just fucking sitting there ... pardon my language. But I'm mad!"

"You have a right to be mad. The group hasn't found its way forward yet. You're part of the group. The group needs you."

After more of that kind of dialogue, the football player went back to the group, and I resumed my facilitator chair, trying my best to channel the Buddha. "It's the group's work to do," I reassured myself. "I'll keep praying for them, and see if I can keep everyone in the room."

The period that followed seemed like hours, filled as it was with painful attempts by various participants to bring the group together. The attempts were mostly reasonable, and none of them worked. "Let's try forming small groups to generate ways of moving the group forward," one student said.

"We need more unity, so let's hold hands and sing," another suggested.

Another student challenged someone making jokes: "Stop being such a clown — you're distracting us!"

Students launched a dozen initiatives to try to get the group out of its stuck place, and all of them failed.

The informal leader of the group, a quiet student who had been trying to maintain the morale of his despairing friends, finally threw up his hands. "I don't know what to do!" he said with anguish in his voice. He began to cry.

The energy shift was palpable. Suddenly, the group was a community. Participants circled around their sobbing leader, touching him and each other. Tears were in many eyes. Facial muscles relaxed. The tension ebbed. I noticed the football player smiling with relief.

The storm was over.

As often as I've been through this, there's no way I can be jaded when I watch a group put itself through pain in order to become a high performance team. Bruce Tuckman's theory (1965) has been widely useful: a group begins to form (a honeymoon period, with participants trying to fit in), then begins to storm—*chaos*, M. Scott Peck calls it—and with any luck it moves into its last stages of norming and performing. Peck (1988) calls the last stage *community*.

Groups don't always take hours to storm. One small group I was in zipped through in ten minutes! Storming is as unpredictable as, well, the weather. Even though I facilitate groups where this sometimes happens and I know the theory about it, when I'm a participant in a group that moves into chaos, I'm just like the rest: frustrated, disgusted, angry. And like the others, I come up with bright initiatives that don't work. Duh—the theory says they *can't* work while a group is storming, however well those interventions might work at another time! At that moment, however, I'm not in theory-land. I'm gripped by a kind of group spirit, and the group is playing for bigger stakes than theoretical models. The group wants community, and this is its way of getting it.

If the reader was brought up in a pain-avoiding culture like I was, you might ask for some easier route to becoming a high-performance team. The dark night of the soul is OK for medieval Christian mystics, and the mantra "no pain, no gain" is OK for athletes, but why can't groups just slide into community, or find a guru to do it for them, or find a consultant to mold them via PowerPoints into a high-performance team?

Once again, when we make this complaint, we're in the land of social construction. The pain associated with becoming a community is only judged negatively if we believe there "ought" to be an alternative. Right—just as there "ought" to be an alternative to the law of gravity!

The gravitational force involved in team building is the belief individuals have that they can fix things. A positive force, surely, and related to the self-responsibility for learning that motivates so much growth! But just as gravity is a positive force (we like it that basketballs fall through the hoop), it is also a source of pain, as anyone can tell you who is old and is toiling up a steep hill. The thing about the law of gravity is, we don't complain about it. We work with it, and play with it.

The football player and his fellow participants were frustrated because they spent hours trying every way they knew how to move things forward, as if they could get to where they wanted to go through *doing*. When their informal leader, the person who most of them held in high esteem, threw up his hands and surrendered, he unknowingly surrendered for all of them. The experience of community, it turns out, is not about doing, but rather about *being*.

And once participants experience themselves as a team, then many kinds of doing become possible, which is why we call that last stage a "high-performance" team. The football player's group, which spent at least four hours in chaos instead of attending to the curriculum, learned a day's worth of material in the following three hours. I could barely keep up with them; they were like babies, like an open system, with a growth curve you would die for.

Well, they did. Die for their growth curve. What died was ego's insistence that we can control the most valuable aspects of life—connection, happiness, enlightenment.

I bring up this group development model here because it relates to the secret life of groups. For one thing, the decision to throw themselves into chaos is below the consciousness of the participants; it is secret to them. As a facilitator, I sometimes miss it until the drama of it becomes crashingly obvious. (My friend Betsy Raasch-Gilman has a better nose for it; I remember her cooking for one of my workshops and telling me in the kitchen, to my great surprise, that the group was getting ready to storm.)

Another reason this theoretical model relates to the informal life of groups: facilitators sometimes give participants lots of hours of free time at workshops with the assumption that participants use this informal time to "create community." Maybe, and maybe not. Participants may be doing good work in pursuing their learning goals, separately and together, but that's not the same as creating community, as one can find by uncovering the cliques and factions that arise during this time out of the room. To understand the distinction between "free time" and "community-building" fully, we need to look more deeply into the question of diversity in groups.

Part II

Diversity, Difference, and Emotions in Group Learning

Acknowledging Difference
to Accelerate Learning

A learning community, also called a high-performance team, has a steep learning curve. Facilitators and teachers want all our learning groups to have a curve as close to that as possible. We'd better understand what enables a group to go there.

The good news from the group development model described in the previous chapter is that what makes the chaos phase so intense is that people are fighting over difference. (They are also storming over the authority of the facilitator—more on that in Chapter 21.) When members of the group surrender, they are accepting the group as it is—*including the differences it contains*. In other words, when a group goes beyond its superficial phase of politeness to a deep acceptance of the differences within it, it frees itself for accelerated learning.

The only trouble is, many cultures strongly resist difference. Resistance to difference may become clearer through the following case.

Williams College has a history of support for tolerance and liberal values. I was asked to lead a workshop for students who wanted to take a next step in their own acceptance of diversity. I asked them to do a mingle.

"This will be a series of one-on-one encounters," I explained. "Just walk around and when you meet someone, shake their hand. One of you will say, 'A difference between us that I notice is...' and fill in the blank. The other will say, 'Thanks for noticing,' and you'll go on to someone else. See how many people you can greet with this formula. Let's practice it one time. The initiator, whoever it is, will say what? And the responder will say what? Great. Please, on your feet. Begin!"

With much giggling, the students moved around the lounge, expressing some of the differences they noticed. I was happy to see them outside their comfort zone, but they didn't seem to stray too far. After most students had gotten to everyone, I ended the exercise.

"What was that like?" More giggling and murmurs. "That was hard!" someone said, and heads nodded vigorously. "I found myself only saying the most obvious things, like somebody was wearing earrings and I was not." "I felt ridiculous because I couldn't say some of the things that occurred to me, and I just went for the hair style or color of their sweater."

"Anyone have any guesses about what makes that hard for you?" I asked. "It's no secret that we have a lot of differences here. Why not just say what they are?"

A thoughtful silence followed the question. A black student spoke up. "I'm the only black student here tonight," he said. "Nearly every one shook my hand and said something. Not one of you said you noticed I was black. I began to feel crazy!"

I asked students to turn to each other in small groups and wrestle with this question: What's at risk when we identify our differences? When they reported back, the discussion continued long into the night with an explosion of insights. What they didn't see as young people, however, and what is very important for their teachers to understand, was the historical context that makes an apparently easy task so difficult.

What's at Stake for a Society Troubled by Difference?

The 1950s in the United States was largely a period of cultural stagnation; one wag said the population was "God's frozen people." An exception was the emergence of a mass movement for change by African Americans. The ice pack melted in the '60s, and toward the end of the decade the center of the black struggle shifted from a freedom movement to a civil rights movement.

In 1969 the Stonewall rebellion in New York City launched a movement for gay liberation; as lesbians, bisexuals, transsexuals, and gay men began to break down the barriers in the '70s, the movement mainstream became a civil rights movement, eventually fighting to integrate into the U.S. army and marriage arrangements. The women's liberation movement of the '70s became, by the '80s, largely a struggle for equal rights.

In each case the interaction between the margin's liberation movements and the institutionalized power of the mainstream became an elaborate negotiation. It's as if the mainstream said, "We notice your vision is substantially different from ours and would require far-reaching changes in our economy, politics, and culture. We will consider rewriting the social contract to include your gender, color, or sexuality *if you will become less different*."

And of course those negotiations are not over; some members of the marginalized groups want equality without assimilation, and some members of mainstream groups don't want members of marginalized groups in power positions even if they swear they will, if occasion arises, kill millions by dropping nuclear bombs, just as if they were straight white men.

The societal difficulty about difference is profound and echoes in every classroom, adult education center, and workshop. Here is a place where our interest as educators—in accelerating the learning curve in our groups—puts us on the cutting edge of the culture. Insofar as we give our groups the experience of making peace with difference, we also make a contribution to coping with a fundamental challenge in the larger society.

Stephen Brookfield is a towering figure in adult education. He writes that the most fundamental changes in a learner's frame of reference can't happen unless the question of power is addressed (2000). Direct education offers a methodology for doing just that, by making power dynamics in the learning group transparent. By assisting a learning group to identify its mainstream and its margins and to make conscious choices about the relationships it wants, we promote an alternative paradigm to the outmoded melting pot paradigm. Sometimes a mainstream might invite a margin into itself, and other times that might be exactly the wrong thing to do—the group as a whole would become the poorer for it.

The vice president of a major corporation once told me about the wall that his company built between the research and development division and the other divisions of the organization. "In R & D," he laughed, "staff members work odd hours, dress outrageously, and do bizarre things we'd never allow in the rest of the company. Other workers shrug their shoulders and dismiss R & D people as 'those creative weirdos.' But we senior officials know we need to protect them and maintain their boundaries: R & D is our future."

"Jabbie" Williams, my high school social studies teacher, used to describe U.S. populists and socialists in glowing terms, even though he was teaching in the '50s when Senator Joe McCarthy's movement was inveighing against all differences including those presented by the left. "Those people on the fringes, outside institutional power, were the creative lifeblood of our democracy," Jabbie used to say. "Where do you think President Franklin Roosevelt got his best ideas?"

Differences Within the Margin

Margins have differences within them; many of us can get to work with those in a way that can accelerate their learning. African American colleagues Judith C. Jones, Ph.D., and Daniel Hunter decided to create a new Training for Change workshop that would support effective collaboration among black Philadelphians. They believed that the divisiveness they saw around them often sprang from the internalized oppression that usually shows up in marginalized groups.

Their workshop spotlights ways that black people stereotype each other, and themselves, and the role of judgment in that process. Knowing that you can't replace something with nothing, Judith and Daniel encourage their participants to replace judgment with curiosity. When participants see a behavior or an appearance that spins them into judgment, they're asked gently to set it aside and replace it with a different mental operation, generating questions to begin to reach into the experience of the other.

Judith and Daniel followed their own advice when working with a core theoretical piece of their workshop. They honored the classic racial identity model in the field, which is developmental and proposes that black people can move from stage to stage (Cross, 1971, 1991). However, they found some difficulty in using it for their workshop, because the model seems to assume that the stages go from "less than" to "more than," an arrangement of inferiority/superiority that could be problematic for Judith's and Daniel's goal of unity.

Asking themselves the Mindellian question, What's right here? they reframed the stages into strategies that black people use to cope as a margin dealing with the white mainstream. They used language that is relatively neutral—*fitting in, rebelling, building group pride,* and *bridging between margin and mainstream*—so that workshop participants could debate the pros and cons of each under particular circumstances.

The result? An adaptation of a well-known theory so that black people can acknowledge their differences, fight about them, and get curious about what led each other to their strategy. The learning accelerated.

What's a Mainstream to Do?

All of us carry some mainstream identity or other, even if we mostly identify with a marginalized identity. An African American may also be heterosexual, a woman also able-bodied, a transsexual also college educated, a Jew also a man, a Muslim also a professional. In our mainstream identities, though, we can be amazingly unaware of the experience, and sometimes even the existence, of the margin.

Mainstreams are indispensable—they do a lot of the work of holding a system together, whether that be a city, a co-op, a department, or the learning group we're facilitating. What makes trouble is that the mainstream is by nature clueless about the experience and perspective of unfamiliar margins. That wouldn't be a problem if it *understood* it was clueless, because then it could get curious, and ask what's going on in the system for the margins, and open itself to a different relationship.

The challenge for us as teachers and facilitators who want optimum performance for our learning groups is to assist the mainstream to see how clueless it is. I had this challenge some years ago when a city government asked me to give them a hand with a rapidly polarizing situation. Street confrontations between anarchist protesters and the police were escalating and the city was in an uproar. The staff member of the human relations agency who called me proposed that the anarchists use me for a workshop and that I give a separate workshop for city officials. He said it wasn't possible yet for both sides to get into the same room.

Having worked for many years with anarchists in various countries, I looked forward to facilitating the workshop for the city's anarchists on how they could make nonviolent direct action effective in reaching their goals. I was more puzzled about how to assist city officials to gain a new perspective and change policies that apparently were not working. I'll tell the story of that workshop in some detail so you can catch nuances that take longer to describe in expository writing.

The training room included the mayor, several city council members, the chief of police and other senior police officers, and senior staff from the managing director's office. They didn't look as if they wanted to be there, even less so when I formed them into small groups.

"Please remember an early time in your life when you were an outsider, when you weren't really in the center of a group. Maybe it was in elementary school, or Girl Scouts or Cub Scouts, or on the block where you lived. For some reason, you experienced yourself as not one of the in crowd. If several times like that come up, please choose one for this activity that you're willing to share. In your small group I'd like you to take a few minutes to tell your story."

The room buzzed nicely. We were over the initial hurdle; a container was beginning to be built.

"Now that you've all shared, I'd like you to remember what the in crowd looked like to you. What was their behavior like, those who were the insiders?... Please share."

The room buzzed louder, and laughter erupted here and there. When they were finished, I had them shout out the characteristics that they saw in the in group while I listed them on newsprint: arrogant, uncaring, self-obsessed, monolithic, superior, not knowing how powerful they are, out of touch with people not in their circle, clueless.

As I usually do after I harvest a list from participants' experiences, I suggested, "Take a look at this list as a whole. What do you notice?"

Silence. Then one of the officials gasped: "That's us!"

Animated chatter erupted around the room, which I had no wish to discourage. Then, "Do others see this list of characteristics as a mirror of how you might be perceived?"

"Perceived?" another official burst out. "That's how we often are: *arrogant, not knowing how powerful we are, clueless*. That's why we brought you here — we need to change!"

They worked hard the rest of the day to come up with policy changes and begin new initiatives that reflected genuine interest in the margins rather than demonizing them.

Mainstreams are simply that way, by nature. Whether it's city officials or the board of the co-op or the insiders in the university department or the leaders of a street gang or the in crowd of the local anarchist community, mainstreams show up as that list of characteristics! When individuals join mainstreams, they go unconscious and forget large chunks of what they used to know about life. No point in blaming them. It happens.

Our job as facilitators and educators is to maintain a perspective that supports everyone, margins and mainstreams alike, to stop hurting each other, to drop the judgments and get curious, to struggle cleanly for their points of view, and to learn, learn, learn.

But What About Oppression?

Shouldn't the group be confronted when oppressive behaviors emerge?

In most cultures, if you're not doing conflict, you're not doing diversity work. That's because most cultures suppress other than superficial differences, as we've already noted, and support their mainstreams in their cluelessness.

Back in the day, I believed it was my job to *incite* conflicts. As a white person, I was especially happy to name white racism when I saw it happening in the group and launch a confrontation. I also remember the satisfaction of being a man and confronting the men in a group over an incident or pattern of sexism that I saw being acted out. I liked proving to myself and hopefully others that I was truly an ally of oppressed people, since I was standing up for people of color when I called out other people on their white racism and standing up for women when I confronted other men on their sexism.

When I started using this confrontational approach, I was in the mainstream of anti-oppression trainers, so I had lots of company. However, when I took a hardheaded look at results I began to wonder how effective it was. Did this approach motivate proactive behavior or give people new skills? I stayed with the "calling out" approach for a while longer, because it really confirmed me as a fierce advocate for my cause. As a gay working class man, I especially appreciated chances to call people out in a workshop when they expressed homophobia or classism. This, I believed, was activism in the learning group: exposing the ugliness of oppression right in the here and now.

Evidence continued to mount that such confrontations led to little more than some behavior change, and often not much of that. Participants would visibly sink beneath the waves of their shame and feel too unworthy to call out for a lifeline. I could be obvious or subtle; it didn't matter: people reared in a shame-based culture went to shame no matter how subtle I was. Having been shamed will motivate people to try to behave better (so as not to get exposed again), so it does serve the goal of control. Does it move people to become proactive and creative in acting for liberation from the "isms"? In my work I wasn't finding the evidence that supported confrontation.

Sooner or later I also had to look at myself and the role confusion I was in. I tried to be an advocate, but I was in fact the teacher; I had the highest rank in the room. Confronting participants from the place of facilitator or teacher takes unfair advantage; it loads the dice because of people's learned attitudes toward authority. Participants who habitually deferred to authority would simply defer to me, no matter what actually moved within them. Who can call that a learning process?

Then there was the other reaction to authority: rebellion! Some participants became angry when I confronted them and shouted back at me, but I began to understand where that anger partly comes from: the scolded child, the teenager caught breaking a rule, the worker chewed out by his boss. At such a delicate, freighted moment when we need to pick our way through the scattered confusions of oppression, do I need to elicit the never-resolved rage of the harshly punished child?

And who is "minding the store" while I'm being an advocate—who is holding the container? When I leave my post as facilitator to lead the charge against evil, who will love the participants (and facilitator) so that emotions can be expressed within secure walls?

Many of us have, in every class we teach or workshop we lead, the goal of the empowerment of the participants. How do participants become empowered by witnessing the teacher calling out some students? If I'm a male facilitator calling out other men, I'm not actually modeling for anti-sexist men the skills of confrontation because my intervention is intimately linked to my authority as group leader, unless they can use these skills when they in turn take the role of boss or other authority figure. And what a model that is! I'm remembering the college where seniors call out juniors on oppressive behaviors, who in turn call out the younger students. The collegiate culture has one more pecking order, reinforcing dominance and submission, in the name of working against oppression!

An abundance of reasons fell into place once I accepted the evidence that trainer confrontations fail to reach their objectives—unless the objective is simply to modify public behavior and drive the attitudes underground.

And yet the trainers' intuition back in the day, that conflict is necessary, is correct. In direct education our alternative to *inciting* conflict is using activities and interventions to *elicit* the conflicts present in the group. How this works may be clearer with another example of the "speak-out" tool described earlier.

The University of Pennsylvania of the 1970s, when I was teaching there, was a socially segregated place. There were few African Americans, and those few protected themselves against pervasive racism by clustering together. My course came to be known to students of color as a safe and diversity-friendly place, so their numbers rose to one-third of the students. Each semester I took the whole class on a weekend retreat about halfway through, providing an even stronger container for the mainstream-margin conflict that needed to be expressed. The speak-out became one reliable method for eliciting the conflict.

I particularly remember one Saturday night when a dozen black students did their speak-out to the two dozen or so white students. The black students went all out, expressing their deep anger at the racism they encountered on campus and their determination to do what it took to maintain their dignity. The minds of the white students were blown, and I had the usual teacherly concern about how the class would reunite. After spending considerable time debriefing the white students, I touched base with the black students, caucusing on their own in the breakout room. I found the blacks deep into laughter and congratulations.

"How was the speak-out for you?" I asked the black students.

"Oh, you'll see" came an answer. "We're going to party *tonight.*"

I brought all the students together for a closing circle. The ritual was barely over when hot music blasted and the black students were calling the whites to dance with them. And of all the student parties I've been to, I've never seen people have a better time.

The rest of the semester revealed in multiple ways the deepened understanding of the white students and the increased assertiveness of the blacks.

To choose appropriate tools for eliciting conflict and accelerating learning, however, it will help to understand more about conflict styles, the subject of our next chapter.

7

Diversity and Conflict Styles

Cultures differ in how they teach people to relate to conflict. Some people are socialized to be fairly relaxed around open conflict while others are taught that conflict is dangerous; still others are brought up to accept some kinds of conflict and not others. Facilitators and teachers can navigate the issue of difference in their groups more skillfully if we know something about the cultural attitudes toward conflict that might be present.

This is particularly challenging for us white facilitators with professional identities, because we are part of the cultural mainstream, we get our norms and values accepted in nearly all settings, and we get to be clueless about how marginalized cultures operate around conflict. Our very understanding of what it means to lead and control a group is biased, so the way we typically do it is to allow white mainstream communication rules to dominate, typically shutting down the voices of other people who have a right to be heard.

In this chapter I will focus on the gap between African Americans and European Americans. Equivalent chapters need to be written about other groups, but my own experience is far stronger between these two, since I am a European American who lives in a biracial family with African Americans.

Regarding the issue of difference, the communication gap can be easier to manage for teachers when whites are not in the majority.

In a workshop where most participants were of color, I facilitated a first-session exercise called Maximize/Minimize the Value of a Learning Experience. The tool elicits self-responsibility and encourages mutual self-disclosure. When we came to the list of minimizing behaviors, one of the participants offered: "I let a condescending attitude shut me down."

At that point I said, "It occurs to me that condescension is an attitude I sometimes show as an expression of my racism. Sometimes my white racism shows up in a kind of patronizing or condescending way."

The group began to buzz with questions and concerns. Participants of color argued about what it might mean to them that the trainer was acknowledging his racism. White participants became silent, realizing that the work of the people of color needed space.

The participants of color gradually reached a consensus that I was OK as their facilitator and there was benefit to my being aware of racist dynamics.

The workshop went extremely well, with free and lively interaction by the participants of color as well as the whites. At the evaluation period in the end of the workshop, several participants of color remarked how refreshing it was to have racism addressed in the beginning, so the issue didn't come up again and again as it often did in other workshops they'd attended.

The fact that the majority of participants were of color plus my public acknowledgment that racism exists ("the elephant in the living room") opened up the workshop so that no one communication style dominated.

When whites are in the majority, however, it can be difficult for white teachers and trainers to support black participants to be authentic, if authenticity for them includes a traditionally black communication style. For one thing, most black people in the United States know how to adapt to white ways and fit in when they feel they need to. Some are experienced and comfortable in that style, while others adapt with an effort and feel relieved when they can return to their cultural home base and be themselves. When the late Barbara Smith was giving leadership to Training for Change, she would often come into weekend workshops that I facilitated and do the Saturday evening session. She was African American. We found that participants of color in the workshop relaxed and engaged in a fuller way when she facilitated.

What *Are* Our Cultural Assumptions About Communication and Conflict?

Ethnographer Thomas Kochman (1981) has brilliantly discerned widely different assumptions in his book *Black and White Styles in Conflict*. Much of his research was done in the city of Detroit, where he taught at Wayne State University. Kochman notes, and I would underline, that there is overlap with class in the analysis; assumptions labeled "black" are particularly true in working class black culture, while assumptions labeled "white" are particularly true in middle class white culture. An implication of this is that when we learn to teach in a way that fully empowers blacks to operate in learning groups, we'll also be relaxing the constraints on working class whites. I for one like that, since as a man brought up white working class I've often found myself hemmed in by the style common among white middle class people. Kochman is of course generalizing and the observations don't apply to everyone. I'll share some of his observations here.

Black culture prefers spirited, animated dialogue—argument— to get to the truth. Participants are expected to be right out there with their views, to take a stand, to show emotionally that they care, to listen to different views—discarding the points that were rendered invalid and coming right back with whatever pops up next. White culture prefers separating the person from the point of view, making statements in a more neutral and impersonal tone. Especially when an issue is controversial, whites often like to be low-key and blacks often like to be high-key.

The assumptions underlying these preferences are quite different. For blacks, assertive, vigorous, and emotionally rich argument is likely to result in greater truth. If we express our points of view strongly, we'll more likely get them either affirmed or discarded. Whites more often assume such argument results in ego-attachment and defensiveness. Then, whites fear, the proponents won't be willing to discard what's not valid in their points of view. Blacks generally assume that this kind of high-intensity dialogue builds greater unity between the arguers. Whites usually assume that such argument will result in separation.

The different ways that many blacks engage in controversy and that many whites do both make perfect sense given the very different assumptions that are being made. However, both sides tend to interpret the other's behavior in terms of their own ethnocentric assumptions. When blacks begin to argue strongly about some issue in the group, whites may assume the blacks just want to sound off and don't even care if the group or organization divides. When blacks hear whites talking in a low-key style about major issues like racism or poverty, blacks wonder how anyone can be so clueless or uncaring.

Another typical gap shows up in the length of time speakers take for their statements. Blacks tend to make one point at a time in discussion, because once the point is made, its validity needs to be tested in debate. Whites tend to talk longer because they often make a series of points, even analyzing in the style of a lecture or of a lawyerly brief. If the issue under discussion is important, blacks can get very impatient with a white "hogging the floor" and will finally interrupt, while the interrupted white becomes indignant and feels disrespected.

Kochman makes more points of the same sort in his chapter on classroom dynamics, which I wish every classroom teacher would read. The stakes are high for teachers and workshop facilitators because we are constantly making judgment calls when these communication styles collide.

If we consistently make our calls on the side of white cultural preferences, we've in effect taken sides in a culture conflict and given our backing to the dominant group in U.S. (and global) society.

Accusations of Racism in a Learning Group

Black participant: "I've been feeling a lot of white racism here and I'm sick of it. I don't know why I didn't leave by now."

Several white participants, sure they aren't to blame (heatedly): "What do you mean?" "I haven't done anything racist!" "How can you say that?" "Tell me what I did that was racist!"

Black participant, thinking to himself: "Well, I must be right, judging from *that* reaction."

Another black participant (who at first didn't feel the racism so sharply): "Come on, you guys, when are you going to face it—it's obvious."

In my experience this isn't such an unusual moment in the life of a group when it passes its honeymoon stage. Kochman helped me to see a whole new level of the interaction, however, in terms of the completely opposite interpretations that white people and black people tend to make of the very same behavior.

The characteristic black attitude toward an accusation made in the black culture, Kochman found, is "If the shoe fits, wear it." The expectation is that the person accused will show by their behavior whether the accusation is accurate. If they put up a big defense, they most likely *did* it. If they don't, they probably *didn't* do it. If they didn't do it, the accusation is like an arrow that missed its mark—there's no response needed because the accusation just didn't apply.

However, the characteristic white attitude is "If I'm accused of something and am innocent, I'd better raise a hue and cry, conducting a major defense. This is how I show that I'm not guilty as charged. If I don't defend myself, the implication is that I'm guilty, and even if others are guilty, I'd better show I'm an exception." The charge of racism may be directed toward white teachers and trainers, and how we respond may be assessed according to the black assumption "A big defensive protest means he's guilty." Kochman quotes the black proverb "If you throw a stone into a pack of dogs, the one who yelps is the one that got hit."

An exchange between blacks and whites can get heated quickly with completely different assumptions being made about the same behavior! We need to be able to assist people to sort out these differences. Once we understand the different assumptions underlying communication, many interventions will work.

A favorite method of mine is to move to the level of meta-communication, "talking about the talk." "Let's take a minute to notice what's happening here," I might say. "We seem stuck somehow, as if we're talking past each other. Anybody ever get to this place before?" (Hands.) "Well, let's slow things down a little bit to feel what's happening. It's OK with me to have a conflict—that's natural enough. Both sides have a lot to say, and I think it's great you want to say it. Is something getting in the way of hearing each other? Who has an idea about how we're communicating?"

An intervention as simple as that can assist the group to begin talking about the talk. The key is to have built the container carefully enough and created a norm of self-responsibility strong enough that participants will be able to work it out with each other, with our assistance. My part as trainer or teacher, I believe, is not to take sides with either culture but to hold out the possibility that there is room for a diversity of authentic reactions. On a good day, participants will get curious about each other. Then the learning starts.

Social Class and Diversity

Curiosity is abundant in small children. By the time people are adults, judging seems to have replaced curiosity as their primary mental operation. As an impediment to intellectual development, the loss of curiosity is particularly marked whenever difference appears.

In this chapter I'll share my suspicions about the influence of social class in making this happen, and challenge the role of academia in the process. I'll show how the loss of curiosity burdens adult educators, and what we can do about it. First, though, a case will bring us to the heart of the matter.

The college students said they wanted to go outside their comfort zones and do something tough, so I took them into downtown Chicago and had them take turns standing on a box on the sidewalk, street speaking.

The sun was behind the clouds that day and the tall office buildings didn't seem very welcoming. Pedestrians quickly walked by as we set up our box on the corner. Initially the students were terrified, but as they warmed up, they got into it. A crowd of passersby gathered. One of the white students spoke against racism, and I noticed a white member of the crowd becoming increasingly involved. "You guys don't know what you're talking about!" he said loudly.

"What do you mean?" asked the speaker.

"I've been driven from two neighborhoods by black people," the man said. "The first was the neighborhood where I grew up. Black people moved in, the crime rate jumped, the schools got bad — it was terrible! We had to move to another part of town, and then the blacks came and did it again. We white people are the ones who are oppressed."

"That's racist!" said the student. "You're completely overlooking the history of slavery. Do you realize that black people were brought here in chains?"

"Yeah, but that was then and this is now. If they can't live right, they shouldn't come into a white neighborhood," said the man.

"Millions died in the slave trade," continued the student, "and then they were forced to work and whipped when they wanted to rest."

"You don't know what it's like to have to worry about your kids going to a school where the black kids don't even know to shut up and study."

I began to wonder how to break the impasse. This was going nowhere.

"But you know who benefits from all this mess," the man continued. "I'm a member of United Auto Workers, and we know that this crap keeps the bosses on top. So in our union the blacks and whites work together because it's our necks if we don't."

"And even after the slaves were freed, they didn't get the 40 acres and mule they were promised. We whites have to take responsibility for . . . ." The student went on in the same vein.

A puzzled expression came on the face of the man, who shook his head and walked away.

Not until the students got back to the training room and debriefed did the student begin to see how locked in he'd been. In contrast, the heckler was ready to go to a layer of analysis where real dialogue could happen. Completely lacking in curiosity about this working class white man, the middle class student couldn't find a way to connect and learn from the difference between them.

It's not so puzzling that the student couldn't connect; all his life he'd heard that middle class people know more than working class people do. His college is busy training him to take his place among Those Who Know Better—not at all the same as the spirit of inquiry that his professors might hold as their ideal.

It might help to look at an adult education setting where another high-stress situation unfolded but the outcome was far different. Again, the details of the case are important in understanding the dynamics at work.

Community leaders came to an all-day retreat after the 2004 national election to learn about trends that would affect their work in the coming years. At midday they created a huge balance sheet on the wall: What social forces were pushing toward a more just society and what forces were pushing against? Everyone had already placed on the wall the forces as they saw them. Now it was question time.

"Someone has placed 'progressive white organizations' with other forces that are *obstacles to* a better society. Isn't that a mistake?"

"Who put that one up?" I asked.

A young black man in the back row, Kevin, put up his hand.

"I meant it to be there," he said. "Progressive white organizations are racist and even though they talk a good game, they're actually holding back the overall movement."

Silence. Kevin was a respected activist who'd given leadership in a number of campaigns. I looked around at the mostly white crowd and saw defensive faces, people trying to figure out how to challenge his provocative statement.

"That would be me a year ago," Markus said. I was intensely curious about what he would say. Markus was new to the area, an upper middle class white college graduate who had been doing community organizing in a poverty area with mixed racial composition. I knew he'd been working hard on his racism.

"Yeah, I can relate to what Kevin's saying," Markus went on, "because I've been part of mostly white or all white progressive groups and it's true, you know, we do put out a kind of atmosphere of exclusiveness. Nobody says to working class people or people of color 'Stay out!' but it's more a matter of tone. It's the way our organizational culture works; it's just not welcoming. And we do love the comfort of our white activist culture. It's painful to give that up, but we need to. Kevin's right. I definitely find it hard."

The discussion that followed was the most grounded conversation I have ever heard among whites in that kind of setting. It was thoughtful and probing because of Markus's intervention, his readiness to identify as part of the problem rather than defend white activists or, on the other hand, to point the finger at other white people. His curiosity about the possible truth in Kevin's statement led him to his comment.

One danger of talking about classism and other limiting beliefs is that we can easily lapse into stereotyping. In this example Markus showed us that it *is* possible to rise above class conditioning (maybe it's easier for a community organizer) and to honor one's own curiosity.

"Calling Out": A Classist Intervention?

Facilitators and teachers have an interest in dissolving practices that diminish learning. For that reason I increasingly challenge calling out when it shows up in courses and workshops. By "calling out," I mean publicly correcting someone who has said or done something that might be oppressive. In the past decade or two the typical young activist has learned to deal with issues of racism by confronting someone who is saying something that is in some way incorrect. It's especially important for a white to call out someone in the presence of people of color, because a white person needs to show that she is a worthy ally of people of color and can confront racism without the person of color needing to take that battle on herself.

In the workshop I just described, let's imagine that Markus hadn't been there. The more typical sequence of interaction would have been Kevin's statement followed by the defensive statement of a white person, followed by a confrontation with the defensive white by another white person who would explain how racist the defensive white had just been. Others would have leapt in to defend the defensive white who was called out, and around and around we would have gone—lots of heat, little light. Because, of course, zero curiosity. The spirit of the Judge would have had the full attention of the court.

Through looking at an organizational culture where calling out is rewarded, we can take another step toward understanding how classism undermines learning.

When I came to a small liberal arts college to lead a couple of workshops, I found a considerable focus on anti-oppression work. Students were eager to unlearn the "isms" that they'd been brought up with and to challenge all oppressive behaviors in sight. Their prevailing mode of challenge was, in their words, to "call out" the person who had by omission or commission done something wrong.

Before I facilitated a workshop for the student group White Allies, I asked them informally what they thought of the practice of calling out. The mainstream was quite sure that calling out was the right thing to do.

In the workshop itself I asked participants to form small groups and tell each other stories of a time when someone they knew had assisted them to a next step in giving up racist behavior. After they'd told their stories, I asked them what methods the other had used. At the top of the newsprint I printed: "What worked?"

They came up with the following list: humor, listening, being patient, being affirmed, giving me the responsibility for change and in that way showing trust, honesty, a balance of listening and sharing, showed faith in me, intervention in context of relationship (not just an incident), the actions and life of the person intervening, companionship instead of feeling alone, being pushed beyond what was believed to be limits, being pushed to explain what was going on, being called out, making a small change and gaining confidence to make bigger changes, staying with a long process that went from honesty to embarrassment (feeling stupid) to caution to being able to deconstruct racist beliefs.

Contrary to the students' belief and practice, their own experience gave a very different picture of what most often facilitates change. Where, then, did the belief come from that was guiding them?

Well, what is the system that is preoccupied with sorting, screening, correcting, and grading, to make sure that people get in line?

One system I know like that is class society. Economies created by class societies require a great deal of sorting, screening, correcting, and grading of people. In class society the job of the middle class is to manage the workers. "Somebody has to do it."

I watch this class expression unfold in workshops time and again: activists who sit alertly watching and listening for someone to slip up, ready to correct them at any moment for an oppressive behavior. In one seventeen-day workshop I worked with a few participants for fifteen days before they finally gave up the managerial role, relaxed, and took responsibility for their own learning!

The participants who most often take on this role are, significantly, from middle or owning class families or, if working class, have graduated from college and absorbed the values of management and control.

The abstract character of the norm of calling out is itself a giveaway. The calling out norm is not based on life experience about what works, as the students in that middle class college discovered in our workshop. Calling out is based instead on the *supervisor's duty of correction.*

I don't know any working class cultures in which people work against oppression in this way. Argument, yes—working class people are often more OK with conflict than middle class people are. But correction, no. I was brought up in my working class family to react to a smug or righteous correction with "Who do you think *you* are?" Meaning: "Who do you think you are—my boss?"

Despite the enormous contribution to the work of anti-oppression that goes on in academia—black studies, women's studies, gay studies, and so on—colleges also seem to be sending waves of young people into civic life who bring the entitlement of a boss's style of correction, with the disempowerment that goes with it!

Making Learning the Priority

Direct education's approach to what historically has been called anti-oppression work is to support conflict between mainstreams and margins and to go outside the participants' comfort zones, where curiosity has a chance once again to emerge. Some of the methodological elements have already been described in the book; more will follow.

Here are methods we've discussed so far:

- Build a container strong enough to hold the conflicts and don't suppress them through ground rules.

- Although we work steadily with the mainstream, we need to be an ally to the margins so they can find their voice and state their demands. Assist the mainstream to renegotiate its relationship with the margins and move toward equality and mutual respect.

- Assist all to identify with their mainstream identities and their marginal identities; introduce them to the complexity of the real world. Don't use complexity to short-circuit polarizations, however; stalemates are not growth-producers.

- Be aware when you are privileging mainstream communication styles and customs, and be transparent whenever possible. Acknowledge differences, even inside yourself when appropriate. Model a pro-diversity, pro-conflict, pro-discomfort attitude.

- Remain confident that storms pass and high perfor- mance may follow. When in doubt, strengthen the container through activities that support mutual self- disclosure.

- Trust the secret life of the group, and build bridges to it.

- Let go of the management job that class society assigns you, and instead mobilize your curiosity. It's a great way to live.

9

Authenticity, Emotion, and Learning

In all the cultures where I've worked or lived, laughter is the most socially approved form of emotional release. When participants laugh, they may be expressing a range of emotions: humor, pain, anger, grief, embarrassment.

If the curriculum of a course or workshop is relevant to participants' learning goals, they will feel feelings. It's inevitable. Participants only want to learn new knowledge or skill because there's something not working in the way they've been operating, and what didn't work has left some residual feelings.

One convenient test of the relevance of a design or curriculum, therefore, is how often participants become emotional. Other things being equal, *the more relevant the curriculum, the more emotional will be the learning group.*

Will the emotion be expressed? That question reminds us of previous chapters, because it has to do with the strength of the container. It is also a question about the culture of the mainstream in your course. A complex set of rules governs the social etiquette of emotional expression. Knowing these rules influences the effectiveness of a teacher or facilitator. I often depend on the sensitivity of someone who is a mainstream "insider" to help me plan activities that might elicit emotion.

In the '90s I worked in Russia with a Moscow-based training collective called Golubka. Any kind of experiential learning was new in Russia in the early days, and Golubka's workshops on democratic leadership and decision making were hot items.

I could tell, though, that most participants had ambivalent feelings about learning democratic practice. On the one hand, they were eager to put the bad old days of Stalinism and the Brezhnev stagnation behind them, with their corruption, power-over, and pretense of democracy. On the other hand, many felt some humiliation about losing status in the world of nations while the dysfunction of their country was exposed. Yes, they wanted to learn how to practice genuine democracy, but how could they know it would work in their culture?

We didn't have the container yet that would support direct work on the ambivalence, but it would have been foolish of my Russian colleagues and me to ignore the resistance to learning that was present. The participants needed to release feelings, soon! How?

I turned to the Golubka collective. "Let's do a skit with two parts," I suggested. "You sit in the middle of the circle, like a fishbowl that participants can observe. In part one, I'd like you to mimic the features of the worst meetings you've ever attended. If people start to laugh, exaggerate some more. You do need to be serious and stay in character. The more *they* laugh, the better. Then in part two, show them what a genuinely democratic group process looks like. Then we'll debrief. OK?"

The Russian participants nearly fell off their chairs laughing when they saw a lifetime of painful meetings unroll before their eyes. My Golubka friends were born comedians, and they played it to the hilt. After part two, we debriefed for the differences, which allowed the group to return again and again to the funniest parts of part one, with fresh gales of laughter.

The discharge of feelings opened the way to a high-impact workshop. The wet-eyed hilarity of those Moscow participants made space for something new, and they eagerly tried out practices in the workshop that might support democracy.

I happen not to be a comedian, and yet my workshops usually include a lot of laughter. I've found that groups will generate whatever they need to in order to laugh (to release tension if nothing else), and all I need to do is encourage it and affirm it when it shows up. Sometimes in the introduction of the workshop I'll ask: "Is it OK with you if we also have a good time?" That plants the seed, which blossoms with some watering and sunshine.

One group in a Vancouver workshop began to drop lines from popular songs into discussions to get laughs. I said, "You mean Hollywood has it right? People really do burst into song?" Without missing a beat, a participant gestured at the snow-capped mountains seen through the window and sang, "The hills are alive with the sound of music." The rest of the workshop, when we weren't taking scary leaps out of our comfort zones, was reminiscent of a classic Hollywood musical!

Suppression of Emotional Expression

Suppression of emotional expression comes from many sources. The teacher or workshop facilitator may not allow it. The mainstream of the group may suppress its appearance among the margins. Whole groups of people learn as children to repress their feelings to the point where they might not even know what they feel. An enduring archetype in the United States is the Tin Woodman in *The Wizard of Oz,* who suspects he could be real if only he could feel. An archetype in England is the owning class man who went to private boarding school during the height of the Empire and has as his prize his stiff upper lip.

Observation in hundreds of workshops leads me to the generalization that those who most rigidly hold back their feelings, who have most thoroughly mastered self-control, are those whose social position puts them in control of others. Whites (especially from parts of Europe that dominated other parts), men, heterosexuals, and members of the owning class are a few of the groups who have been required to learn to keep a lid on their feelings. Part of their preparation for controlling others (heterosexuals controlling homosexuals, owning class people controlling middle class people) includes stiffening their ability to control themselves.

In fact, their success in making emotional expression unavailable becomes a badge of honor and proof of their right to dominate. Historically, a white American man needed to keep the lid on his emotional expression (except for anger) in order to allay suspicions that he might be gay. Now that power relations are shifting between straights and gays, heterosexual men can begin to relax their vigilance and can go to gay men for makeovers and generate a more open style of self-presentation called the "metrosexual."

The habitual stifling of emotional expression is about control and domination. Those who enforce suppression tell us they are teaching us to be "appropriate." The habit of suppression is not, however, about appropriateness; parts of our population are taught from childhood that it is *never* appropriate for an adult man to cry or for an adult woman to express anger. It's exactly that rigidity which makes this issue huge for classroom teachers and for workshop facilitators. Rigidly holding back emotional expression prevents authenticity. *And authenticity is essential for deep learning.*

The accusation of "touchy-feely" is, therefore, a diversion, entirely beside the point. The question for learning groups is not simply "Can we feel here?" but rather "Can we be *authentic* here?" Authenticity supports learning, and pretense prevents it.

A generation gap that fractures many faith groups, civic organizations, and adult education centers is related, I believe, to this issue of authenticity. At first I was mystified in my multigenerational workshops to get feedback from young adults that they experienced the course as a "young people's workshop." I was surprised because I didn't do anything special to make it so. Then I remembered that one of the most frequent grievances of young people is what they experience as the pretense and woodenness of the older generations. Because direct education supports authenticity, the young adults felt the workshops must have been designed especially for them!

How to Support Authenticity Among Participants

Strengthen the Container and the Mini-Containers in the Group

I invite buddy pairs who want coaching to come to me during meal break to get assistance in building a stronger relationship. In gay men's workshops, depending on the workshop goal, I sometimes create small support groups and explicitly call them "families" to assist them to bring forward and work on family tangles they had while growing up. I coach the support groups as needed to strengthen their usefulness as containers for the men's work.

Participants' decisions to behave authentically in a learning group are strongly influenced by their perception of safety—not comfort. If participants feel safe enough, they will go *very* far out of their comfort zones, as you can see when you take a quality high ropes course or other adventure-based learning activity.

Support Projection of Feeling onto Objects

There's a variety of activities that do this; for example, ask each participant to draw on large sheets major events in their lives using the metaphor of a river, or ask each participant to bring an object into the training room that represents something important for their learning goal. As participants explain their drawing or object, feelings often rise to the surface and the container is strengthened.

Former Greenpeace trainer Nadine Bloch asked a group in which I was a participant to form small groups and take turns creating group sculptures. "When it's your turn, you will be the sculptor, so use the other members of your small group however you want. Lift their arms, arrange their torsos, show them with your face how you want their faces to be. Do it in silence. Take this chance to re-create, for example, a breakthrough moment in your learning to be a leader. After you are satisfied with the sculpture, thank them, sit in your small circle, and tell them the story which they represented with their bodies." Depending on the container present in each small group, deep feelings can rise to the surface.

Give Permission

One convenient way I give permission is to encourage yawning in my workshops. Contrary to myth, yawning can help people stay awake. We can use the fact that yawning is impolite to our advantage in building the container: giving permission to yawn increases the safety for other expressions deemed impolite. If a workshop has gone a little while with no one yawning, I'll yawn myself. That gets other people yawning, gets still others protesting at the violation of a social rule, and gives me the chance to give blanket permission to all to yawn at every opportunity.

Draw a Cognitive Map to Reassure Those Who Need Some Theory

I use the "comfort zone" diagram, explaining that learning actually happens when we're *out* of our comfort zones. I bring back the comfort zone concept here because those who have been conditioned against showing feeling will be uncomfortable, however pressing the feeling is. They deserve support to be real.

Watch the Margins in the Group and Encourage Them

Mainstreamers are rarely the first to be authentic in a course. This seems structurally obvious; the mainstream is the power center—in fact, part of the definition of a mainstream is that it ordinarily gets its norms to be accepted in the group. And those who would maintain control need to be in control of themselves, as we noted earlier. I've found the growing edges of authenticity, therefore, to be in the margins of workshops.

I certainly wouldn't tell the margins that they need to take on that job—the facilitator need not lay extra burdens on the margin. I nevertheless know that margins are the growing edges of any group, so I encourage their activities when appropriate so the whole group can shift. Toward the end of a break, for example, a few teenagers are dancing around the boom box as the other participants start taking their seats. "That looks like fun," I might say. "Care to teach us a little bit of it?" Then I'll invite a few of the more open older people to join me with the youngsters in making the moves, and then a few more until most of us are dancing. For some of the mainstream, getting out of their comfort zone with no disastrous consequences is an invitation to a next step of their own making.

"You Made Me Feel This Way!"

I was brought up to believe that other people can create and maintain my own emotional state. I've heard a thousand popular songs insisting, for example, "you make me feel so young" and "you made me love you—I didn't want to do it." This still widespread belief complicates a facilitator's navigation of the world of feelings in a workshop, as we work to create a safe place for authenticity.

Is it true that others can make a person stay in a particular emotional state?

No. We see evidence to the contrary constantly. Consider those masters of emotion, the movie directors. One person comes out of a movie with tears still in his eyes while another is saying, "What corny bullshit!" It appears that individuals make unconscious decisions about how to react to the same emotional stimuli. Even a dramatic crisis can't determine emotion. A disaster unfolds before the eyes of bystanders. One person freezes with fright. Another leaps into the situation, busily assisting.

In the classroom or training room we can easily observe how false the belief about controlling emotion is. You offer Stimulus A (a joke, an instruction, an open question). Observe the group. Some participants smile, some laugh, some are in pain, some are angry, some are curious, some are judgmental, and some are just bored. Maybe all of them can claim that you "made them feel" what they're feeling, but you know better. You offered Stimulus A. Each of them is responsible for her or his own reaction, and the reality is that she or he can change it if she or he chooses to.

The reason many people don't change their feeling states at will is because they believe they can't—they bought the idea that someone else can make them feel X or Y. Because they believe they aren't in charge of their emotional life, they appear not to be. For those of us committed to empowerment, this is a remarkably dangerous illusion that society labors to teach its members. If I still believed I am at the mercy of others' control of my emotional states—as I believed when I was a child—I would be giving away my power and shirking my responsibility for myself.

This fact is a closely held secret in many societies, where people have bought the fiction that others are constantly controlling them by managing their feeling states. People may not give up that belief easily; there's some comfort in not believing in our own power. For many it takes unusual self-awareness, years of psychological or spiritual training, or a large degree of self-confidence. A learning group's design and facilitation, however, can make a big difference. If we emphasize self-responsibility and build a container safe for a *range* of feelings, participants more easily see through the cultural hoax that they are puppets.

Warning: The Caretaker May Appear Along with Authenticity

The Caretaker role can show up in any workshop along with the Rebel, the Know-It-All, the Goody-Two-Shoes, the Earnest Puzzler, the Enforcer of Political Correctness, and other typical roles people play in learning groups. These typical roles play out more dramatically when the container isn't strong enough and when the participants haven't realized yet that this is their chance to go for a breakthrough on their learning goals. However, if you decide to encourage the participants in your learning groups to be authentic, when feelings start showing up, someone is even more likely to do a star turn as Caretaker.

Caretakers fill up so much space with taking care of other participants that they sabotage their own learning and that of others. Typical acting out includes touching another participant who is crying (When did the crying one ask to be touched?) or rushing across the floor with tissues. It may include staying up late nights taking care of others, getting overtired, then getting sick. It may involve preoccupying themselves with whether the workshop design and facilitation is meeting the needs of others. For example, I remember a workshop in which a caretaking mainstream went into an uproar about the facilitators' perceived neglect of two participants who used wheelchairs, and, finally, when someone thought to ask those participants for their own perspectives, we learned that the people using wheelchairs were doing splendidly!

One thing we can do as teachers is to model our belief in the participants' own power and individual ability to take care of themselves. When we do that, however, be aware that Caretakers may become irritated, disappointed, or perhaps even angry that facilitators "aren't taking care of people." I suspect an unconscious game being played by Caretakers that implies a contract: "If I make my central purpose the taking care of others, then I will be taken care of by others. My needs will be met, therefore, because others (especially the facilitator) will take care of me. I'm entitled to being taken care of because I have chosen Caretaking as my role."

I remember a chorus of protest that erupted in a leadership workshop of mostly women when I, the facilitator, admitted I didn't *care* if the men were overparticipating and talking over the women!

"This is a leadership workshop," I said, "and the women here need to learn how to stand up for themselves in the face of male domination. You can do it. And if you choose not to practice, it's on you." The women and feminist men in the room spent fifteen minutes raging before they got to a place where they could see that my facilitation choice was actually on the side of women's empowerment.

Caretakers often get support from other participants when they try to reorganize the workshop into the contract they like best: "Instead of self-responsibility, let's all take care of each other." One reason other participants may support Caretakers is the prevailing assumption that "I am at the mercy of others' emotional control of me." Actually, if I believed I am powerless about my emotional life, I would want a Caretaker, too!

The fact that Caretakers sometimes tap into other participants' illusory belief encourages me as facilitator to reach out to potential Caretakers from the start. I often place in front of the room the guideline "Take care of yourself so you can take care of others." That plus "Use everything for your advancement" gives me leverage for clarifying when the Caretaker starts to undermine the learning of himself and others.

The other thing I do as soon as I realize we have a Caretaker among us is to find out from him what his learning goals are, and then frequently check in and redirect his attention to what he came to learn. That's his real job. And mine to support.

It's also important to ask whether the Caretaking role may be acted out because the container is not yet strong enough. Inside myself I sometimes thank the Caretaker who is like a canary in the mine shaft, pointing out a lack of safety. I can then shift my design to strengthen the container and invite the group to do so as well.

To promote authentic behavior and therefore optimize learning in your class, build a strong container and support people to express their emotions. Boredom will be a relic of history.

What About the Facilitator's Emoting in Front of the Group?

At times a teacher is deeply moved by something that comes up in the course. If it is ever appropriate for us to show strong emotion in front of the group, when and how might that be? A specific case reveals in detail the considerations that guide me.

The leadership development workshop included a large cluster of welfare mothers, from an anti-poverty organization in Boston. I was glad the workshop was designed for an entire weekend: the container took time to build because of the contrasting styles and life circumstances of well-off suburbanites who were also in the workshop.

By Sunday morning we'd moved into the zone where both container and self-responsibility were in good shape, so I suggested we have an Open Sharing, which is a time when participants can share whatever is in their hearts. Open Sharing is a tool that usually takes the workshop deeper and, diagnostically, reveals what most needs to be addressed in the remainder of the workshop.

"This isn't a discussion time," I explained, "and it's fine if we sit in silence for a good while. It's OK to share insights, or gratitude, or puzzlements, or disagreements. Just so it's coming from the heart. Let's see how well we can listen."

"I'm sitting here thinking about my son Jeffrey, who's twelve," said an African American woman from the anti-poverty group, after some silence. "Really, I want to be strong for him. I want him to grow to be a man, and so many of our boys don't make it."

My gut clenched. My own son, an adopted African American boy, was one of those who didn't make it.

Tears came into the eyes of another African American woman. "I was thinking just the same," she said. "We're here learning as fast as we can how to take leadership in this dumb-ass society, and I just hope it can make a difference for my boy. So many boys I know are in jail or drugged up or just dead."

Mom after mom spoke, not to discuss others' comments but simply to share their worry and grief. Most of the group had wet faces. "Our boys … our boys." By that time my heart was breaking. I'm a grieving dad, but I'm also the facilitator.

I do a rare thing, for me. I let myself cry along with the group, keeping a diligent watch the whole time on how things are going with the mainstream and the margins, the possible emergence of someone who — fearful of this intensity — will try to distract the group. I find I can maintain eye contact with everyone and still allow the tears to run down my face. I'm careful to cry less intensely than most of the others: it's their group and I don't have the starring role.

By staying in touch with everyone, I can see that a meta-communication is now needed: "It may be that the deep and generous sharing this morning helps those whose children aren't in such danger to gain new understanding."

The heads of suburbanites nod.

"We don't always sign up for a workshop expecting to get to this place," I smile, wiping my eyes. Grins break out on faces of the African American women. "You got *that* right!" one of them said, and laughs surfaced.

Tissues were passed around. "It's Sunday morning and wouldn't you know we'd be having *church!*" someone said.

More laughter and jokes followed. "Time for our break," I said, stretching. "Might be useful to check in with your buddy."

This story reveals how I navigate those moments: my first priority is facilitation, not self-expression. If I'm clear that I can do both, I'm careful that my expression of feeling is low-key compared with the others.

I don't expect these circumstances for a facilitator to happen very often. I'm grateful when they do.

Part III

Designing Learning Experiences

10

Structures for Organizing the Content

The late Harvard sociologist George Casper Homans once remarked that we gain our understanding of the world through a series of successive approximations (1950). He was certainly describing how I learn about complex phenomena. I first get a very simple and superficial picture. I then add more aspects and the picture grows. With new angles and connections, the picture gets closer to how things really work. As I play with it in varied contexts, my image becomes still more complex, and I'm able to make sense of more and more of what it is I'm trying to understand.

I'm happy with a series of successive approximations, even grateful! Intelligence is making connections, and I make the connections as I'm ready to. It's OK with me that, in my first encounter with a body of knowledge and concepts, I don't immediately get it all.

When I first began to teach college-level courses I didn't see the value of *teaching* through successive approximations, even though that was in fact how I *learn!* I used to identify the body of knowledge at its appropriate level of complexity for the course, and then I organized the information by abstract categories that were in some way logical.

I relied quite a bit on logic. I often started with definitions. That way of starting suited me personally, because my theoretical mind understood the multitude of considerations that go into choosing a particular set of words as a definition.

Unfortunately, that choice was all about me, not about the students. There was no way the "field's" definitions could make sense to most students at the start of the course. I would give a bit of reasoning to support particular definitions, but to be honest, I was asking them to accept my definitions on faith. And, indeed, even though I believed at the time that I was engaged in a very rational exercise, in fact I was inviting the students into a venture of faith: faith in me, and in the field, and in the institution that backed us up.

Finally I discovered the joy of teaching in alignment with how I—and others—actually learn! I gave up faith-based teaching. I rediscovered the delight of encountering a body of skills and knowledge led by my curiosity, *as someone who cares about some aspect of a field for my own reasons and wants to extend my knowledge of it.* There's even a classical phrase that describes this natural human process: "the pursuit of knowledge." Someone, somewhere must have known that what goes on in education when it is real is not the *receipt* of knowledge, but the *pursuit* of knowledge!

"Peeling the Onion"

A metaphor could be useful here. I like "peeling the onion." It's a working class image and avoids the possible pretentiousness of "a series of successive approximations." It taps the kinesthetic learning channel as well as the visual. It's active, not passive, and invites discovery. The metaphor affirms us when we humbly start at the beginning, because we can be pleased that we are starting: the top layer is worth peeling for its own sake, and it also presents the next layer for scrutiny.

In a diverse learning group—as I've argued earlier, all groups are diverse—the metaphor also levels the playing field. Each of us, no matter how much or little experience we have with the topic at hand, is still challenged by the layer of the onion we're wanting to peel at the moment.

The onion is not only a metaphor for a complex, multilayered body of knowledge; it is also a metaphor for the self and our own layers of resistance and passion as we encounter the juiciness of the quest. It assists participants in a learning group to understand that if there are thirty participants in the room, there are also thirty workshops, and they have the responsibility to peel their own onion to discover how to fully empower themselves in relation to the knowledge in this particular field.

Building curriculum around the onion metaphor opens the teacher's mind to catch "teachable moments" that inevitably show up in a group with a strong container. Using the onion metaphor explicitly in the group opens a pathway between the participant's private and public work in the class. The teacher or facilitator might offer to assist a participant "to peel her onion" in front of the group through a series of open questions; participants don't usually find it intrusive once the metaphor is out there. Onion peeling is a homely metaphor, and it elicits the interest and solidarity of the other participants. They know that each has an onion to peel—layers of incorrect beliefs and energy needing to be liberated in order to reach a learner's full potential in using the field's concepts and skills.

This way of thinking about curriculum excites me because it invites empathic imagination: What *are* the successive layers of approximation through which participants' understanding of reality becomes ever more accurate and complex? Then, how to design activities that will lead to deeper layers of the onion? And how can we tap into the corresponding layers of the participant's own challenges and goals?

How does such designing work, in practice? A brief adult leadership seminar for the United Nations will show how thinking through successive approximations of content yields a concrete design. I knew that the participants would have different amounts of knowledge and experience with the subject matter. I wanted all of them to get to "peel the onion."

The United Nations Institute for Training and Research (UNITAR) asked me to fly to Geneva, Switzerland, in 2001 to lead a workshop for thirty indigenous leaders from six continents. The subject: nonviolent strategy. The time allotted: three hours. I've taught a graduate course on this subject and considered I'd only scratched the surface! What could usefully be done in three hours?

I decided realistic content goals would be for them to understand what distinguishes nonviolent action from other forms of struggle and mobilization and also what are the three different applications of nonviolent action, since such an understanding could be useful for their making — in their own situations back home — the beginning steps of strategizing.

I flew to Geneva one day early so I could get to know the participants, who were already at work on other modules in a UNITAR seminar on conflict. I interviewed most of them informally regarding their own experience of struggle; I discovered there was already the beginning of a container. Thus prepared, I could create a design; I'll italicize the layers of the onion to help track the levels of approximation.

First we played a game, to strengthen the container and acknowledge the kinesthetic learners who had been marginalized in the seminar up until then. (I prioritized the previously ignored kinesthetic learners throughout the design.)

We then created an experience in which I stood next to the flip chart and the participants shouted out any images and associations they had with the phrase "nonviolent action." I wrote as quickly as I could. We reflected on the list. I circled and linked some images and noted that those related to Gene Sharp's definition (1973), which I didn't claim was correct but only that it would be convenient if we used the same one for this workshop. The more multicultural the group, the more lightly I treat definitions, which are a swamp even in homogeneous groups. This generalization step narrowed and sharpened their initial images and associations — *the first layer of the onion.*

In small groups, participants then shared nonviolent cases they'd heard of, including in their own history. We harvested the results of the small group work in the whole group, then did some work comparing and contrasting — a kind of generalizing step. A debate ensued on some of the cases, which of course I welcomed. I allowed the rising energy of disagreement to spur us on, rather than offering closure through giving my expert opinion. And so we reached the *second layer* of the onion. We might tag it "There are many cases in our histories as indigenous peoples of this thing Gene Sharp calls nonviolent action!"

In the whole group of thirty we returned to experience, doing a Parallel Lines role play (sometimes called a "hassle line") with one of the lines acting out abuse. The other line's job was to halt the abuse nonviolently. After reflecting on which were the most effective of the tactics they tried, we generalized this form of action and gave it a name: "third-party nonviolent intervention," one of the applications of nonviolent action. What made this the *third layer* of the onion is that it introduced a new cognitive step: characterizing a particular kind of conflict that nonviolent action can be applied to.

The group container was growing rapidly (thanks especially to the role play), so I grabbed the momentum and generalized some more; I explained that, in addition to the application of third-party nonviolent intervention, there are two other applications: social change and social defense (*fourth layer*).

We'd now reached my curriculum goal — intellectually — but it would be illusory to believe that the concepts were now internalized. Participants need to work with ideas to get them; as John Dewey said, "We learn by doing." We needed a step of application. In this case, as so often, the application is a new experience. Continuing my concern to reach to the neglected kinesthetic channel, we did an activity I invented for this workshop, the Applications Relay Race.

At the end of the previous day's conversations with participants, after learning about the conflicts that they were facing in their own localities, I formulated their conflicts into situations of one or two sentences each and came up with twelve situations. I put each one on a separate card. Because I decided to divide the group into six teams to run the race, I made duplicates of the cards so that each team would have the same set of twelve conflict situations.

Six teams of five formed into lines for the relay race. Each team chose a name, and the names were reported to all, accompanied by some cheering. A race is exciting in many cultures! The target of the race was the series of four posters placed on the far wall, headlined Social Change, Social Defense, Third-Party Nonviolent Intervention, and Unclear. I gave each relay team the set of situation cards, with the challenge: "In this situation, would you use a nonviolent change strategy, nonviolent defense strategy, third-party nonviolent intervention, or isn't it clear?"

On a signal from me, the first card was read by each team. As soon as the team made its choice, its first member dashed to the far end of the room, attached the card to the appropriate poster, and raced back to look at the next card. Again the team rapidly decided which application would fit the situation described on the card and dispatched a new runner to dash to the wall.

The teams competed energetically despite the heat of the afternoon and finished within a short time of each other. All cheered, and I asked them all to go to the far wall and note which cards had been placed in which category. After some buzz at the wall, I led a discussion in the whole group standing at the wall that compared and contrasted the different choices, generalizing and sharpening theory. We reached the *fifth layer* of understanding the three applications and their relation to each other.

Returning to their seats, participants eagerly listened to my own judgments about which situations go with which nonviolent applications. Sometimes I was challenged about my own choice, and through discussion we realized that strategists can sometimes choose different applications for the same situation, depending on how they choose to *frame* the struggle in light of a variety of variables (*sixth layer*). Interest was high as participants considered what to do next when they returned home.

In a three-hour seminar we went from a vague scatter of images of what nonviolent action might be to a working conceptual framework that analyzes nonviolent action into three applications. Further, we discovered there was not always an automatic match between situation and application — useful to the strategist's fundamental task of framing.

We peeled six layers of the onion, and the group had fun doing it.

Modules Versus Threads in Curriculum Design

In longer courses in adult education, or, for that matter, higher education, the content of a course can often be divided into modules and threads. Modules, often called units, are the rice and beans of curriculum design. When Daniel Hunter and I organized a prototype three-week curriculum funded by the United States Institute for Peace for training unarmed civilian peacekeepers, we assumed that we would use the module approach (Hunter and Lakey, 2004). We happily began to organize the curriculum into modules, then found, to our surprise, that some kinds of knowledge are not best learned that way. Some chunks of theory and practice have two more requirements: they need time to "simmer" on the back burner of consciousness, and they need the addition of other ingredients (knowledge chunks) to reach the textures of wisdom required for application.

In our particular curriculum we considered that, for example, exploring issues of culture and rank, learning the state of the art in team security, and developing conflict skills in immediately threatening situations are not best taught through a module. Treating such subjects as "units" assumes they can be explored and sufficiently digested in a single unit of time. All the content needs to be learned through a series of successive approximations, of course, but we found that some content needs to be addressed, then set aside while other, related content is addressed. When the learners have gained the larger context through learning related content, they can then revisit the first subject with a larger cognitive map. Then we can build in a stronger application step through simulations and lab work. The result: more internalization of nuance and complexity.

We call such areas of content "threads," as in a tapestry in which a certain color thread appears, disappears, then reappears in another figure, thereby enhancing the meaning of the whole. (You'll notice that I, in trying to describe our process, use different metaphors to try to reach different kinds of learners among the readers. Deriding mixed metaphors, although popular and fun, ignores learning theory!)

Although inserting threads is a complicated way to organize a curriculum—relying simply on modules is much easier—Daniel and I found it stimulating and at times even exciting to thread the various content areas at intervals through the days and weeks of the course. It was intellectually exciting because the connections the participants were invited to make became more abundant and also more accurate in terms of real-life situations. It enabled us to go beyond the onion, which as a metaphor takes us designers to a much better place than linear logic does, but still leaves "content" conceived of in an epistemologically simple way.

One of the values for the learner that we saw in trying out our threads was confidence building. We saw how the periodic reinforcement of gains made, for example, by a conflict-aversive participant trying to learn immediate conflict skills, could increase her confidence and deepen her creativity in dangerous situations.

The curriculum ended up with four modules and seven major threads. In the facilitator's manual we are very transparent about the curricular structure so that other educators can try the module-and-thread approach for creating their own curricula (Hunter and Lakey, 2004).

The Model of Experiential Education

Peeling the onion provides a model for organizing the *content* so the participants gain, step by step, a deeper and more complex understanding. That model doesn't, though, explain how to organize *learning activities* that deliver the content. For that I rely on the classical four-step model of experiential education developed by David Kolb (1984). Training for Change facilitator Betsy Raasch-Gilman describes how she used this model in a short workshop with the goal of teaching collaboration skills in a team. I'll insert the labels to identify which of Kolb's steps she's in.

[Experience] I invented a simulation exercise around playing poker. The game is simple and brief: I make a chart of the winning hands in the card game of poker and post it on the wall. I then divide the participants into teams of four or five and deal each person two random cards. The assignment is for each team to come up with the best possible poker hand, given the cards they hold. They have to do so in silence, however. I don't set it up as a competition among teams, although if the group gets competitive, I debrief that, too.

[Reflect] My "unpacking" questions highlight the ways in which people work together: "Did anyone have an ace to start off with? Did you think, 'Oh, good! I have the highest card! Everyone will be glad to see my ace!' That's kind of like coming into a meeting with a really great idea or proposal, isn't it? And then what happened?"

Usually participants report that the ace is only valuable in combination with the other cards — if it's an ace of spades and everyone else has diamonds, it's no good. "So has that ever happened to anyone in a meeting?" I ask. "That you came in with a good idea, but it didn't really fit where the group was at? How did you let go of your idea and work with the rest of the group to come up with the best solution to your problem?"

I also use questions about leadership — who seemed to decide on the final hand and how did they check for final agreement, especially without using words? I can also highlight group maintenance behavior: "How did you know that others welcomed your ideas and were taking them seriously?"

[Generalize] I often follow the poker game with discussion and handouts about democratic group process, inviting participants to tell stories and play "stump the facilitator" with their worst experiences.

[Apply] Then I move into a role play, so participants can try some of the skills they just learned. I generally write out roles for the role players on little slips of paper. Most people are not particularly confident about acting, and I want to give them as much support as I can. I don't put in every possible negative or troublesome role; in a group of six or seven players I try to assign three substantive roles and tell everyone else to play themselves as they would normally act. The situation I choose for the role play is moderately challenging and not terribly complicated, so that they have room to improvise.

This sequence—experience, reflect, generalize, apply—is relied on increasingly by teachers and trainers around the world because it produces the most consistent results for empowering the participants to use what they've learned. Activist and professor bell hooks (2003) has pointed out that much of the early anti-oppression educational work has been disappointing because it is based on the assumption that if participants change their picture of reality, behavior change will follow. Not true. Stopping with the third step in the model leaves the learning incomplete. Add the application step in order to increase the chance of behavior change.

In the workshop for indigenous leaders in Geneva, Switzerland, for example, starting with the word-association exercise, the cycle went experience-reflect-generalize; experience-reflect-generalize-*apply* through the relay race, where the concepts were used in relation to concrete situations from the lives of the participants. We then treated the application step as an experience and proceeded to reflect and generalize from *that*. The four-step experiential education model, it turns out, can be a cycle.

At the end of the UNITAR session, the participants and I went outside to relax in the shade under a large tree with immense spreading branches. A conversation immediately started about the role of women in society. It became animated and then heated, as some participants sprang to their feet, gesturing vigorously, verbally attacking the women and the one feminist man who argued for gender equality. There was no backing down on the feminist side, and the arguing became so loud that a staff member came out of the building and rushed to my side.

"George," she said, "please stop this. You see, it's becoming violent!"

I, a relaxed witness to the fight, explained to her that there was no danger, and that the group was simply doing good work.

The dinner bell interrupted the group, and we slowly turned toward the dining room, joking and laughing about the argument, with a few people getting in their last digs. I asked a couple of participants for their analysis of what was going on. "We've been building up to this struggle about gender for a couple of days," they said. "It needed to happen."

"But why *now*?" I asked.

"Obviously because of your workshop," they laughed. "We were just putting it into practice!"

The Four-Step Model Is Essential
for Multicultural Groups

The experiential education model levels the playing field for multicultural groups. Consider what a generalization is, such as "Elites are rapidly integrating economic activity on a global basis," "Social classes develop cultural characteristics deriving from their life situations," "Homophobia is closely connected with sexism," "Power-over (domination) fails to mobilize the full productive energy of a group." The core of generalization is, of course, abstraction. Abstraction is a wonderful thing. It anchors the knowledge in the cognitive map of the learner. Once the concept is anchored and located in the learner's way of seeing the world, it becomes more accessible, both for recall and for sharing.

The way we communicate about abstractions in learning settings is, though, through a language. That's exactly the problem! Clarity of language is up for grabs in a multicultural setting. What words mean is strongly influenced by cultural background, and your understanding of a set of words might be different from mine if we're from different cultures. The more we teachers care about precision, about really accurate understanding of a concept—sometimes it becomes a matter of life or death to trainees—the more we have to face this unhappy reality about language: it is a murky swamp!

The experiential education model gives us a big hand with this problem. Starting with *experience*—the common ground of the learning group, because it's something they go through together—the teacher can work with reflection (Step 2) in a way that maximizes the chance that, when the generalization step arrives, the group is linguistically on the same page. It doesn't mean that disagreements are to be avoided in Step 3, that participants won't have splendid arguments about the utility or even rightness of a concept. However, it does increase the chance that they will be arguing about the same thing.

Application: Where the Rubber Hits the Road

The fourth step, application, serves the participant and the facilitator. Both find out whether a concept was internalized. If not, the concept can be addressed again in a different way. Some teachers want to race ahead to the next item in the curriculum no matter what, which sinks motivation for everyone; it sends the message "That last chunk wasn't important enough to learn thoroughly, and probably this next chunk won't be either." The notion that a syllabus needs to be covered—no matter what—might be the single greatest delusion in traditional education and a major reason why so few adults recall much of what they learned while they were in school.

Application also builds the skill linked to the concept. In adult education, knowledge nearly always has some use; otherwise we wouldn't teach it. Using knowledge involves some skill or other. Solid educational designs provide an application step for skill development.

The application step itself becomes Step 1 again—an experience—which for full value requires reflection and generalization. Paolo Freire (1972) insisted that it is in the alternation of action and reflection that we learn best. People get stale when they either act without reflecting or reflect without acting. When we use the experiential model for design, we are teaching on a meta-level one of the most important lessons of all: a methodology for lifelong learning.

Applying Experiential Education Now, to This Book!

A book is a limited instrument for learning. I love books, and at the same time I am aware as I write this one that words on a page don't serve well those with other learning styles.

One thing I *can* do, though: I can use the experiential model's insistence on putting the experience first in the sequence. Instead of leading with the generalization step, I can introduce the concepts in this book through recounting stories; after all, the story is an experiential teaching tool used since ancient times, and successful teachers still rely on it. The story as Step 1 not only offers vividness and sometimes drama; it usually conveys more detailed information than expository writing in the same amount of space! That's because a story can be layered, implicit, suggestive in its details.

A story invites the reader's reflection, for nuances and shades of meaning not immediately apparent. When I read other people's case accounts, for example, I find myself asking, "What was going on for the facilitator at that moment? What impact did that first move have on the participants' responses later? What diagnosis led to taking that risk? What might have been the downside of that move for a margin, or for the mainstream? How might I have done that differently? Given my cultural and other background, is there an equivalent kind of move that I could have made to get that result? Here the facilitator is using a tool familiar to me but tweaking it in an unusual way—what impact might that have?" And so on.

For some readers the rest of the book might become harder to read; they might find that deconstruction of the stories is challenging, although I hope they will find it rewarding. For other readers the rest of the book might be easier to read because they like getting "launched" into a concept by a story. For both kinds of readers, I hope the stories will result in your wish to try out the ideas for yourself to see how they work for you. Just as the model suggests, I hope that starting with experience will bear fruit in application.

11

Building on What the Learners Know

"Now that you all have glasses in your hands, I will take my big pitcher of water and give you some," said Ouyporn as she moved into the crowded workshop.

Ouyporn Khuankeaw is a facilitator who breaks new ground in leadership training in Thailand. She's pouring water into glasses held by the participants.

"Ah, I see this glass is empty. I will give you some of my water. And your glass, too. I am so happy to have such an abundance of water to give you. You, too, may have water from my pitcher. Another empty glass — I will fill it."

She continued with her patter until she filled the last one. "Please go inside yourself right now and be aware of your feelings.... What was that experience like for you?"

She waited. "There is a second part to this exercise. In this second part, you have permission to give each other water from your glasses. Please stand up. Now begin."

At first hesitantly and then with growing confidence, the participants moved around pouring water in each others' glasses. Smiles appeared, then giggles. The room came alive with participants smiling and pouring, some more, some less.

"Please stop where you are. Go inside yourself again and be aware of your feeling state.... What was this second part like for you?"

She waited. "Still reflecting inside yourself, I'd like you now to compare the second experience with the first experience."

She waited again. "Now you may sit down."

A tremendous buzz emerged as participants found their seats, carefully holding water glasses, some of which were alarmingly full. "What did you notice?" Ouyporn asked.

The debrief was animated and full of insights. Finally, Ouyporn asked, "And if this little exercise had anything to do with education, what would it be?"

After accepting a number of comments, she said, "I started the workshop this way because so many of you believe education to be worthwhile has to be the teacher lecturing, pouring to you from her pitcher. I want you to know that, in this workshop, we'll use the second method. I hope you will be willing to pour and to receive from each others' glasses."

During the break I asked Ouyporn about her experience with this exercise. "I nearly always need to use it," she said, "because Thai education has been corrupted by Western imperialism even though we were never a colony. My people have been brainwashed into thinking that they are just empty glasses. That's the educational model in the West. But in this exercise they are reminded of their real-life experience. In Thai communities we do rely on each other, and collectively we are very smart when we share. My task is to legitimate what participants already know, and build on that."

I'll risk a bold generalization. In my country, as in Thailand, *participants in a learning group already know much of what they need to know in order to move ahead.* We teachers and facilitators will do our best work when we proceed from this assumption.

The value added from the teacher is only partly the content we present in the course. Our larger contribution is in our ability to assist participants to access the knowledge that is already present in the group, to generalize from it, and apply it. This principle may be my most outrageous contradiction to the assumption most educational institutions make. Fortunately, I have experience being outrageous.

Does this mean that an effective teacher can be ignorant of the subject? No, her or his knowledge matters a lot. Contrary to conventional thinking, the best way to use our knowledge is usually *not* to present it. Its best use is to inform ourselves how the participants are doing as they pursue their learning goals. Based on this diagnosis, we can devise the additional activities that will enable their success. We can't assess how they are doing and assist them to reach their goals if we don't know the field.

"Knowledge is power." That's precisely why it is the knowledge held and discovered by the participants that leads to empowered action. This is direct education.

A teacher's warming up her or his own knowledge and dispensing it once again is indirect education, Part One of the Water Glass Exercise. Indirect classroom education is not famous for leading most participants to empowered action—or even being remembered a year later.

Who Holds the Knowledge?

Does this principle mean that each *participant* has most of the knowledge that's needed? No, it means that the knowledge is *within the group*. The reader may know of the NASA Moon Survival training game, a simulation in which small groups work simultaneously to solve a problem that might be encountered by an astronaut on the moon (see Appendix D for more information). Before the small groups set to work, all the participants try to solve the problem as individuals. The small groups then tackle the same task, to be done within a time limit, and each group is required to reach consensus in solving the problem.

At the end the scores of the small groups are tabulated and compared with NASA's solution. The individuals in the small groups also compare their results with the NASA solution. The individuals then compare their scores with the consensus-based score of their team. What they find, in the large majority of cases, is that a group is smarter than the smartest individual within it!

The boldness of our maxim—the group, together, holds most of the knowledge it needs to move forward—raises another question: Does this principle mean that the group can access the knowledge it needs before taking the workshop? Not likely. For one thing, groups rarely know how to access fully the knowledge and skills that lie within in the group, often because of poor mainstream/margin relationships. For another, the facilitator/teacher generally notices something valuable that's missing, often on a conceptual level. The indigenous leaders that the UN brought together wanted to know how to strategize about nonviolent action and had a lot of information already, but they didn't know that nonviolent action has three different applications with implications for strategy.

Direct education is centrally about assisting participants to share powerfully and affirmatively what they already know and to make new discoveries and inventions supported by a collaborative group process. Direct education uses the group's momentum to add needed pieces of the teacher's knowledge to it. In this chapter we'll focus on activities that build on what learners.

Elicitive Tools: The Instruments That Make It Possible

Guided by knowledge of the field, the learning goals of the participants, and the obstacles that get in their way, the experiential teacher or facilitator works with a large and growing collection of activities that elicit

- knowledge

- skills

- wisdom

- curiosity and wonder

- creativity

- humor

- empathy and solidarity

- rebellion

- critical thinking

- action

The oldest elicitive tool is probably storytelling, which might have been used around campfires in Neolithic times. The most complicated elicitive tool may be the simulation, done elaborately by modern armies in their war games.

An array of elicitive tools that I've found travel well across cultures is available for free at www.TrainingforChange.org. Each chapter of this book draws from the elicitive tool chest. See Appendix D for more leads to effective tools.

Open-Ended Questions: The Bread and Butter of Direct Education

In other cultures the elicitive question might be called the rice, or pasta, or cornmeal of direct education. It is a staple because the other elicitive tools usually need questions to function well, especially for debriefing in the reflection and generalizing steps. Questions also work fine by themselves.

An elicitive question is *not* a probe to get the "right answer"; it is not your seventh-grade teacher asking what year the American colonists declared independence. In direct education the facilitator asks the question knowing that understanding involves peeling the onion, so various answers are entertained to support the group's peeling. One way to support the process is by making a list on newsprint.

A facilitator might ask, "How can leadership make a difference when a group or society faces a crisis?"

The group offers answers: "By reassuring them because some people are scared." "Offer creative solutions to the problem." "Negotiate with those who are posing the threat." "Confront and punish whoever is threatening." "Promote unity." "Get people to do research and develop a plan." "Remind people of their biggest values." "Mobilize people to act." "Prevent scapegoating." "Get people headed in the same direction." "Lead rituals that help people feel their feelings so they don't dump on each other." "Organize resources and channel them to the priority places."

The group goes on and what at first seemed a fairly straightforward opportunity for leadership to step up has become highly complex. A participant asks, "How can all that be done immediately?" The group has begun to peel the next layer of the onion. The facilitator gets to throw in concrete examples like the U.S. response to Hurricane Katrina; pieces of theory; connections to the group's own experience when electricity failed for a few minutes during the previous session; and an observation that so far it's been mostly the men making the suggestions on the newsprint list.

This example shows how intimately the elicitive question is related to the curriculum. The stronger the container and therefore the freer the group is to be its diverse self, the more the responses will include some that are out of the box and provoke deeper thought. A feminist might say, "This shows that one leader can't do it all—nobody can handle all that. Our culture sets us up with wrong expectations—it's the patriarchy again!"

Usually the elicitive question that launches the group is followed up by questions that prompt the group to take on another layer of the onion or, if the group deflected itself to a different subject, to guide them back to the onion they were peeling.

I usually prepare my major questions ahead of time so they will elicit a juicy group search for knowledge and elicit other behaviors on my list above including creativity, humor, and critical thinking. I've found questions that use the word *why* can more easily elicit premature philosophizing than *how* or *what* questions (What are some characteristics of …? What lessons could be learned from …?).

Elicitive questions accelerate learning because they prevent the teacher from going over material that most of the group already knows—participants teach each other much more quickly than logic-controlled teachers do—and they help keep the group alive rather than tuning out. They also provide a powerful diagnostic opportunity for the facilitator: we find out where the group is in several respects, including who might be on the margin at the moment.

Tools for Challenge

Adventure-based learning (ABL) is an elicitive toolbox that shows what makes direct education so direct. The activities are also called "group challenges." They are mainly used for leadership development and team-building, but variations of them can be used to teach an astonishing variety of content areas (Nadler and Luckner, 1992).

In a group challenge the facilitator gives the group a task to accomplish along with the rules. Often the task is to get the group from one point to another, in a particular formation, through a set of hazards. The group needs to organize itself, develop a strategy, and implement it in order to achieve success. All along the way there are multiple opportunities for the group to show its skills and effectiveness, and also what it needs yet to learn.

Adventure-based learning tools empower kinesthetic learners. In most learning groups kinesthetic learners expect to be marginalized and may not work hard because they don't see how they will be able to achieve excellence. ABL plays to the strengths of kinesthetic learners and supports them to participate more fully in all aspects of the course.

Challenges are attractive to direct educators because they enable the facilitator to bear down on the specific learnings that *this* group needs to gain. In traditional education, groups are expected to cover a chunk of knowledge even though they may already understand half or more of it; that's one reason why traditional education is usually slower than direct education. I've been with groups that have raced through a particular challenge because the task didn't put the group on its edge and then taken a long time with another challenge because the group acted out what it most needed to learn—how to acknowledge diversity, for example, or how to communicate clearly, or how to access within itself the expertise in spatial relations needed to solve a problem.

As the teacher gets to know the group and what its growth edges are, the teacher can choose ABL activities that will challenge the group to learn more. The activities also provide flexibility for the teacher to use different metaphors in the debriefs, which in turn lend themselves to different aspects of theory when the generalization step is reached. The activities provide perfect opportunities for the teacher to build on what the participants already know.

12

Learning Difficult Material

The United Mine Workers called all their field staff east of the Mississippi to West Virginia to help lead the part of the Pittston Coal Company campaign that took place in the coalfields in 1989–90. Although this was one battlefront among several, West Virginia would be the site of the mass participation by workers, their families, and their communities. I was learning their history as rapidly as I could and discovered that just after World War I there had been an open war between the miners and the U.S. army, with violence escalating to the point of bombing from the air. Miners I met were proud of their history of standing up for themselves.

The union hired a motel to be the site of the training for the field staff and other leaders. It was early spring and the weather was still raw in the early morning when I arrived. I knew the union was counting on my colleague Nancy Heskett and me to do a good job with these fifty people, because they would in turn work the seventy-hour weeks persuading the rank and file that nonviolent strategy was worth an all-out commitment.

"Honestly, I'm resisting this training, George," a senior UMWA staff member told me during breakfast. "I went into the mines as a teenager, and you know mining coal was not a sixteen-year-old's idea of fun. In the winter I'd hardly see daylight, because by the time we got out of that hole in the ground it was dark."

"We youngsters used to look forward to a strike," he continued, "because we could really have fun. We'd throw rocks at the scabs, sabotage the company trucks, start fires, keep our squirrel guns handy, and basically raise hell." His eyes were sparkling with the memories. "I loved that kind of strike, man, with the violence in the air. For us that was a relief."

He paused and shook his head. "But I know those days are over. That kind of strike doesn't work any more. So,"—he looked me straight in the eye—"teach us nonviolence."

"OK," I grinned. "Nonviolence as a last resort."

We both laughed.

The hardest material in the workshop was the strategic concept that nonviolent struggle is political rather than a fight over turf. I tried my metaphor of guerrilla war versus conventional war, pointing out that guerrilla war strategy isn't about holding the hilltop once captured but is instead about winning the hearts and minds of the people. Nonviolent struggle is in that way like guerrilla struggle, I said. Even though most of the participants were military veterans, to them the metaphor was like hearing an abstraction trying to clarify an abstraction — hardly compelling.

As it turned out, the role playing was how they opened to the theory. First we role-played sit-ins in the company offices. The "sit-inners" were to be neighbors in coal-mining towns. Other miners played the roles of company office workers, police, and media. The sit-inners did a great job in their role except for one thing: when the police came to arrest them, they grabbed hold of desks and wrapped legs around chairs. As the police tried to disentangle them and pull them away, the scene degenerated into confusion. Obviously, in the minds of those role-playing sit-inners, this struggle was about turf!

In the debrief, Nancy and I asked every elicitive question we could think of that might assist the participants to discover how turf-bound they had become. I resisted my urge to share my knowledge about strategic theory, a big urge for a published author. Just as I was about to give up and give them a mini-lecture, one of the miners playing a TV journalist said, "You guys gotta know that, from me lookin' through my TV camera, you didn't look nonviolent at all."

Howls of disagreement erupted. "You don't know how much I wanted to slug a cop, buddy! I was definitely nonviolent."

"That's the point," rejoined the "journalist." "I *didn't* know. All I could see through my pretend-camera was what looked like a fight. And that's what people will see in their living rooms."

Silence. From that point the discussion turned to the importance of keeping the Pittston campaign focused on winning allies rather than holding turf. I saw them sharing their insights with each other, but suspected the learning was still superficial.

"Let's go outside!" my co-facilitator Nancy said. "It's time to explore another situation."

We went into the motel parking lot where we had prepared a couple of miners and a truck. "That truck will represent a Pittston truck sent to pick up some materials. Your job will be nonviolently to stop the truck from reaching its destination, which is over there."

The truck proceeded toward us and, without discussion, the participants rushed to the front of the truck and leaned against it. Picture over forty former football players, still in shape, pushing against a pick-up truck. Smiles appeared when they realized they were winning as the driver gunned the motor. I heard someone count, "One, two, THREE!" and the men grabbed the truck, picked it up briefly, and moved it a few inches. Now they were grinning broadly.

"One, two, *three!*" Again, a few inches more. The men were actually turning the truck around!

I've never seen people more elated than those miners after they'd turned the truck around 180 degrees to send it back where it came from. Slapping backs, laughing as the sweat poured off them, they headed back inside the motel for the debriefing. I was exhilarated and also in a state of mild panic. How do we extract from their "victory" the strategic dysfunctionality of obsession with turf?

Of course the first step had to be self-congratulations, and we had a prolonged and lusty cheering session. I was as thrilled as they were at this demonstration of coordinated teamwork, even though worried about what they would conclude from it. We encouraged more reflection on what they did well, punctuated by jokes and sidecracks, knowing that what Arnold Mindell calls "the primary process" needed to be honored before anything else could happen.

Finally one of those role-playing the media spoke up. "You guys, I know it was fun and all, but I gotta say you didn't use what you learned from the office sit-in."

This time a bit of shock entered the silence, as though this miner was spoiling the party.

"Be honest," the miner continued. "You know Pittston can get its damned truck in even if it takes the National Guard to do it. We're not going to win this campaign by stopping a truck here and there."

"He's right," another miner said after more silence. "We gotta remember we're in the spotlight. We have to play to an audience and win them to our side. What we did was fun [a chorus of laughs] but let's think again how to stop trucks so people get what we're about."

That was when I knew we'd done our work, by setting up the role play so there was a "media" representative who could feed back to the group information about the message — important to any group that is trapped inside its own perspective. The container was strong and the participants were taking responsibility for their learning. The UMWA had a good chance of winning because, in consultant jargon, they'd become a learning organization.

And they did go on to win.

What Is Difficult?

For most adults difficulty is not just about complexity or level of abstraction; it is related to how well the thing to learn fits within their belief system. In fact, there are points of theory that can be expressed in clear, plain language and still be tough to learn, even by people with advanced degrees. Many of the highly educated foreign policy experts in the U.S., for example, found it nearly impossible to learn during the Vietnam War what the coal miners in the workshop learned that day of our training. Even after reading theory held by North Vietnamese leaders, many U.S. experts still failed to grasp that the struggle in Vietnam couldn't be reduced to "turf."

During that war I was told about a revealing party conversation in the U.S. Embassy in the South Vietnamese capital of that time, Saigon. A U.S. military officer was bragging to a French journalist about the number of battles the U.S. was currently winning. "Yes," replied the journalist, "and I've noticed that the battles you are 'winning' are closer and closer to Saigon."

The journalist was using a metaphor to try to catch the attention of the officer: it's time to learn why, in your "winning," you are losing! The U.S. power holders did lose their Vietnam war and set up, a generation later, another round of mass death and destruction in Iraq and Afghanistan. Their priority to "control the turf" went awry yet again. The discourse of the experts supporting the invasion of Iraq even ignored the importance of nationalism—hardly a new concept for understanding the world for the past couple of centuries. The belief system shared by most U.S. foreign policy makers simply does not support the learning curve that they need.

My experience teaching at Swarthmore College helps me see a different source of difficulty. Super-bright people (my students are brilliant) can fall into a habit of apprehending a theoretical point without going on to *comprehend* it, that is, without connecting with its implications.

At first I was impressed by my students' eagerness to seize new principles ("Nonviolent action can overthrow dictators") and file them away for easy access during testing or discussion. Later I realized that their quickness also allows them to avoid considering the fundamental assumptions and attitudes they walked in with. For the students who can mentally run around the block four times while I'm walking around it once, what's difficult for them is to confront their own worldview, to ask, for example, "How does this proposition contradict what I've been told since I was a child about the nature of power? What does it mean for foreign policy decisions by my government? What does it mean for my own conduct as a citizen where up until now I've been amazingly compliant?" The same mental quickness can encourage a student who values equality to leap into political correctness without opening to liberation.

The advantage the mine workers had that day over foreign policy experts and academically bright students was a container that supported them to struggle deeply with a hard lesson and listen to their peers break out of the old paradigm. Struggle—we come to that again. The need to struggle for a hard learning poses yet another question for the facilitator, a question illuminated by the following stories of success and failure.

What Does It Take to Learn a Hard Thing?

The Russian human rights group wanted to become stronger to face a growing climate of repression in the period after 2000. My job was to use team-building tools to increase cohesion and democratic participation. I thought the most important piece of theory for them—and most difficult to learn—would be Arnold Mindell's mainstream/margin (1992, 1997). In this book I introduced that concept in Chapter 4, even though I realized that many readers might respond with a quick "Right, of course, it makes sense that groups don't thrive by ignoring their margins." Readers might not push themselves deeply to *comprehend* the theory and apply it to the groups they are a part of. It was vital for these Russians to internalize this theory deeply, however, because the continued existence of the group might depend on it. They would need to struggle.

Because direct education points us first to the materials the group brings, the opportunity was plain as day: the workshop included a "hard core" of participants who had been in the human rights group from the beginning, and also a bunch of "newbies" who had been in the group for only a year or two. After opening with a diversity welcome, I acknowledged the existence of the veterans and the newbies, and asked the former to come inside the larger circle and sit down. "I will make a challenge," I said. "You in the middle have the job of inventing some way to take account of the difference in the group between you and the others."

First the protests: "We want unity, not division." "Why should we make a point of our difference?" "Give us exercises that will enable us to move on." "We hired you to build our unity."

Then, since I remained unmoved by their protests, they faced each other. "Let's just move back into the circle and show we're together." "But it doesn't take account of the difference, which is what George said we should do." "Let's give them a history of what we've done together, so they'll feel more part of things." "But that's just about us, not about them."

The discussion in the inner circle went through cycles of creativity and boredom, hope and despair, with seemingly no ability to agree on anything. The outer circle largely stayed engaged in watching and listening, although of course the margin had its own margin. Finally, after an hour of frustration, a subtle shift took place. Shoulders relaxed and a suggestion was made that found ready support. The core members rose and moved to be parallel to the others, then circled around, greeting and welcoming each person and asking questions of them. The behavior of the core for the rest of the weekend was highly responsive to the newbies, because they had been through a struggle and made a decision.

The amusing part for me came a couple of hours after the opening struggle. I pretended I was a lecturer, walked solemnly to the flip chart, and said, "I want to inform you that every group has a basic dynamic: it has an inner group, called the mainstream and an outer group on the margin." The participants burst into laughter, began to banter with me and among themselves, and showed in every way that here was a fundamental piece of theory—finally named—that now lived within them.

My next project on that Russian trip was to gather with nongovernmental organizational trainers from the eleven time zones of the former Soviet Union. Knowing that there was also, in this loose network, a core of more experienced people and a periphery of newcomers, I decided to do the same exercise.

It flopped.

Frustration rose as the mainstream resisted the task, and the margin grew ever more alienated. On one level, I realized that the mainstream was replicating the behavior of the larger system: Russians were warring with Czechnya and, in sometimes less brutal ways, refusing to renegotiate their relationships with the margins. On the workshop level, however, I watched the mainstream, composed mostly of people I'd known for years, refusing to try something new. I finally realized that the challenge was too big and devised an honorable way to move on.

It took me a while to figure out the critical difference between these two groups, both composed of culturally similar NGO workers. The first already had a substantial degree of cohesion, a high stakes mission, and a menacing threat on the horizon. The second did not have those sources of motivation. The mainstream in the second case just didn't care enough to create a new relationship with its margin.

My mistake as a facilitator in that situation was *overlooking the importance of motivation in sustaining a struggle to learn hard material.*

Perhaps if I'd waited until after a couple days of whole-group bonding through exercises and sociability, the mainstream would have motivated itself for the struggle. It was another lesson for me about the trickiness of what appears to be a simple concept; what looks easy to apprehend on the printed page can be much harder to comprehend in a way that makes a difference. For another thing, I clearly had more to learn about the art of sequencing in supporting learning.

13

Sequencing for Maximum Impact

"I want you to design an unusual kind of retreat for the Women's Prison Association," Ann Jacobs, the executive director, said. "The consulting firm that does most of my work won't do it. They say it can't be done, but I believe it can, and I believe you can design something that will work."

Puzzled at the request, I looked at the phone's handset as if the answer was there. Why me? New York is full of consultants; I'm in Philadelphia. "What's so unusual about the retreat you want to have, Ann?"

"Well, I want the board to be there and the senior staff of course, and beyond that I want a slice of the entire rest of the staff: program staff, support staff, even kitchen people and maintenance staff. That will include former clients, because we hire former clients when possible."

Ann's agency assists women who've been incarcerated get back on their feet, and that requires a range of services including temporary dorm living, day care for the children, case management, and advocacy. I began to understand what her consultants didn't like about this.

"Not only that, I want a representative number of current clients there, and also a couple of senior people from rival agencies, and an independent expert or two from our field. Forty-five, fifty people."

I responded with a low whistle. "Let me guess. Nobody can put that much disparity of rank in a room together, all the way from wealthy board members to poor women of color clients, and from senior staff to maintenance, and make anything productive happen. Right?"

She laughed her agreement.

"I can give it a shot. But why me?" I needed to know this because Ann loves trainings and participates in a range of them. She knows how they work and what's possible. We'll be working very closely together if this actually happens.

"That weekend training of yours that I went to in East Village," she began, "you remember that you put us in practice groups on Saturday afternoon? I was shocked when you told us later that you went out of the building and went browsing in bookstores while we worked in the practice groups! Then when I thought about it, I realized you knew that we'd turned onto our sense of responsibility, and we didn't need you. Out of the box, right? That's why I'm turning to you now. I need your belief in what people can do under the right conditions."

Designing a Workshop with Rank in Mind

To create this design I didn't use a different process from what I do to prepare a two-hour workshop in the neighborhood—I just did each step more elaborately, to prevent differences in rank from shutting people down. I did a series of interviews with a cross-section of the staff and clients to find out how much they were on the same page with the retreat idea and what they wanted out of it. I spent more time with Ann to understand her goal, which was to gather the wisdom of the whole system to inform choices needing to be made for the future of the agency. In a way, it was the pre-work you might want to do before creating a strategic plan. She wanted the diverse perspectives of the stakeholders, but she wanted those perspectives to interact with each other, all in about half a weekend! And knowing the tremendous cultural diversity in her agency, she wanted the people to interact freely, so the flavors of their differences would have room to mingle.

After clarifying the goal and interviewing a number of participants, I did what I usually do: I brainstormed a list of favorite tools/activities that might be relevant to this design. (Sometimes my list doesn't look long enough for this particular task, and I skim my favorite sourcebooks for more activities that might possibly be useful.) Once I have my list, I feel more confident, even for a daunting workshop. To me, the list says "abundance." I'm always more confident when in touch with abundance.

The next step is sorting, which is an invitation to myself to be powerful and make choices. As the reader can see by now, designing is a creative process, and each teacher may go about it in an idiosyncratic way. The way that works for me is summarized into a series of steps in Appendix D. The principles of design, however, are valid no matter what our individual style. This story illustrates some of those principles.

I sorted my list by some key criteria:

- Are there activities that will give everyone a chance to shine, no matter what their background or rank?

- Are there activities for auditory, kinesthetic, visual, and emotional learning channels?

- Are there activities that can be adapted for the differently abled?

- Are the container-building tools suitable for a variety of cultures?

- Are there activities that invite participants to self-responsibility?

- Are there activities that allow for expression of the emotions people have going into the retreat, especially anxiety?

I drew a blank when it came to one of Ann's objectives, which was to get perspectives on the macro political picture of criminal justice trends. I knew of no activity for this objective that wasn't academic in tone and wouldn't put half the group to sleep. Fortunately, my Canadian colleague Karen Ridd teaches a method for inventing new tools for moments like this, so I invented a new activity that included a tug of war, eliciting participants' understandings of the fierce conflict that rages in the field of prisoners' rights and so-called criminal justice.

Satisfied with my massaged list of tools, I took the next step: putting the tools in sequence. Some trainers like this step the best. Veteran facilitator Betsy Raasch-Gilman writes, "What I love the most about design is letting my imagination roam. If I ask them this question, what do I think they'll come up with? What if they don't?"

Another experienced facilitator with Training for Change, Matt Guynn, writes, "Workshop design is one of the activities in life in which I am able to become most absorbed and lose myself! In design, I become completely focused on the intention of the workshop and the needs of the participant group. The most powerful design incorporates each activity into a powerful sequence that has intentionality in every choice. How can the introductions, the opening activity, the closing for the first evening all contribute to the goals of the workshop? I love it!"

Where to place which activities in a sequence is a judgment call, and teachers and trainers can enjoy debating the pros and cons of each placement. Some criteria are fairly clear, however: put high-energy activities after lunch and dinner (when group energy sags), put easier activities earlier, and put harder and more uncomfortable ones later when the container is stronger. In this design I need to pay extra attention to the container, because of the huge differences of rank in the room.

Although the unfolding of the content of the course or workshop (or, in this case, the retreat) has an influence, I'm not very interested in a sequence being logically sound! I'm extremely interested in its being *psychologically* sound. If participants are strongly engaged, working with the material on a deep level as they go, there's time for linear integration (logic) later. It's something like life: now that I'm an old man, I get to integrate what I've learned in my life and make sense of it, for example, by writing this book.

In preparing for Ann's retreat, I checked for variety in the design:

- Am I overusing one size of small group?

- Is there variety of placement of kinesthetic, visual, auditory, emotional tools rather than a clustering together?

- One especially emphasized by Judith Jones: Is there a pacing of self-disclosure, so participants won't worry about feeling overexposed? Differences of rank will show up on this one, too.

- Am I addressing the typical energy curve of a workshop (begin medium, go up, then go down to reach its lowest point in the middle of the event, then go up again)?

Now I'm close to finishing the design. I still need to think about rhythm, however. As Duke Ellington wrote, "It don't mean a thing if it ain't got that swing."

The Rhythm of Differentiation and Integration— and Rank

Learning groups need times when the participants are all together and times when they are divided into subgroups (or individuals). The first is integration; the second, differentiation. Those two phases are so natural I see them wherever I go, even in dinner parties and car trips.

Every group needs this rhythm, just as much as the individual needs to inhale and exhale. Differentiation is expressed in small group activity, pairs, individual work, and even sizable caucuses. (In a group of two hundred, a caucus of fifty is differentiation!) Integration is expressed in whole group activity.

If a teacher doesn't provide for this rhythm in the design, the group will create it anyway. A teacher who tries to hold a class in its whole group format will, if sharp enough to notice, see that participants start to zone out after a while—they simply need to differentiate. Asking humans to inhale exclusively is a fruitless enterprise!

Because of the huge differences of rank in this group, I took special care with the rhythm of differentiation/integration. After the brief introductory part, the design went right into differentiation, to give the various categories of people (wealthy, white, Upper East Side board members; formerly incarcerated, poor Puerto Rican women) a chance to experience safety with others of their kind. After exhaling, the participants would be ready to inhale and do a substantive whole group activity.

The activity was mixing it up with people of different ranks to do a task, so it was integrative in nature—"inhaling." To make it easier given the meager container, I put them into small groups to accomplish the task. The small groups presented their product to the whole group in the form of skits, and since skits reliably encourage a measure of fun, the atmosphere of safety built rapidly.

The next morning opened with mixed small groups—again, that blend of integration on an easier-to-handle level—then went to a whole group exercise to further develop the integration of the whole. I recognized that the design had included a couple of integration moves in a row, so I planned that immediately we would move to differentiation. After that activity we turned again to integration through a whole-group kinesthetic activity that included tension and drama (the tug of war). The design continued to alternate the rhythm of differentiation/integration to the end, when the retreat closed with a circle of integration.

Using the Resource of Days and Nights

I persuaded Ann to start the retreat Friday with supper, ending Saturday at the end of the afternoon, rather than an all-day-and-evening Saturday format. On Friday evening, then, I placed the anxiety-releasing activity: creating skits on "my worst fears about the agency." The small groups that invented the skits were a mixture of the various kinds of participants, so they could do a task together that didn't privilege those with more schooling or other sources of social rank. The skits turned out (as usual) to be hilarious, and the laughter provided a useful (though partial) release of anxiety.

During the design work I drew in from Training for Change Dr. Judith Jones, who agreed to co-facilitate the retreat. There was no way I could facilitate such a complex retreat on my own, and Judith is a great match for me: we have different styles and because of our race and gender differences we see and hear different dynamics in the room. Our differences also mean that more participants are able to identify with at least one of us and give us the benefit of the doubt as we take them further and further out of their comfort zones!

Judith and I were outside our own comfort zones as we watched the large group gather for Friday supper, and it didn't help when we met one of the regular consultants to the agency who had turned down the job because "it couldn't be done." He told us he planned to stay the whole time to observe. No pressure!

As it turned out, the participants were ready to share, and open to discovery. The design principles revealed in this chapter allowed the potentially threatening issue of social rank to go from foreground to background, and board members and clients alike participated enthusiastically. Ann got the outcome she wanted: wisdom from the whole system for planning the future.

Goals Determine Design and Facilitation

It's useful to post the goals for a course on the wall for the first session. I explain that the participants may have their own learning goals, and I hope they do, so my stated goals simply make transparent what guided me to my design.

Some participants will understandably ignore my stated goals; at that point the container is thin, after all, and participants are wondering how they fit into the group, not what might be going on in my head. Later some will get upset because I haven't included this or that which they imagined that I would. It helps to be able to point to my statement of goals hanging on the wall.

I'm careful not to set more goals for a course or workshop or retreat than I can easily carry in my head as I facilitate it. If I'm running low on time, the goals influence which activity needs to be dropped to end gracefully and not out of breath. Goals influence how much I might choose to prolong a debrief in order to make sure that the group has a chance to "get it," or whether I'll add another activity to give them another chance to internalize the learning.

I hold myself accountable to the stated goals of the workshop, whether negotiated with a client or created by me. The goals support my inner sense of confidence and authority when the group is acting out in some way. I also need the goals to evaluate the workshop. I read participant evaluations in light of my goals. I experience my goals as my friends rather than my taskmasters; I wouldn't want to design without their support.

The next layer of the onion called "accountability" needs peeling, however. A commitment to working outside the comfort zone—designing for edginess—raises further questions about the teacher's accountability, the subject of the next chapter.

Accountability in Direct Education

I happened to be at the door when the young doctor arrived. We were about to start a workshop in the large living room of my house, one of my favorite training venues although I don't facilitate there often. The doctor and I met in Zimbabwe, but he is from the United States. Enthusiastic about medicine, he's also enthusiastic about training and had long planned to come to one of my training of trainers workshops.

"Stephen," I say, "welcome to the workshop—I'm so glad you're here. But you look exhausted!"

He manages a grin even though he is bleary-eyed. "You'll never guess the week I had," he says, "extra shifts in the ER. But I was determined to come this weekend. Where's the coffee?"

I catch up with him over supper and suggest he take a nap before we start. "No, no," he says, "I'll be OK. You'll see."

What I see when the training begins, however, is everyone getting off to a good start except Stephen. He's the margin. I decide to make an intervention.

"You may find that the format for this workshop is strange for you," I say to the group. "I believe that we learn best when we move into being authentically who we are in the moment."

Heads nod, including Stephen who is propping himself up on a sofa between two other participants.

"Take Stephen, here," I go on. "What might represent his authentic self in the moment would be taking a little nap."

A startled Stephen struggles to sit up straighter, and I see in him a tired little boy in third grade on a warm day in June struggling to stay awake!

"I'll be fine," he says to the group. "Just haven't had much sleep this week."

"Stephen, would it be OK if I worked with you a little bit about this? It might help all of us to learn more about the group container and optimum learning."

"OK," he replies.

"What would be the worst thing that could happen if you took a little snooze right now, right where you're sitting?"

"Well ... nothing bad would happen, except I would miss some of the evening's content."

"Can you think of a way that you could make that up?"

"Yeah, sure, I could ask someone to take some notes and share it with me after the session."

Both people sitting on the sofa quickly offer to do that.

"But, really," Stephen goes on, "now that you're pressing me on it, I realize that I'm embarrassed to go to sleep here in front of everyone. I mean ... that's a no-no! It's beyond acceptable behavior!"

"I realize that you weren't brought up to do this, and it would be out of your comfort zone. Would it be *safe* to take a nap here in the room?"

"Of course it would be safe. So ... I get it." He laughs and looks around. "You want me to go outside my comfort zone and sleep right here in front of everyone while you go on with the workshop. Is that it?"

"It's not about what I want, Stephen; it's about what you want. I got a lot of sleep last night and I'm doing fine. Do you want to go to sleep now?"

"Of course!" He laughs again. "I'm sitting here torturing myself trying to stay awake!"

Everyone laughs. "Well, maybe you'd better ask the group if it's OK with them, if that's still on your mind."

"Is a nap OK with you?" Stephen asks with a sheepish grin on his face. He looks around. Heads nod. "OK." Stephen shrugs his shoulders, lays his head on the sofa back, and is asleep in seconds.

We continue the workshop agenda and Stephen sleeps at least an hour before waking up, tension lines gone from his face. "Oh, man," he says, "that was sweet."

The group breaks into happy cheers.

Design for Discomfort

When participants see a member of the group they can identify with step successfully outside her or his comfort zone, they breathe a sigh of relief, as Stephen's group did. As a margin he was, in fact, sleeping for the group, expanding its sense of safety, building its container. That was one reason I spent so much time with him on his issue—also because we had rapport and I expected that he would trust me. The result was that the group's container was far stronger by the end of that first session than it ordinarily is, which paid off for the rest of the workshop in the risks people took in pursuing their learning goals.

Teachers sometimes worry that designing for discomfort turns learning groups into grim events. Then they come to my workshops and are surprised by how much fun they have. The humor in direct education grows out of engagement, edginess, risks that work out—a little like the funny stories we tell about scary camping trips or protests or blizzards.

A lot of zest gets unleashed when people give up pretense and get real. As the container strengthens, people give themselves permission to get silly or make puns or do the funny things they ordinarily are too self-conscious to try. All of this going into the pot makes for workshops that have people sometimes laughing till their sides hurt—and an optimum learning curve.

When a teacher or facilitator forgets to design activities that take participants out of their comfort zones, collusion is the likely result. The unstated contract goes something like this: "We'll pretend to learn and do what you ask us to if you just don't ask us to do anything that is uncomfortable." A pleasant time is had by all—and precious little learning, much less breakthroughs to a new level of knowledge or skill.

Remember the Introverts!

Working the discomfort zone doesn't mean our goal is to increase suffering. Temperamentally, some percentage of human beings need solitude in order to regroup, refresh, regain their motivation. For them a learning group is a very different experience from that of the extroverts who breathe in energy from others, who need almost constant interaction, who often discover what they think as they express it to others.

Workshops can be wearing for introverts, therefore, and even invite suffering if we don't take account of them in our design. Build in journal-writing, meditation, the option of solitary walks rather than walking with buddies or support groups. Remind them that it is OK to eat alone, and support their growing ability to assert their needs in a group atmosphere that may be compulsively chummy. Once again, we get to support the margin.

Raise the Issue of Commitment from the Outset

Ninety-five percent of my trainings include the rule, well publicized ahead of time, that the workshop is an experiential package that requires all participants to attend all sessions. Without such a policy, some participants will give themselves an out; if the workshop becomes, according to them, (a) too boring, (b) repetitive of what I already know, (c) full of jerks, (d) weird or strange, or (e) all of the above, they will bolt.

Holding this kind of reservation has several consequences. It reduces their commitment to the workshop and reduces the chance that they will learn anything at a deep level, even if they stay to the end. A participant with reservations also reduces the engagement of other participants in the workshop, because they pick up the signals of reduced commitment and they experience less safety to do their work. In addition, in my experience the participants who give themselves an escape clause believe that they cannot tolerate being out of their comfort zone—a belief that provides for lifelong nonlearning.

If someone does quietly slip away mid-workshop and then returns for a later session, I simply refuse to let him back in. To allow him back in would be colluding with a behavior that damages the container, hurts other participants' chances to learn, and undermines his own ability to grow. I have too much self-respect to allow that. I also pray that he will someday see the game he's playing and develop too much self-respect to play it any more.

Because U.S. middle class culture has made comfort a god above most other gods, U.S. facilitators face this potential threat to the learning group fairly often. When I smell its potential in the room already in the beginning, I'll simply put on newsprint, along with the other guidelines I shared in Chapter 2, "Complete the training." I ask if participants are aware of the advance publicity about the workshop and the rule about full attendance. If some didn't read it, I explain the reasons for that rule, and ask if anyone is unable to make that commitment.

If someone says they can't, I'll sometimes ask a series of elicitive questions to assist them to "peel their onion" and discover whether, in fact, they are unable to attend all sessions or whether it's something like the privately held escape clause. I then state that a break will be coming up soon, and that will be the point at which anyone who can't attend all sessions needs to say goodbye. I hope they'll find a way to make it work, but it's OK if someone needs to leave at break.

Expressing openly and clearly the authority of the facilitator raises the question, Where does our authority come from? Worried about authoritarianism in education, I was one of the activist trainers in the late '60s who preferred a very different model, one that I hoped would express our values of democracy and equality. In 1970 I would have been horrified at the thought of doing what I've just described in the previous two paragraphs! It would have appeared to me power-over, a kind of leadership without accountability (Starhawk, 1990).

Let's take a close look at an alternative model still popular among some facilitators: what I call negotiated design.

Negotiated Design

When I use negotiated design (which I still occasionally do), I begin with newsprint on which I've written the proposed goals and design, with the design broken down by stated times and activities. I do that to encourage buy-in—if the group discusses thoroughly and modifies the goals and design, they in the process become co-owners of the workshop as a whole and develop a vested interest in its success.

In the '70s I hoped such a process would prevent a mid-workshop rebellion (what we now call a storm, or chaos), which in those days I misunderstood and feared. The ownership model we were trying did not prevent mid-workshop rebellions. If a group wants to storm to become a community, it will do its best to storm.

The negotiated design model has several merits. The model announces boldly that this will be a different paradigm from traditional schooling and encourages those who hate school to give this way of learning a chance. It gives oppressed people the experience of a kind of democracy in which the highest-rank person in the room (the trainer) is forced constantly to negotiate with those of lower rank. The model gives practice in negotiation skills and in reaching consensus. Negotiated design increases group awareness by participants who are self-absorbed, since they have to look around and be aware of their impact on the working consensus that up until now has been achieved. In the negotiated workshop model, the question Who is the facilitator accountable to? has a clear answer: the group, in the here-and-now.

Accountability to the Group or the Goals

I still use the negotiated design model from time to time, depending on the goals, the nature of the group, and other circumstances. Mostly, however, I've moved to the direct education model, in which my accountability is to stated workshop goals, along with my commitment to assist participants to reach their own learning goals whenever possible.

The differences between negotiated design and direct education are substantial. In the direct education model, the goals are worked out ahead of the workshop through agreement with the sponsor of the workshop, or the goals are publicized to attract individuals to sign up for the workshop. Once the goals are set, they remain the goals for the workshop, and in the direct education model I hold myself accountable to them.

One reason why I no longer prefer to hold myself accountable to the group in the training room is that, when it comes to decision making, "the group" usually turns out to be the *mainstream* of the group. The mainstream in the training room, just by acting as its typical self, tends to suppress the margins. Sadly, in the negotiated design model I've often watched the margins lose their voice. The following situation will illustrate.

Four participants are speaking up before the group breaks for lunch:

"Some of us think that after lunch we should not go street speaking, even though it says so up there on the newsprint."

"Right, because it will take too much time away from the other skills we want to learn."

"Right, and I'd like to follow up on this morning's discussion, which really only just got started."

"I agree that street speaking is not a good idea for today, and maybe we can go tomorrow."

These four who spoke in rapid succession happen to be part of the mainstream of the workshop. If there were a voice on the margins that wanted to explore street speaking, would that person want to speak up under these circumstances? Especially when at three previous points in the workshop, the agenda broke down while long discussions were held about what to do next, and those discussions were mainly conducted by members of the mainstream, while the margins checked out?

What I found in a variety of negotiated workshops was that the negotiations I was having were almost entirely with the mainstream, those who felt most confident, most assertive, and most entitled. When I gained a fuller understanding of the subtle power dynamics in groups and realized that every group/workshop/retreat has a mainstream and margins, my interest in negotiated workshops declined considerably.

Of course I would have liked to catch the moments of negotiation as "teachable moments" regarding the mainstream and margins of the group. It would be tempting to assist the mainstream to become aware of its unaware exclusion of the margins, and assist the margins to speak up for themselves.

But those times of proposed shifts in the agenda were not genuine teachable moments! The participants in my illustration above had their attention on the substance of the debate (street speaking), and they were in no shape to explore simultaneously such a subtle thing as their own group dynamics. *Individuals* can explore seriously more than one topic at a time (although with difficulty), but *group mainstreams* rarely can, especially if the mainstream has no wish to look at itself, which is an inherent part of a mainstream's condition!

Facilitating Risk and Understanding Resistance

Resistance itself—a normal and expected dynamic in learning groups—is an argument against negotiated trainings. Participants normally resist going outside comfort zones, resist considering a radically different point of view, resist doing something with a real risk of failure, resist naming a self-limiting belief, and so on. If some part of a group is given veto power over all activities where real learning can take place, what's the point of teaching?

Now that I've learned how intimately risk and learning are connected, I want to put my energy into trainings where people can feel their resistance, express it, and go ahead and risk. That's what produces transformation.

"All right," says Dr. Judith Jones at a typical moment near the beginning of a workshop, "I know that some of you are used to watching out for the groups you're part of. You take the job of caring for the group, noticing conflicts, being alert for oppressive remarks. I have a gift for you in this workshop. You will not have to take this on! Instead, for a change, you will have a chance in this workshop to go for what *you* want, to pursue your own learning goals. You don't have to be the guardian at the gates this time—it's not that kind of workshop. We facilitators will track the group and take care of the facilitation. You can just breathe a sigh of relief and take care of your *own* self!"

In my mind mainstream participants get credit for the leadership they give in serving group goals, and when activists are the mainstream they are often willing to sacrifice their personal goals to keep the ship afloat. Direct education—in contrast to negotiated design workshops—gives these mainstreamers a break. They deserve it. And they need it for their own growth and development.

I've dedicated my life to values that include democracy and equality, and I grew up with more than my share of anti-authoritarian spirit, as my teachers could tell you. There's a part of me that would hate to be considered authoritarian. Asserting strong authority in the training room, as when I insist that someone leave the training because they skipped a session, sometimes leaves me second-guessing myself.

It seems that every time I start to become confused about this issue, a movie comes along that clarifies it for me. In *Remember the Titans* (2000), white racist football players resist their black coach's insistence that they become genuine teammates with black students. The coach, played by Denzel Washington, is not negotiating. The white players have a breakthrough on their racism. If the coach had been "democratic" and negotiated with the white players, they would have learned nothing about their racism. The movie was based on a historical situation.

In *Billy Elliot* (2000), the working class boy studying ballet reaches a point of furious resistance to his teacher's instruction. The teacher, played by Julie Walters, doesn't back down. Billy burns through to the other side and achieves his learning goal, magnificently.

In both movies, empowerment for the participants required having a teacher who was willing to see the resistance for what it was, and strong enough to be on the side of the students even though the students completely misunderstood. I recommend both films to trainers. Many coaches and teachers have favorite stories in which tough loving made the difference in supporting people to achieve their learning goals. The methodology of direct education makes this possible in our learning groups.

And for Those Who Don't Identify with Sports Coaches?

Fortunately, for those who don't identify with athletic coaches and dancing teachers, there's an alternative image available—the tour guide in a museum! Where does a museum guide get her or his authority? Is it from knowing more than the participants in the tour? No. The tour may include Ph.D.'s in art history, outstanding artists, or the granddaughter of Miró! But the tour guide has a particular kind of expertise: knowing the museum. The guide knows that if the group gets so excited that it wants to spend an hour in the room with the Matisse, it will run out of time and miss the gallery with the African sculptures. (And then get angry with the tour guide.) The guide's authority is based on knowledge of the museum, the journey for which the participants have signed up.

We teachers and facilitators, who may know much less than the participants do about many things, have legitimate authority based on one fact: we know the course or the workshop. We know the journey that the participants have signed up for. We know what will support or distract them in the course of that journey. It's our job to guide them.

15

Emergent Design
Facilitating in the Here and Now

ACT UP arose in the 1980s as a lively network of groups in the United States protesting against government inaction in dealing with the AIDS crisis. Many of its members at that time were HIV positive or had AIDS. ACT UP was famous for pushing the envelope in its tactics of nonviolent direct action.

When a federal official came to speak in a city near Washington, a local chapter of ACT UP mobilized to confront him. The police were out in force and prevented the protesters from entering the building, at which point the members of ACT UP pulled out whistles and blew them to make themselves heard. The noise was unbelievable; that plus some pushing incidents resulted in the police losing it and attacking the demonstrators. Many ACT UP members were hurt in the police riot, so ACT UP sued the city and won a cash payment for damages.

ACT UP leaders called me and asked me to present a nonviolent civil disobedience workshop at their next meeting. They said that the police riot had been a sobering experience, and they wanted to calibrate the militancy of their protests more carefully. They knew me as a gay activist who deeply respected their work.

I carefully designed the workshop based on the group's history and the leaders' goals. When I walked into the room in the church basement jammed with ACT UP members, I felt an angry vibe.

I started to wonder if the workshop was the idea of the leaders but not the members. To check out my diagnosis, I asked for a go-round in which each person would say in a word or phrase the attitude they wanted to take to their next protest. One after another the participants responded; "angry," "fighting," "in their face," "no holds barred" were typical responses.

I mentally let go of my plan and decided to let the design emerge from the needs and wants of the group. The first thing to do was respond to what Arnold Mindell calls "the primary process." I took a deep breath and started.

"As you know, your leadership asked me to lead a nonviolent civil disobedience workshop tonight, and the thing about nonviolence is — like so many concepts — it's got its upside and its downside. Let's take a few minutes to notice what some of those are."

I placed on the newsprint, in the middle, "NONVIOLENT ACTION," and put a plus sign on one side and a minus sign on the other.

Immediately the minuses came flying at me, and I wrote furiously. The list of minuses became longer and longer. I added more paper. I checked my watch as I wrote to see if there was still time to get to the movies, since it looked as though we were going to bag this workshop.

Then someone suggested a plus. I wrote it down, and then quickly wrote the minuses that followed. Then came another plus, and another, then another. By the time we were finished listing, there was a respectable number of pluses along with the very long list of minuses.

"So," I said in a neutral tone of voice, "looking at this list you've made, what would you say? Does it make sense to continue with this workshop?"

Silence.

Someone in the back of the room, leaning against wall, said, "OK you guys, I can see which way this is going. I just want you to know I just can't stomach a nonviolent protest at this point in my life, after what the police did to us, so I'll come to the next demo but I'll stand across the street.''

A woman sitting near the front got up and talked in a similar vein: ''I'm in solidarity with you and if you want to do nonviolent civil disobedience, go ahead. I just won't be in the middle of it.''

After a few more statements of that sort, I asked, ''Does this mean that you want to do the workshop?''

Dozens of people shouted ''Yeah!'' as if I were the most clueless person they'd seen all day.

Realizing that this activity represented ''integration'' in the rhythm of group life, I dropped the preliminary steps that are usually part of this workshop and immediately got them into subgroups for role playing.

The rest of the workshop followed this procedure: while debriefing one activity, I was also planning the next, following my usual design principles but needing to think on my feet. More than once I wished I had a co-facilitator!

The group was easy to work with because they had (a) expressed their rebel energy in the go-round and (b) resolved their ambivalence through the ambivalence chart of pluses and minuses. Looking back, I'd say it was one of the best civil disobedience workshops I've ever led.

The proof of the pudding, however, is in the eating. I went to the next ACT UP protest to see how it would go. The protesters were strong, clear, grounded; Dr. King would have been proud of them.

At one point I saw one of the ACT UP leaders in intense discussion with the police captain in charge; I moved close enough to listen. "Look," the captain was saying, "I want us to figure out how to do these arrests so nobody's hurt, you know? I'm near retirement. I'm just trying to get out of this thing alive." The ACT UP leader stared in the police captain's eyes. "Well," he said, "now you know what we want. We want to get out of this alive."

The Mechanics of Emergent Design

Emergent design is not usually so dramatic, but the process is the same: the shaping of activities and facilitation to respond to the immediate needs of the group in a way that reaches the learning goals. The flexibility of "designing on your feet" means that we have a chance to be much more accurate as teachers—the activities we insert can be closer matches to the unique journey the group is taking.

How much of a design is emergent can vary. Dr. Judith Jones and I often lead workshops in which 85 percent is predesigned and the last 15 percent is left open for decision as we get to know the group better and its special wants and needs. In some workshops I plan the first half of the workshop and create the last half out of my observation of the group in the first half. Sometimes I'll plan only the first session of a five-session course and let the rest emerge from my growing knowledge of the group. And of course I do at times have the entire workshop planned in detail, and the only tweaking I do is at the level of facilitation.

Emergent design is not "winging it," at least not the way I've seen facilitators wing it. Longtime Training for Change trainer Matt Guynn describes the process well:

> Emergent design prompts me to be impeccably prepared, personally and as a trainer. I need to be well rested, on top of my material, and ready on all levels. I love it because it keeps me on my edge.
>
> I have approached emergent design several ways. One extreme is to intentionally overprepare, thinking through activities and creating a kind of menu for myself, where things are completely scheduled, but I have five extra activities to substitute when needed. I do that especially when I am newer to content or to a group of people.

My other extreme is to go in with only goals and no preset agenda and to work in the moment based on intention and intuition. For me, this takes immense focus since I am relying on my moment-to-moment diagnosis of the group. It also requires having an ample toolkit of activities and elicitive questions at my disposal. I have done this more often with shorter workshop sessions; for example, a one-hour session on healing from the wounds caused by institutional religion.

A middle road that is most common for me at this point is to create goals and an overall trajectory for a workshop's design. In a five-session workshop I often leave the last one or two sessions to emerge as the workshop unfolds. Leaving the final sessions open from the start allows the sessions to emerge from and complete the work of the group.

Where's the Accountability?

As Matt says, emergent design is an art, relying to some degree on the facilitator's intuition. The question naturally arises, What is the accountability system? Someone with the power and rank of a teacher or trainer always needs some mode of accountability, lest they be so swept away by the excitement of dancing with the group that the training gets lost in a welter of feelings.

The announced workshop goals provide accountability in emergent design. One reason why I prefer no more than four or at most five goals for a workshop is that I can always keep them paramount in my mind as I make choices about interventions and activities. It's something like sailing a boat: because of changing winds, the sailors may not be able to sail in a straight line toward a destination, but may need to tack, proceeding in a kind of zigzag. The sailors are still guided by the destination. They don't, in a burst of intuition, begin sailing for a different port!

Emergent design, then, allows the facilitator/sailor to go with the weather conditions of the moment, to take time with teachable moments, to take account of mainstream/margin relations, always keeping in mind the final destination. If a tour guide used emergent design, she would begin the tour without a prescribed route through the museum, following the interests and excitements of the tour group but nevertheless making sure that by the end of the tour the participants would have seen the highlights that were promised!

The "end of the tour" is worth emphasizing. I never let emergent design interfere with the ending time of the workshop as a whole. In a weekend workshop, for example, I prefer not to state an ending time for Friday and Saturday evenings—it's best to stay open to group dynamics and the teachable moments which sometimes emerge late in the evening. But if we've said the workshop is to be over Sunday at 6 p.m., then 6 p.m. it will be. This is a matter of basic respect for participants, who have the rest of their lives to look after.

Stumped in San Francisco: Needing a Diagnosis

One reason I often choose emergent design is that it challenges me to continuously sharpen my diagnostic skills. What's happening in this group this morning? What are the shifts from yesterday? Which themes are emerging? Which areas of content are meeting what kinds of resistance? When Training for Change teaches emergent design, it emphasizes diagnostic tools and gives the chance to practice them.

I remember using emergent design in a workshop for adults in San Francisco when, two-thirds of the way through, I drew a complete blank on what was happening in the group. I'd been careful to stay in touch with mainstream and various margins, participating in many conversations during breaks, but I suddenly realized there was a very strong atmosphere in the group that was impossible for me to name. I had no clue what to do next.

Fortunately, I remembered that the learning group is itself a resource. After all, it's their workshop more than it is mine! I didn't want to ask the participants directly, however, because mainstream/margin relations were not great at that moment and I didn't want my diagnostic quest to turn into an incoherent argument based on power relations.

I turned to the group and said, "It seems that there is a very strong dynamic in the room just now, but I'm quite puzzled about what it might be. I'd like your help by participating in the following activity. Please form small groups, choosing people to work with that you are not friends with and haven't worked with much before."

They did that.

"I'd like each of your small groups to create a sculpture, using all your bodies, expressing what might be happening now in this room."

They willingly set to work and in ten minutes were ready with their sculptures. One at a time the groups showed their sculptures to the others. We were all struck by the similarity of theme in all the sculptures, and participants named it immediately: fear of risk.

I thanked the participants and declared a break. With a few minutes to myself, I found in my toolbox a container-building learning activity, appropriate to where the group showed me it was.

Part IV

Facilitation

16

Setting the Tone and Building Safety

Gay artist and trainer Skylar Fein got a call from a Catholic college that wanted a gay sensitivity training for its resident advisors (RAs). Here's how he tells the story:

> I realized it would be challenging, especially when I found out that many of the RAs were religious, and the college had never done any kind of gay training before. I went to the campus ready for anything.
>
> I found the room and waited for the RAs to arrive. And in they came: huge, white tough guys, one football player after another. Coming in the door, one yelled to another, "You faggot!" Then one of the students called out, "What's tonight's training on?"—and I realized that the college staff had been too afraid to tell them.
>
> I said we'd be looking at "lesbian and gay issues" (saving the "bisexual and transgender" part for later), and a thunderous silence ensued. While we waited for the last people to arrive, and the room bristled, I decided to do a quick intervention. I grabbed a pack of index cards and approached the toughest looking guy. I shook his hand, introduced myself, and said, "Tonight we're going to look at gay and lesbian issues from an RA's perspective." I gave him an index card and asked him to write one question—any question—"about gay

anything, and since no one will know who wrote it, really go for it, OK?"

I moved on to the next student, and then the next. I shook each person's hand and we had a quiet moment together. A few minutes later, I went to the front of the room, where I effortlessly got their warm and thoughtful attention.

Fortunately, not all beginnings are that challenging, but all of them do benefit from thoughtful attention. Setting the right tone is among the most important skills a facilitator can learn.

As Skylar's story shows, the two major aspects of setting the tone are to signal the relationship you want to have with the group and to explain the parameters of the situation. Most participants want to fit in, whatever their reservations.

Teachers and facilitators differ on how much bonding they want to do from the start. Some facilitators like to hang out as participants gather for a workshop and register, chatting informally. Some like to design the workshop to start with a meal, so participants can break the ice with each other and the facilitator can begin to build the container before the workshop formally begins. Other facilitators believe that hanging out sends the wrong signals; interpreted as socializing, it might be an invitation to projections (mother, father, my favorite hostess, the organizer at church suppers), and it could increase the participants' attention on the facilitator rather than each other and their own learning goals.

I've gone through different phases on this question during my history, since I consider both points of view to have a lot of merit. My current practice is to be strongly guided by two criteria: How much or little do I know about the participants, and how insecure are they? If I know a lot about them already (pre-workshop interviews or questionnaires, for example, or reports of great similarities to people I've worked with in the past), then I'm likely to make an appearance at the last minute before the workshop formally opens. If, on the other hand, I'm in a lot of ignorance about the participants, including their cultural backgrounds, I want to show up early to take the opportunity to learn about them.

The second criterion, degree of insecurity of the participants, also weighs strongly with me. Because of oppression issues, or because the workshop format is new or content is scary, participants can arrive with a fair amount of anxiety. Relaxed warmth from a facilitator can be immensely reassuring. As a person from the United States, I have the additional awareness that whatever my country is doing at the moment influences participants' perception of me. Even when non–U.S. participants know my anti-war stand, until they know me personally the perennial war-making of my government can influence their perception of me. They usually admit to me their initial worry at the end of the workshop, not at the beginning.

Energy and the Initial Encounter

The gilded proscenium and huge chandelier of the Academy of Music was matched by the elegance of the crowd in their furs and cashmere coats. Most of the three thousand who'd come to hear the Rev. Dr. Martin Luther King Jr., in Philadelphia's most beautiful venue were dressed to the nines.

I'd heard Dr. King speak only once before, at a youth march for integration in 1958, and there he'd sounded like the southern Baptist preacher he was. What, I wondered as I looked around, would he do with Philadelphia's black and liberal glitterati?

He began by talking about Hegel's philosophy, in the slow, measured tones of a scholar. I was astonished, and I also saw that he was meeting most people exactly where they wanted to be met. As he went on, he gradually increased the pace and heightened the tension, breaking it occasionally with a quip that enabled us to laugh. About halfway through, I began to hear responses to his calls: "That's right." "You're telling it like it is." By the end of his speech, people were at the edge of their seats, smiles on their faces and wetness in their eyes. I realized we'd been transported to a Baptist chapel in Alabama.

Users of direct education have no need to be charismatic preachers to learn from Dr. King's astuteness. "Meet them where they are" is as much about *energy* as about anything. If the group is stiff and somber, go to your stiff and somber place and, after spending time with the group in that energy, move gradually to where you want to go. If the group is boisterous and silly, go to your silly and boisterous spirit and laugh it up with the group for a while until you gradually move them to an energy more appropriate to the next learning activity.

I learned from a presentation by John Grinder, co-founder of Neuro-Linguistic Programming (NLP), that groups are more likely to be successfully guided when they are met where they are, *energetically* (Bandler and Grinder, 1979). NLP calls it "pacing and leading." I've found it a major principle not only for the beginnings of a learning group but throughout the course or workshop, especially when participants get back together after a break.

Start Where *They* Are, Not Where *You* Are

The preoccupation of participants when they gather initially is "Who are these people and how do I fit in?" so it only makes sense to start with participant introductions. I've seen teachers and facilitators waste the first valuable minutes by talking about the course or the goals or the site or themselves while, from the back of the room, I notice participants stealing quick looks around, trying to orient themselves to their peers, hearing hardly a word from the person up front.

The first step, therefore, needs to be to allow participants to bring themselves into the room through presenting themselves in some way. There are many tools for doing this, with varied consequences that serve various design goals. I minimize the facilitator self-introductions and usually avoid them altogether. Of course if the group's culture is so formal that avoiding a self-introduction is read as disrespectful, I'll meet the group's norm on this.

Since groups especially in the beginning need support in focusing, I eliminate empty chairs in the circle. I believe an empty chair is an energy drain; two or more empty chairs invite scatter. (This is also true later in the workshop.) I also dress in brighter colors for the first session, to assist participants with scattered attention to hear and see me better. I also never let a wall with windows be the "front of the room"; a solid wall is the best backdrop for the newsprint and least distracting for the participants.

Visual learners need information on wall charts and handouts throughout the course or workshop, but especially in the beginning. When a group's attention is scattered, pointing to the wall benefits everyone. I post my workshop goals and emphasize: "These are the goals that guided the design of the workshop, but they are not necessarily the same as your own learning goals. I hope these goals will serve your goals, but they are no substitute for the very specific objectives that you want to achieve while you're here."

Signaling self-responsibility is part of setting the tone. Additional tone-setting signals are the guidelines "Take care of yourself so you can take care of others" and "Use everything for your advancement."

I don't post on the wall a list of the learning activities we'll engage in, unless I'm following the model of the negotiated design. I usually put on newsprint the main blocks of time we're working with and the topics we'll explore, like this:

12–1:30	Lunch
1:30–4	Democratic leadership in teams

With this format I'm suggesting two things: Yes, especially for you participants who learn better if you have some rough idea where we're going, I'm thinking about you and will tip you off when I can. No, for you who want to co-facilitate this workshop by keeping track of the learning activities and their timing, I don't need your help on that. The facilitation is handled. I'd rather you focus on achieving your learning goals.

The natural nervousness that teachers and facilitators often feel in the beginning of a new learning group is sometimes translated into worry about time: "There's not enough time to get everything done in this workshop!" This is quite an intrusion, because participants typically feel in the beginning of a learning group that there's all the time in the world. Veteran Russian trainer Igor Ovchinnikof's comment helps with this issue. Igor told me that early in his career as a trainer, he believed there was never enough time to get everything in that needed to be covered. "As the years and the workshops have gone by, my perspective has completely shifted. I now find that there's plenty of time to get the important things done, so now I let the less important things go and just relax."

In short, most of what we do in direct education in setting the tone is to remind the participants that the workshop is about them and their goals, not about the facilitator or teacher.

The First Session

As the first session unfolds and you're engaged in container-building activities, your facilitator behaviors continue to set the tone. Make sure the comments from participants are accurately paraphrased on the newsprint—check with them from time to time. Refer back to things participants said, and use their metaphors whenever possible.

Recall the water glasses exercise from Chapter 11: some or most of the participants believe that *you* believe in the first model of education (The Teacher Is the Fount of All Knowledge). Most come into the room having surrendered to this model; they do not expect to learn anything from other participants. It's your job—from the beginning—to show by your actions that you believe in the second model (The Students' Glasses Have Water All of You Need). Quoting or citing participants shows the paradigm you're working from.

Giving permission is important, since throughout the first session, participants are either assuming that politeness is The Rule or are wondering whether there will be a point when they can stop pretending and become real. I continue in the early part of the workshop to make little permission-giving comments: "It's OK to stand in the back and walk around if you're feeling sleepy." "I was once given a buddy by random assignment and I thought he was the biggest jerk in the room." "Some of the things you hear in this course may strike you as obvious and others as outrageous. Controversy is OK here."

The Mohawk First Nation near Montreal invited a group of trainers from Peace Brigades International to lead peacekeeper training. A major powwow was coming up on the first anniversary of the 1990 struggle over the extension of a golf course into Mohawk ancestral lands at Oka. The Mohawks' defense of their land had become a national issue that had escalated to military involvement and a death. The Mohawks blocked the golf course but were concerned that now, a year later, the powwow might be infiltrated by provocateurs who would stir up violence and mar their victory.

Early in the workshop I noticed a high degree of attentiveness from a young man, and I remembered that I had noticed him before the workshop walking with unusual grace and centeredness. He seemed to be 180 pounds of solid muscle, and I wondered if he had training in martial arts. When it came time to cast the next role play, I asked if he'd like to volunteer. He came forward and volunteered to be the one who a provocateur would scream at and hit, trying to get him to respond violently.

The role play had about eight characters and was slow to warm up to the point of confrontation, and then suddenly the provocateur lashed out. The young man stopped and looked at the ground for a second, mobilizing himself, and then straightened, spread his feet, put his hands at his side, and gazed directly into the eyes of the provocateur with an expression of fearlessness. The provocateur tried to regroup and attack him again, but he got nowhere, reporting in the debrief later that he felt like he was attacking a mountain.

The behavior of the young man became the workshop's reference point for nonviolent peacekeeping. His example was far more powerful than a story could be, because the participants had witnessed it and he was one of their own. There was also no question that he could have violently nailed the provocateur, so the fact that he obviously chose an alternative added to its power.

Two important tone-setting goals were achieved with this intervention. First, the exemplar for peacekeeping was not an exotic Gandhi or a white guy named Lakey; it was one of the Mohawk's own. Second, the workshop's method was that Mohawks would explore options together, drawing on their own wisdom and strength.

Those Awkward Moments When the Group Is Regathering

I used to dislike the moments between when the group was called back and when everyone was present. I don't start until everyone is present, so I usually would let people know when ten minutes remains for the break, and then five minutes. At the five-minute point, I would go back to my chair in the front of the room to model readiness to begin, but then I didn't know what to do for those five minutes before the seats were filled.

Since learning "pacing and leading" from NLP, I now find an abundance of things to do, because I tune in to where participants are at that particular point. I almost always engage with a few of those who have returned, informally asking how their break was or wondering about the weather. Taking cues from their energy,

I support joke-telling or complaints about outrageous politicians or bemusement at the craziness of the world.

I consciously don't try to get group attention (that would be "starting") but just chat with a few of those who seem available. Not only does this help me reconnect myself before launching the next activity, but it also gives an incentive to participants to return from break in a timely way. Participants quickly make judgments about all sorts of things in a learning group, including "It's boring to go back early after break because all we do is sit there and wait for the latecomers. I'd rather be a latecomer." By sitting in my chair engaging in amiable companionship, I'm supporting the group to be "doing something" as it gathers; returning to the group is returning to "where the action is."

Managing Small Group Activities

Some teachers and facilitators undermine their positive, confident tone by allowing themselves to worry about transitions from small group to whole group. Here's how I think of the reluctance of small groups or buddy pairs to stop working and return to the whole: they are having a good and/or meaningful time and don't want to stop! What's for me not to like? I should prefer that they're finding their group (or the task) useless and are *eager* to return to the whole?

To make it easier for small groups to let go and join the whole group, I ask the participants to acknowledge their partners, which gives them the chance to do a brief ritual giving closure: "Please acknowledge your partners however you'd like to, and return to the circle." Participants will do a range of things, from a brief nod to warm hugs, depending on what's been going on in the buddy pair or small group and where the container is.

It also helps, of course, to give them a few minutes warning: "In two minutes we'll be drawing this to a close." That gives them more freedom to make sure they share the highest priority thing that's left to share.

A jolly argument among facilitators is whether to tell small discussion groups or task groups how much overall time they will have to accomplish their work. Some prefer to announce the amount of time to assist them to be self-steering. Others agree with that value but honestly don't know how much time it will take to get a particular task done, especially if they're using a new tool or working a group whose culture they don't know well.

When I don't announce an amount of time, I watch instead the energy curve of the groups. Typically, it starts fairly low, rises to a crest, then starts to decline. I'll announce, "Not much time left on this task." Immediately the energy rises to a new crest, at which point I say something like "Just two minutes to wrap this up."

In some small-group sharing activities, it helps to regulate the time each person has within the small group. Sometimes small groups can be self-regulating, sometimes not. If not, I simply announce that I'll be micromanaging the time to make sure everyone has the same amount of time to share. I ask the groups to figure out without talking who will go first, second, third, and so on—they enjoy that challenge (an easy one). If there are more than three small groups, I always check to make sure they've accomplished the task: "OK, please raise your hand if you're number one in your group ... number two ... number three. ... Each person will have _____ minutes to share. You get the full amount of time until I call on the next person, so please let's stay together on this. I'll let you know when you have only half a minute left. OK, number one, you have _____ minutes!"

Supporting Safety

It's important that we teachers and facilitators do our part in assuring that the group is a safe place for learning, working with the group and the participants' own sense of self-responsibility. There are many things we can do to increase safety.

Be rigorous in following through on what you say you will do. If you announce a break as fifteen minutes, make it fifteen minutes. If you say you'll return later to a question that is raised, make sure you do. Acknowledging your own facilitator mistakes can also be helpful, briefly and matter-of-factly, because it models your view that you are an accountable person, and that reassures others. The more rigorous you are in such matters, the higher your credibility will be, and that leads to an increased sense of safety Further, it models a norm of accountability (because one place where many people are sloppy about accountability is to themselves). The more normative accountability becomes in a workshop, the safer it is.

Positive reinforcement supports all kinds of growth. Sometimes I'll invite participants to affirm themselves for a specific achievement right away. I usually allow a little time to elapse before I affirm participants, because people with shaky self-esteem are usually well defended against a direct affirmation; they discount it as a "mere compliment" or "manipulation." Referring to it the next day might have even more impact: "Last night I realized you really pulled something off when you. . . . Sometimes it's surprising when we find ourselves being that sharp."

Facilitator credibility is also enhanced if you model OK-ness. Get your emotional, spiritual, physical support needs met outside the group, from co-facilitators or a support person you've brought along. During breaks, spend your time with participants one on one to build your credibility through listening and giving support.

Inviting participants to a high standard of responsibility for themselves increases safety. This can often be done conveniently around cleanup, for example. In general, a sloppy and disorganized classroom or workshop space lowers the safety in the group and invites sloppy and disorganized behavior, which can become downright dangerous. If your design includes adventure-based learning activities or an invitation to emotionally risky self-disclosures, you won't want such activities in a messy and thoughtless atmosphere.

Structures build safety, which is one of the strongest arguments for ground rules/group agreements. Other structures that build safety include frequent use of buddies/support groups, opening and closing rituals, the expectation that the trainer will guide the process rather than work it out with the group through negotiated design, and having participants write their learning goals and then revisiting them.

Creating a norm of "challenge by choice" builds safety if you're doing activities from the discipline of adventure-based learning (which includes ropes courses and group challenges). According to this norm, participants can choose whether or not to participate in a particular activity and also at what level.

Outside the Comfort Zone

"I don't know if I should say this," she said, fighting back the tears, "but I've always felt like an imposter as a leader. It always seemed like someone else could do it better, if they were around. But they weren't. I was the only one there. So I'd do it, but ... I always feel like a fraud. Like someone could unmask me and tell me ... I don't deserve to be holding this position."

"How many others here have sometimes felt that way?" I ask, putting up my hand. A number of hands go up.

"Look around you," I say to her. "What you're feeling is not so unusual. If you'd like to, you could tell us more about the messages you got that you weren't good enough to lead your people."

That's the kind of moment that happens when a group is safe enough for people to venture out of their comfort zones. Sometimes it is that visible to me and to the rest of the group; sometimes I find out only when someone tells me during a break about the risks they're taking.

The irony is that *when participants can tell me how scared they are, I know that the room is safe!* The container is strong enough for them to be aware of the risks they're taking and the nervousness that goes with it. The safety supports participants to go outside their place of comfort or familiarity.

In the discomfort zone, which is the zone of learning, people may laugh a lot to release tension, or cry, or yawn, or even shake. These are expressions that go with discomfort. When we are safe, we can express our discomfort physically.

If the room is unsafe, people may go out of their discomfort zone into their alarm zone—and shut down. In the alarm zone, they are too scared to laugh or cry or sweat. They freeze, like deer in the headlights. They shut down their expression of feelings.

On those rare occasions when participants go into their alarm zone I change the energy decisively. I send them back to their buddies or support groups, declare a break, play a game, or do something else to shift the atmosphere. Groups are resilient and usually respond quickly. I then do a couple of activities that strengthen the container, since entering the alarm zone simply means that the container isn't strong enough and participants don't feel safe to take the risks they need to take to learn what they want to learn.

Most of the facilitation tips in this chapter have had to do with managing the learning activities and the atmosphere of the room. In the next chapter I'll share approaches that support the participants to go to where learning accelerates.

17

Edgy Interventions to Accelerate Learning

Dr. Judith Jones was leading a two-part activity in which participants tend to get balky during the second part. In the first part Judith draws on newsprint a large circle labeled "We" and writes inside the circle what the participants identify as characteristics of the group. Most participants happily identify the group's characteristics because the workshop is two-thirds of the way through the course and the mainstream has fallen in love with itself. On this occasion the characteristics named are overwhelmingly positive, although a couple of marginal voices dare name attributes that are limiting, like "middle class," or "white," or "very polite."

In part two, participants are asked to name characteristics that are "not-we"; Judith writes those characteristics outside the circle. (Those, of course, are the behaviors and qualities that are marginalized in this workshop.) From the back of the room I watch a few participants trying to game the system by just naming the reverse of whatever is inside the circle, like "rude." I also see participation drying up as people intuit the stickiness of the task: Do we name "working class" or "black" as not-we? Where will that take us?

Of course this is the resistance that is productive of learning, as resistance is meant to be, and Judith expects it. She waits for courage to emerge in the group, for some brave souls to start naming the hard stuff. On this particular night, courage is in short supply. The waiting grows tedious. Judith then surprises me.

"Well, I'm getting tired of waiting for you to get real here. If you don't soon start talking, I'm calling it a day and going home."

The group gave a shocked laugh, and the tension dissolved. Person after person stepped out of their comfort zones and named things they were ambivalent about exploring. The activity shifted into high gear.

The Freedom to Make Powerful Interventions

Interventions often function to invite participants out of their comfort zones so they can learn. Arnold and Amy Mindell and their colleagues in Process Work think of a group as having an "edge," a place where the mainstream fears to go further. The breakthrough courses are those in which a group finds itself going over its edges to accelerated learning.

Where do Judith and other highly skilled teachers get their ability to use interventions to support a group over its edge? I've been fortunate to watch many such, and found that there is a "method to their madness."

They are aware of timing. Judith knew that she couldn't have effectively made that kind of provocation early in the workshop. Not only was the container not strong enough, but she has to deal with the load of projections that are placed on her as an African American woman. She may be a Ph.D. sociologist who teaches at universities, but she knows that, unconsciously, middle class white people still see her as "mammy," the woman who used to adorn the Aunt Jemima box, always ready to smile and reassure. Judith's anti-racist work includes a decision not to conform to that stereotype, so in the beginnings of workshops with a white mainstream she presents a neutral affect, not playing into the mammy role even though she knows some participants will project it on her anyway because the culture has taught them to.

Direct education itself builds rapport, so Judith develops a strong relationship with the group even though she avoids a warm, outgoing exterior. By halfway through the workshop, the group knows she is on their side—she really does support their learning goals. This gives her the freedom she needs to threaten to leave—an edgy intervention, when you stop to think about it. She means it—the participants realize suddenly that she is not about to stay and waste her time—and at the same time she did allow a smile as she said it: the spoonful of sugar helped the medicine go down. The mainstream rose to the occasion (the margin was already eager) and the session proved to be the most powerful in the weekend, where participants learned the most about oppression and liberation.

Two sources of powerful interventions are an awareness of timing and an awareness of the main projections that are laid on the facilitator. At least since Sigmund Freud's work (1989), psychologists have observed that adults as well as children project. Knowing what participants project on you gives you the freedom to be wise in choosing interventions. Freedom is important because it also leads to creativity—participants often remember longest the moments that are most surprising, and then remember the cognitive pieces that went with them.

Training for Change colleague Erika Thorne describes the power of surprise:

> We were two-thirds through the last day of a three-day strategy retreat. People had worked very hard, and at this point they were weary. Grinding out the last goals and objectives in their prioritized program areas seemed like the last thing they wanted to do. Yet I knew they would be disappointed later if we gave up this section and went on to what they were looking forward to: brainstorming a name for their new network.

I asked the next question in the strategy task list: "OK, what are the concrete things we know must be done under Goal #2?" The side conversations, glazed eyes, and turgid atmosphere told me I wasn't about to get an answer.

So I flipped my markers, tape and sticky-note pads high in the air so they'd land all over the room. I put on a look of mock resignation, playing out the "beleaguered facilitator" role.

People woke up, sat up, a few got "bonked" by markers, and everyone cracked up. Then they started applauding me for my "performance," laughing and teasing each other all the way.

We nailed our objectives and took a long break.

Here Erika used well her temperamental inclination to be a drama queen, but the story reveals something additional. Erika suspects that participants project on her a seriousness bordering on anxiety, so her sudden breaking of rules of propriety was all the more effective. She also shows in this intervention another important consideration: the optimum distance skilled facilitators establish between themselves and the participants.

Close, But Not Too Close

Fortunately, personality styles differ among teachers and facilitators, adding diversity to the field and an important criterion for choice of co-facilitators. I prefer to choose a co-facilitator different from me not only in demographic and cultural characteristics but also in personality. Together, we support a wider range of participants to pursue their learning goals. Each style, though, brings its own issues to the question of powerful interventions. Sometimes we need to develop work-arounds to be effective.

My personal style is to want closeness in relationship, whether at home or at work. Sometimes I want to be too close—I can get confused and lose the big picture as a teacher, and my interventions suffer. When the educational trends of the '60s included forming participants in a circle with the facilitator included in the circle, I found that the format exaggerated my difficulty. Instead, I needed to set up the chairs in a U formation, placing myself as a dot between the ends of the U; that format provided physical/emotional space between me and the participants, thereby working around my difficulty with boundaries.

Other teachers might have the opposite problem from mine—a style that is so good with boundaries that they end up too distant from the participants to create, and bring off effectively, the interventions that put participants on their learning edge.

Some teachers and facilitators believe that a lunch break is a chance to "socialize" with participants. I don't believe socializing is what happens in a workshop that goes beyond the superficial level. It's naïve to believe that participants take a break from projecting onto the facilitators whatever it is they are projecting. If a participant subconsciously needs to see the teacher as their mother, grandfather, first girlfriend, Great Leader, beloved rabbi who took them through their bar mitzvah, or whatever, the interaction is weighted quite differently from what the trainer may want to believe. Real socializing takes place between people who can actually see the person they are hanging out with, and the facilitator role generally prevents that.

At Loose Ends

Rodrigo looked uneasy. He was in an advanced facilitator training and was leading a practice session with the whole group. He'd just set in motion an activity that involved small groups doing a task, and they were happy campers. As he explained later in the debrief, they certainly didn't need him for the next fifteen minutes while they did their work. What, he asked, is he to do with himself? I thought it was a great question, because too many teachers and facilitators regard such periods as time out instead of an opportunity to support the participants at their edge.

"Well, Rodrigo," I said, "how about cheering them on while they work?"

He returned a puzzled look.

"What's a game you love to watch?" I asked.

"Soccer," he said.

"Do you cheer for your team?"

"Of course," he said, "I shout myself hoarse."

"OK," I said. "Just do that — but do it internally. Inside yourself, root for the participants. Yell like crazy."

Rodrigo's skepticism was all over his face. "That's silly," he said. "That couldn't make any difference."

"Would you try a little experiment?" I asked.

"Sure," he said. Rodrigo was always ready to push himself to learn something new.

"OK," I said, turning to the other participants. "We're going to cheer inwardly for Rodrigo on the count of three. Do whatever works for you. Scream like you're at a rock concert. Pray for him, if you're into that, or visualize him bathed with white light. The main thing is to open your heart and be *for* Rodrigo 100 percent. On the count of three. Are you ready? One, two, *three!*"

I watched Rodrigo as he turned shade after shade of deeper red. Beads of perspiration began to collect on his face as we sat quietly in the room, gazing at him with smiles.

"Please stop," Rodrigo said. We laughed together as we stopped our cheering and praying.

"I can't believe the energy I felt zooming over here in my direction," he said.

"Well," I responded, "that's a whole room aiming at one person, so it's pretty intense energy. Don't worry that when you do it as facilitator you'll be laser-beaming the whole room."

I turned to the group. "Just know that when you're facilitating, one of the more powerful ways that you can support participants to learn at their max is silently to cheer for them, to pray for them. They can always use it!"

Confusion and Hostility as Welcome Signs

Sometimes when an individual or a group reaches its edge, it acts confused. Typically I congratulate participants when they are confused, acknowledging that my own breakthroughs to new learnings are usually preceded by confusion. I ask them to do their best to tolerate the confusion.

Sometimes I reach for the knowledge that is hiding just underneath the confusion: "If you *did* know the answer, what would it be?" The participant usually laughs in response and then simply tells me (and herself) the answer she knew all along but was afraid to admit into consciousness.

Sometimes an individual acts out the edge of the group through "obnoxious" behavior that gets under everyone's skin, including the facilitator's! In a group whose atmosphere is controlled and polite, the difficult participant is rude and interrupts constantly. In a group that likes to go down a very linear and logical path, the difficult participant goes off on tangents. In a group of gentle folk who look on the bright side, the difficult participant expresses cynicism and anger.

The key that can unlock facilitator awareness at such moments is to ask herself the elicitive question, "What's right here? If there were some rightness, some functionality being expressed in this annoying behavior, what would it be? What group edge might this person be pointing at?" Asking ourselves such questions, rather than simply trying to control the behavior of "the obnoxious one," can lead to an intervention that supports the group to go over its edge to a new level of authenticity that supports more learning.

Sometimes two participants will pick a fight with each other that represents an edge for the group. Usually the antagonism shows up in the secret life of the group, so it may take some doing to get it to surface in public. I find that most often someone will come to me with the information, the buddy of one of the antagonists, perhaps. I then work to persuade the antagonists to bring the conflict out in the group with me as facilitator. There's an entire discipline devoted to the work of facilitating and mediating conflicts, so I don't need to describe interventions in this book. (See Moore, 1986.)

There's something striking about mediating a two-person conflict in the group context. When I persuade two participants who are in struggle to work in front of the group, fishbowl style, the work they do usually supports the whole group to go over an edge, an edge that the group was until then too scared to go over!

Handling Deflection

In the four-step model of experiential education (Chapter 10), the first step is of course the activity and the second step is reflection on that experience. Not until the third step do we get to generalization, putting the learning into the context of a theory, locating it in a big picture.

A sign of a group getting stuck on its edge instead of going over it is avoiding the second step. You are asking elicitive questions to support reflection, and members of the mainstream try to take the discussion "out of the room." After a role play, for example, ripe for possible reflections on what just happened, someone will say "This reminds me of a time when we were in a crisis and … ," or "Yeah, what do you do if somebody won't own up to their racism, like this guy in my office …."

The heart of learning (some would say the heart of *living*) is to be in the here and now. Then-and-there statements and questions from participants obstruct learning because (1) what's being reported on isn't a shared experience in the group, so it leaves people out; (2) what's reported on distracts and increases the distance between the activity the group engaged in and the reflection they need to do about it; and (3) the participant frequently has a hidden agenda, such as arguing for hopelessness and despair.

When such deflections come up, I simply return the group to the here and now, to the discomfort zone where learning actually takes place, and make a mental note to think more about the meaning of the deflections for dealing with later. If hopelessness is coming up, for example, I'd want to welcome it as a subsurface reality nearly all groups carry and begin to work on it intentionally rather than in its masked form as a deflection.

Notice the importance of timing in making this facilitator judgment. A participant's story about something outside the room may be deflection during Step 2 (reflection), but may be quite valuable during Step 3 (generalization). Data from then-and-there can be just right when we're generalizing, because we are stepping away from the immediate in-the-room experience at that point in order to make theory, complexifying the cognitive map that learners have in their heads.

Another form deflection takes is to attack the exercise. "That role play we just did was really bogus. I didn't get a thing out of it." "I don't know what we could possibly learn from that exercise. You set it up in a confused way."

One response I sometimes use is to validate the participant's reaction at its face value but put it on a range: "Sometimes there's quite a range of reaction to a particular exercise—for some people it's hard initially to see the learning for them, and for others it's immediately something that works for them. Let's go ahead and explore what some of the lessons might be here."

Another intervention is to begin immediately to ask debriefing kinds of questions about the subject matter that the exercise addressed: "How many of you found in that mingle that it was hard to identify leadership roles you play well?" (Hands.) "What were some of the roles that were named?"

What never works is to try to defend the exercise. Defending the exercise (or the video clip or the handout) colludes with the deflection itself—I'm joining the participant who may be trying to avoid the discomfort zone by going away from the substance of their experience. If they disliked the exercise, the activity is probably twice as meaningful to them in reality, but they won't find that out by debating pedagogy. They might find it out during the group's discussion of the content.

The other thing I remember is that no activity works for everyone. There's always a margin! My job is to design a large enough variety of activities in it so there's something for everyone.

When Only a Few Are Carrying the Ball

I'm remembering a workshop on the environment where I'd clearly lost the mainstream; only a few participants were responding to my elicitive questions. I did what I've done many times before.

"I'd like each of you to write four of the most important things you'd want to remember if you were negotiating with the manager of a store that's selling paper from rain forests."

After five minutes: "Even if you're not finished, take your notes and form groups of four."

I waited until they'd done that. "See if your group can get consensus on the three things most important in dealing with the manager."

After ten minutes: "Please acknowledge your colleagues however you want to and return to the whole group."

I waited until they'd done that. "We're going to harvest the work you've done and put it on newsprint. We'll take one point from each group and go around until all the groups have reported one of their points, then go around again to see if any is left out."

We proceeded to reflect on the activity and then generalize, with wide participation from the group. I was able to add some theory to build on the knowledge the group already shared.

I've never been in a course where this sequence was experienced as overused! The introverts love the chance to do some work on their own, and everyone can benefit from it. The small groups engage everyone in animated conversation. The whole group benefits from everyone's work, not just that of a few, and the harvesting process provides a graceful opportunity for the trainer's own knowledge and wisdom to shine.

18

The Power of Framing

I was scheduled to return to Russia shortly after President Bill Clinton led NATO in bombing Belgrade, Serbia, in 1999. I knew that the Russians were appalled at Clinton's act. No one had bombed Belgrade since the Nazis did it during World War II, and Slavic Russians naturally identified with the Slavic Serbians. Further, if the United States could decide to bomb Belgrade because it disliked the actions of that government, couldn't it also decide to bomb Moscow when it decided it disliked Russian policies? I expected a somewhat frightened and upset group in the training.

On the other hand, a number of the trainees had been in previous trainings of mine in Moscow and had every reason to trust me because of the strong and empowering experiences we'd shared. They also knew that I don't support bombing and I'm not a supporter of the U.S. Empire. Surely, I thought, these particular participants wouldn't project on me their fear and anger against Washington!

Well, they did. They didn't confront me, but instead expressed their upset through defensiveness. The tension was palpable. My every suggestion and invitation got wariness in return. Humor went nowhere. Protests against creating group agreements emerged, because if they made agreements, "George will enforce them." (I later realized that in their minds they were asking, "Who can trust him as an Enforcer?") By the end of the first session I was distinctly annoyed at the balkiness of these participants who had gathered across eleven time zones of the former Soviet Union presumably to learn from me but, it turned out, in fact to wall themselves off from me!

I went to my room to get unstuck. I wasn't thinking creatively about what to do next to assist the group to relax. I prayed for clarity and prayed for compassion for the group. "Please, God, help me to see this from a different point of view." The release came, accompanied by tears, and the fog lifted. Now I knew what to do.

Thirty-five tense participants returned from lunch, took their chairs with closed body language, stared at me as if daring me to try to force them to open up and learn. "I've been thinking lately about how excellent it is that we have the ability to defend ourselves," I started.

As the interpreter rendered it into Russian, I watched the eyebrows go up. "Think of our skin," I continued. "Where would we be without our skin to defend us against germs and disease? And if we do get sick, how useful it is to have medicines to defend against excessive fever or other dangerous conditions!"

Participants were by this time leaning forward, and a few had unfolded arms or legs. I continued in this vein, praising the value of defenses. Then I said, "I'd like you to form groups of four, and each of you will get a chance to tell a story to your group about a time when you successfully defended yourself or family or loved one against an encroachment or imposition. Tell them about a time you successfully stood up for yourself, or stood up for someone else against injustice." Participants lost their balkiness as they looked for the three others that would make them a foursome, and soon launched into their stories with intensity.

When they regathered into the whole group I asked them what the stories told them about the value of defense. Together we made quite a list, and in the process we celebrated defense. The room relaxed, the air softened, humor erupted, smiles emerged, and the group opened. We went on to have a splendid workshop, with the depth of transformational work that is only possible when people make themselves vulnerable.

Framing and Reframing Opens Windows for Learning

My mistake was in framing "defensiveness" in my mind as a negative thing, a framing many of the Russian participants share since they also are trainers and our ideology is one of praising openness. But defense is, like so many human concepts, an ambiguous concept that has pluses and minuses. If we become rigidly attached to one side, we miss the bigger picture. Successful work with groups benefits from letting go of rigid judgment, allowing ourselves to see the "other side" so we can join the group.

I sometimes think the main thing we do to help people learn is to frame and reframe: "That's the position the mayor is taking; I wonder what might be the interest that underlies that position?" "Right, I can easily see what you're saying there, but then I'm a man. I wonder if gender could influence how I see this question?"

Occasionally saying "I'd like to invite you to. . . ." rather than "Turn now to the person sitting next to you" reminds participants that they are responsible for their own learning. "Who has a different point of view?" is a reminder that there are always margins in the room.

Even the names we give to our tools can open or close doors. I no longer call Parallel Lines role plays "hassle lines" because there are many times when the skill I want participants to practice does not require one side to hassle the other. The very name "role play" is itself problematic for many people, and I rarely use the name in my trainings because it arouses needless resistance in some participants. I'm remembering the Steelworkers local union president who had heard that I use role plays and warned me, on the morning of the workshop for the United Steelworkers of America, "Don't try to use role plays with my members; they won't go for that stuff."

The heart of my design that day was a series of role plays! So I said, "Well, we'll see."

I addressed the crowd of participants: "How many of you are veterans?" Most hands went up. "OK," I said, "well, then you know about war games and probably some of you have participated in them. We'll be doing war games today in preparation for the action you're taking next week."

They participated in the role plays with enthusiasm.

Understating: Framing to Increase Participation

When we create elicitive questions to assist the group to access their knowledge, the more strongly we frame it, the more likely we are to leave some people out: "Share in your small group a time when you *completely understood* how racism affects your life." The strong ways of framing sometimes seem punchy and motivating, but they are more likely to invite hesitation and second-guessing.

I personally have an enthusiastic temperament and have been called a drama queen. I love to exaggerate and be a cheerleader. One of the hardest things for me to learn about teaching has been the value of understatement. I sometimes motivate myself with a ringing statement or question like "When in my life did I realize I could make a *big difference* in the world?" Self-facilitating, I ask myself the question because I want to recapture that moment and bring it forward now when I need it again.

When I reflected on the language, however, I began to see how it could leave people out. There are people who may never have experienced a moment when they realized they could make a "big difference," especially among working class and poor people. And so I reframe the question when I use it in a workshop: "Share in your small group a time when you felt you could change something in your life, or change something around you."

The elicitive questions we use have many such choice points. Unfortunately, I personally prefer language that inspires me: "What's something a leader should *always* do?" "What are the *no-no's* in negotiation?" The more assertive participants may be happy to respond. For others, such language demands certitude, and they may not be certain. I can get better results by asking, "What are some things a leader could do that consistently work?" "When you're negotiating, what are some behaviors that might get you into a bit of trouble?" More participants will join in creating a list of responses to such questions.

Understatements work well for probing below the surface, because they elicit less caution. Here are examples of understatements that can be useful for moving the group to discovery of more complexity. Some of them I learned from the facilitators of Process Work Psychology (Mindell, 1992, 1997). The italics show the words and phrases that make these questions and observations understatements.

> How many of you can relate *to some part of* what she just said?
>
> If you knew what you need right now, what *might* it be?
>
> How many of you have ever felt *a little* ... (and instead of *fear*: *anxiety* or *nervousness*)
>
> No right or wrong here, just to notice what *might* be happening. . . .
>
> I wonder what *might* be happening here.
>
> I wonder what that *might* represent?
>
> What else? ... *If* there were something else?
>
> I hear you using the word _____. Would you go into that *a bit more?*
>
> It seems *in the moment.* . . .
>
> I may not be getting this right, but *it seems that.* . . .
>
> Would it be OK to make *a little experiment* here, just *to see if there's something* to be learned?

Naming is framing, but I've also learned to be careful about naming something I see in the group, unless I've decided that a provocative intervention will be useful to move the group forward on its learning goals. For example, I've said, in response to someone asking why I did something, "I thought it wise to deal with the level of anxiety in the group." I then got an argument about whether the group was anxious, not a useful argument at that moment!

Still, it can be extremely important for the teacher or trainer to find some way of acknowledging a reality that is very apparent to the group, lest the participants get worried that the facilitator doesn't see what's right in front of their face. We call it the "elephant in the living room" dynamic, from the image of the social gathering at someone's home where an elephant happens to be in the living room but no one—including the host—remarks on it.

Understatement helps with the elephant in the living room problem, too: "I wonder if anyone else is feeling a bit of tension in the room?" If you are anywhere close to sensing accurately what's going on, participants will let you know!

Framing from the Margin

What keeps me on my toes when teaching adults is knowing, on the one hand, that as I'm facilitating activities and debriefs, I'm primarily working with the mainstream, but, on the other hand, that some of the most profound insights at any given moment might be held in the margin. My job is to move us through the design while staying open to the intervention from the margin. The margin's intervention often takes the form of a reframing. Consider the following story from Canada.

Michelle, a young First Nations woman, was clearly having a hard time of it in the workshop. She wasn't that far from home geographically. But she was far from home culturally, as she explained to me during the break as we stood under a tree. (She took all her breaks standing under a tree.) She told me it was a big stretch, that she was way outside her comfort zone, but she expected to be able to make it to the end of the five-day training.

On the fourth day, the workshop turned to the issue of cross-cultural communication. We made a list of participants' insights based on their experience, responding to the question: "What works?" One participant said, "Don't make assumptions."

Michelle, now more relaxed about speaking up in the group, said, "What do you mean, *assumptions?*"

Other participants assumed that her question might be about definition, so one of them defined *assumption*.

"No," she said, "I know that, but what do you *do* when you make an assumption?"

Slightly annoyed, another participant defined the word. When Michelle looked dissatisfied, still another participant asked, "Well, what do *you* do when you see a stranger coming into your village and she's dressed differently?"

"I do what my people have been taught to do," she answered. "I look at the person with honor and curiosity."

The group sat silently, stunned. I, too, was off balance. The ground was shifting under our feet. None of us with European ancestry had previously been invited outside our paradigm in this particular way.

A few more questions were directed to her as participants strained to enter her worldview, but we soon called it a night. Participants nursing their hot cocoa in the lounge later had very thoughtful looks on their faces.

How deeply can we allow our cultural fundamentals to be challenged? Are there really cultures in which people greet difference with honor and curiosity? How many profound framings of human experience are being lost to us under the global assault on indigenous cultures?

Storytelling and Generalizing

The third step in the experiential education model—generalizing—is actually a kind of reframing. It's putting the reflections of the participants, which are immediate to the activity they just went through together, into a larger context, a bigger frame.

In a simulation called the Elephant Game, for example, the participants wend their way blindfolded through an obstacle course. They go through a lot of stressful moments which test their endurance, their communication skills, their ability to maintain morale, their ability to look out for each other while taking responsibility for themselves, and their ability to create a communication network that supports coherence of the whole. In the reflection step, participants tell what happened in various parts of the obstacle course and notice what worked in supporting endurance, communication, and so on.

The content of the generalizing step depends on the goals of the workshop: teamwork, social change strategy, leadership dynamics, social defense strategy, and so on. If I choose the frame of building healthy social movements, I ask: "How was the experience of the elephant's 'tail' like that of margins in a social movement?" "How did the way your group handle stress resemble what movements do and don't do?" "How did your group's way of choosing leadership relate to how social movements choose their leaders, and what do you think of that?" By asking questions like this, the trainer is assisting the participants to reframe their learnings from the immediate activity into larger issues that impact the reasons they chose to take the course or workshop.

Another tool for reframing that also serves the step of generalizing is telling a story. A classic role play scenario used by the Alternatives to Violence Project is called "Beating the Dog" (http://www.avpinternational.org). It's done in the form of parallel lines: one side is asked to play an angry dog owner who has "lost it" and is beating her or his dog on the street. The other side is asked to play a passerby who decides to intervene nonviolently to reduce the damage to the dog. The role play successfully brings out a number of options which people might be able to use in situations of violence. During the reflection step, those options are listed on newsprint.

Many participants, however, have no conscious experience with third-party nonviolent intervention and are at a loss about how to generalize from the reflections they just made. Because of the cultural message that nonviolent action doesn't work in most situations, many participants even resist the idea that one can generalize from this "trivial" role play of interrupting dog-beating.

To frame the generalization step, I tell a personal story of a time I intervened when a man assaulted a woman on the street. The story combines suspense and humor and shows me as a very flawed intervener; yet the intervention resulted in success, thereby reframing the reflection step into a bigger picture with real-world implications. After the story, the group is usually bubbling with connections they've made to their own lives or something they heard or read about. Later I've heard from workshop participants who put the lessons into action by intervening in fights they ran across in their everyday lives.

Storytelling is one of the oldest teaching devices in the history of humankind and is still one of the most effective. One way to increase dramatically your effectiveness as a trainer or teacher is to develop a repertoire of stories relevant to the content you teach and to be ready to tell them at a moment's notice. Participants in a number of our advanced facilitator workshops have added to a checklist of tips for good storytelling:

> Along with the content-related point to the story, include universal themes (loss, growth, a time you embarrassed yourself, and so on).
>
> Use humor along with memories of being sad, angry, outraged.
>
> Assume that everyone has stories inside them.

Use your range of voice; it's OK to be dramatic.

Body language amplifies and expresses story, as do props (the visual channel).

Your facial expressions also tell the story.

Be in touch with the listeners; don't just focus on the story. Maintain eye contact.

Connect with the mood of the group initially, and once rapport is established, move emotionally more into what's appropriate for the story (pacing and leading).

Connect with how important the story is to you: care about your story and your audience.

Hint where the story is going (some listeners are impatient).

Pauses can be valuable for reflection or to heighten the drama.

Structure the story: make a beginning, middle, and end.

Simplicity of language is effective.

Use details for clarity and to make the story picturesque, sensual.

Set up the story a bit so it's clear to participants that it's not just a one-paragraph anecdote. ("That reminds me of a story, the time when I. . . .") Then change your body position—sit down if you've been standing, or stand up if you've been sitting, or move to a different part of the room.

On a good day you'll tell your story using many of these tips, and participants may be so amused/inspired/enlightened by the story that they might slip into what I call the "entertainment" headspace. You'll need to elicit responses to the story that enable them to make their own connections and underline the theoretical point being made in this generalization step.

19

Sensitivity in Cross-Cultural Issues

Canadian educator Karen Ridd and I were asked by the International Network of Engaged Buddhists to lead an extended strategy workshop for the leaders of ten farmers' movements in Northeast Thailand. That region is in some ways different from the rest of Thailand, with its own history and dialect. The farmers were fighting to assert farmers' rights, to prevent pollution, and to stop the building of dams. Their movements were at various stages of development; some had been working for years and gained substantial victories, and others were just beginning.

Day after day Karen and I put before them the tools of direct education which elicited from them their knowledge and wisdom, and challenged them to discover new options for their movements. The more experienced taught the less experienced, while the less experienced pushed the envelope with provocative questions.

On the way to the Northeast we had met a Canadian representative of a nongovernmental organization (NGO) who had served in Thailand for many years. When we told him what we were doing, he became upset with us and issued a challenge: "What makes you think you can bring the tactics of nonviolent struggle to this country where the culture is conflict aversive, and what gives you the right to even try?" We remembered that challenge when the farmers in the workshop made a list of the action tactics they had been using for years in their movements. Nearly all were tactics of nonviolent struggle.

Once again we confirmed that by using direct education, we're not bringing water with which to fill their "empty glasses." We bring proven formats that assist people to think for themselves more effectively, and we bring the ability to reframe in ways that invite new discoveries. Our expertise is our ability to ask questions, confident that the people who know their situation will also figure out the answers. The Thai inviters asked us to set aside time the next year to return and work with another movement.

Direct education is the most culture-friendly way to teach for empowerment that I know. The main preparation is to become fluent in direct education at home. If we can practice it effectively in our own culture, we are "good to go." We are safe to travel without causing major damage because the approach itself is intrinsically respectful.

Even though direct education is a solid approach for work across cultural lines, some specifics will make your workshops and courses in other cultures more effective, whether those cultures are in another country or in your own. From the experience of Training for Change and that of others, we've brought together some hard-won lessons.

Learning About the Group and Its Culture

When working with a culture not your own, diagnosing the group can be that much harder. Ahead of time, when you seek information about the group, set aside assumptions and replace them with curiosity and honor. Take time with those you are interviewing, listen before speaking, double-check information you're given, and ask "What else?" since what you've learned so far may be only the tip of the iceberg.

When you are with the group itself, listen to jokes for their underlying content, for diagnostic clues—including jokes an interpreter makes to you, if there's an interpreter. Participate in the cultural activities that happen outside the formal workshop, which might be dancing or singing or games, but be sensitive to whether you're invited. The group might want time off.

I've found it indispensable to find a "bridge person" who will honestly tell me what's going on, including my gaffes—the sooner the better. For example, during a workshop held in a Buddhist temple in Cambodia, I suddenly noticed a look of complete distraction on people's faces. My bridge person came over to me and whispered into my ear: "You're committing an obscenity—your feet are pointing toward the statue of the Buddha at the end of the room!" I quickly moved my feet so we could go on.

Fortunately, I had already acknowledged to the group that there was a tremendous lot I didn't know about their culture and their situation, which made it easier for them to forgive me. Acknowledging one's ignorance to the group also encourages participants to come and volunteer information that they might not give to someone who is acting the know-it-all.

When the group begins to resist emotionally something that you're trying to assist them to see, back off. You can find out later what's going on. Pushing when you're in mystery probably won't help. I leave a lot of my riskier interventions at home when I travel across cultural boundaries.

When English is the stated language of the training, check and double-check language skills. I was once part of a team working in South Africa; most of our participants were activists in the African National Congress. Because the mainstream spoke fluent English, we didn't realize until almost halfway through the workshop that we needed to bring in Zulu interpreters.

If you have interpreters, include them in the training team if possible—they are often valuable resources.

Approach each workshop in the culture with freshness and curiosity, rather than assume it will be like the last one in that culture. When we're not in our home territory, it is highly tempting to make premature generalizations.

At one point in my career I viewed myself as a complete klutz, temperamentally unfit to try to cross cultural lines to do adult education. I'd certainly made enough mistakes already to fill a small book. As I kept being asked back by some of the same groups, though, I realized that in my beating myself up, I was making this all about me—exactly the predictable response of a person of privilege! Instead, the way to serve my hosts was to accept, in advance, that I will, guaranteed, make cultural mistakes. All I can do is minimize them, forgive myself, and be grateful for the generosity of spirit in the people I get to work with.

Building Rapport

Sulak Sivaraksa is an internationally respected Buddhist intellectual who has repeatedly been in trouble with the Thai government for his dedication to democracy and the environment. Based in Bangkok, Sulak has built a network of nongovernmental organizations to support social justice and is deeply suspicious of Western influences in the Global South; nevertheless, he invited me ten times in a decade to train adult educators in direct education. From Sulak and his colleagues, I learned much about the specifics of rapport building when crossing cultural lines.

Find an early time to tell some of your story, including your motivation and how this workshop fits into your life. Participants are curious about strangers; if you don't tell them your story, they might make up a story that is far from the truth.

Acknowledge what you do in your own setting back home, and how you try to make it a better neighborhood or city or country. Explain how the work on this trip benefits you and your movement. It's usually helpful if you include some humor at your own expense. And don't try to do all this at the beginning of the workshop. Everything I said earlier about course beginnings matters. In fact, it matters even more, because if you speechify about yourself in the beginning, you will convince them that you have something to be defensive about.

Be aware that you will be tested; participants need to know if you are reliable and if you walk your talk. Be aware of security concerns for local people, and do not ask to know more about the political situation than you need to know to do your work, if security is an issue for them. Be aware of local attitudes toward power holders. Listen in hot political situations rather than express your own opinion.

Show respect with your questions about the culture and in every other way you can think of. Keep remembering that it's about them, not about you. Because this principle is so important to me, I have often hesitated to come out as a gay man in cultures where that would be problematic. I want the workshop to be about them, not about me.

Still, I yearn in such situations to be in solidarity with those in the room who may be a sexual minority. What happened to me about halfway through my decade of work in Thailand was once again a chance to relearn the First Principle: trust the process.

_____

My Thai co-facilitator Pracha Hutanuwatr, a close associate of Sulak Sivaraksa, said he thought the container was strong enough to do some serious diversity work in this workshop. The goal was to explore community building, and he knew many of the participants personally. He said they were somewhat invested in a Thai tradition of ritualized unity, even though everyone knows of the disunity under the surface. He suggested he lead a different kind of ritual, which exposes hidden differences. He asked me to join as participant.

We all stood on one end of the room while Pracha gave us our instructions. ''When I call out an identity or condition,'' he said, "please walk across the room, turn and face those who remained standing at this end, and then return. For example, if I say 'men,' all those who identify as men can walk down there" — he pointed to the far wall — "turn and pause, and then walk back. Of course the monks would not walk in that case because in Thailand they are a third gender. Questions? Remember, this is a silent ritual. No talking, please."

Pracha did indeed start with men, and women, and those who were ordained, and went on through a series of categories. When he came to "ethnic Chinese," "tribal person," and "former Communist," I knew he was intentionally moving to sensitive ground. Suddenly he said, "lesbian or gay."

I was shocked. Pracha knew I was gay. He knew if he named it, I would walk. In his own country, he was inviting me to come out!

While processing the implications, I slowly walked across the room, turned and found beside me a young monk whose face was alive with strong emotions. We took a moment to gaze at the crowd at the other end. As we took our silent steps of return, the monk broke into loud sobs.

I watched him as he rejoined the cluster of monks. I saw by their body language that it could never be the same again. He wept, alone. As Pracha called the next identity, I went to stand beside the gay monk so he wouldn't be completely alone.

At the end of the exercise, Pracha asked us to join our buddy to share about the experience. I joined Pracha, himself formerly a monk for many years. "This will be very big for the monks," he said. "They have a lot of work to do."

I kept in touch with the young monk, who finally found some allies in the monastery while remaining a one-man gay activist alliance in the larger monkhood. The word spread in the underground network of lesbians and gay men that Sulak's network was on the cutting edge of Thai culture. Pracha took a risk, as do all of us facilitators who value liberation. The monk ended up grateful, and so was I.

How the Culture Might Influence Your Design and Facilitation

Organizational development consultant Erika Thorne was hired to assist an immigrant mutual aid group in Minnesota to create a strategic plan. Many Hmong people had newly immigrated to the area, and Erika didn't have strong connections to the culture. Her approach to planning is highly elicitive, so the group was able to engage actively, but Erika noticed that the closer the people got to finishing the plan, the lower the morale became. Once the plan was written and agreed on, the organization almost fell apart from the culture-related stresses associated with achieving the goal!

In retrospect, Erika writes, "It would have been more effective to conceive of the assignment as organizational development with a modest amount of planning. And to approach it as an exploration of empowerment, which would have opened the process to culture-specific activities to reduce stress." Erika's experience also underlines the value of having a bridge person, someone who we can test our design with and look for how culture might suggest needed revisions.

If you have a mainstream identity in relation to the marginalized group you've agreed to teach—even within the same city—a good habit to get into is to use the water glasses exercise near the beginning. It's almost impossible for most margins to look at someone from a mainstream culture and not see an "expert who will expect deference to his or her superior knowledge." The sooner you get out from under that burden, the better!

John Paul Lederach (1995), with his wide experience with conflict transformation training in the Global South, underlines

Friere's emphasis on naming as a way to open the doors of discovery. Lederach found while working in Central America, for example, a place where there are 160 synonyms for *conflict*. He put each on a card, invited participants to organize the cards, and they were soon developing their own theory of conflict from indigenous wisdom.

Lederach also discourages the use of exercises that demonstrate the "correct way" to do something—mediation, for example. The trainer's example is very powerful, especially early in a training, so demonstrating the "right way" prevents eliciting from participants what makes sense in *their* cultural terms. Instead, he uses role plays the way we do at Training for Change: to elicit options that the group can reflect on as it discovers what makes sense for the group's members.

Using the discomfort zone concept can help us to redesign to suit the culture. Most cultures have customary ways of beginning events—a short speech by the host, for example, or a ceremony of some kind. Remember that even coming to a seminar led by a foreigner already puts most people in their discomfort zone. There's no need to move them into the alarm zone by dispensing with the traditional opening and plunging immediately into how you do things back home!

Be sure to ask your inviters and bridge persons about the political situation that surrounds the workshop, especially regarding security. For their own safety, participants may need to be very careful about self-disclosure, and you may need to avoid some learning activities that otherwise would support the workshop goals. In an authoritarian state in Africa where I worked, my local co-facilitator told me that one of the participants was a police spy. He explained that when the debrief of an exercise got to a sensitive part, he would call a tea break. Then I would engage the spy in conversation over tea while the other participants informally milled about and said what they needed to say to one another!

Hard Questions: A Facilitator's Checklist

Intention to do good is not enough. None of us men avoids sexism in his relationships simply through intention; none of us white people avoids racism in our relationships through intention alone. Clarifying intention is helpful, but other dimensions of reality need to be addressed if we're not to do more harm than good.

After listening to people from other cultures for many years, in their tears, anger, amusement, and wisdom, I've come up with the following checklist to increase the chance that I'm doing an honest day's work when I work in other countries or in cultures where I am mainstream in relation to that culture. It may be a useful checklist for you.

Do I know that my struggle is interconnected with theirs?

"If you have come to help me, you are wasting your time. But if you are coming because your liberation is bound up with mine, then let us work together." (This quote is usually attributed to Lilla Watson [1992], an aboriginal activist from Brisbane, Australia, but she requests that the collective origin of the quote be honored.)

Am I fighting on my own front, as well as working with others?

The struggle for change at home is where I know most and where I am most responsible. It grounds me. If I put nearly all my attention in other cultures, other countries, I run the risk of losing touch with the ground, of becoming spacy, losing my authenticity. I cannot teach what I no longer know; I cannot take others places I no longer go.

Am I supporting the domination of U.S. power holders?

Corporations increasingly advertise their products and practices as environmentally friendly; so much of this advertising is exaggerated and even fraudulent that there's even a name for it: "greenwashing." Ethical consultants and teachers don't participate in greenwashing.

I believe that my government and others have a habit of using economic and military power to force and manipulate others into sacrificing for the greater profit of our power holders. Just as polluting corporations don't display their records of environmental destruction, my government doesn't display its record—well documented—of supporting hundreds of dictatorships and compliant warlords over the years. Instead, my government proclaims its devotion to freedom and democracy.

I would consider myself unethical if I were to use my teaching skills to further my government's version of greenwashing, that is, its pretense that it puts first the values of democracy and freedom. I don't want my work to be used to buttress a claim that isn't true. This book isn't the place to argue my point of view, but the reader who wants to work among the marginalized needs, I think, to understand my assertion and consider it seriously.

That said, the fact remains that I am a U.S. citizen and I sometimes work on the ground in contexts where the agenda of the marginalized group overlaps with the agenda of U.S. government agencies. On the ground, it's complicated. Purity is not my goal, but I would like to be as clear as possible. I want an educational outcome that empowers the participants; such an outcome requires that I not be thought to be an agent of one of the armed nation-states who comprise the global mainstream.

I rely on several methods. One is to make it clear to participants that I want to listen to their political views and struggles; I want to understand. Another is to acknowledge responsibility for any ways that I know of that my country has hurt their country. In Cambodia, for example, I have each time included (when the container was strong) an apology for the role that the United States played in making possible the genocidal Khmer Rouge regime.

A third method is to include in my design an activity that opens genuine discussion that my government wouldn't want to happen. I once introduced the simulation Star Power, for example, into a country where the United States hopes that capitalism will some day prevail. The game gives local people a chance to debate whether that is the future they want. A U.S. representative who observed the activity was appalled and attacked me for it; it turned out that her version of "democracy" did not include democratic debate about economic systems.

Teachers and facilitators from the United States and other mainstream countries may find a variety of ways to make their work more fully empowering for the margins. None of us can take a pass on this without colluding with the cluelessness of the mainstream. We can't be ethical teachers and at the same time volunteer to be naïve.

Am I accountable to the people who invite me?

I set it up to make it easy for the inviters not to invite me back, because I'm aware that norms of hospitality and obligation can make inviters less than fully free to decide I'm no longer needed. In the two countries where I've returned most often, Thailand and Russia, it was always clear that the inviter was in charge of whether I would be invited back.

Do I offer appreciative presence?

I learned the value of appreciative presence personally in the early days of the activist group Movement for a New Society. It was very affirming that two "outsiders" came and spent time with us. Elise Boulding and A. Paul Hare were two internationally known sociologists I respected tremendously. Elise and Paul were full of questions and enthusiasm for our experiment and carefully avoided giving us advice. They left us feeling stronger and more confident. I think of them as role models for occasions when I'm an outsider.

An important consideration for me, therefore, is whether the invitation is for a technical role in which I am expected simply to fly in, stay in a hotel and facilitate, and fly out, or whether I can offer appreciative presence. I know that in many countries in the Global South, relationship is valued far more than in Europe and especially in the United States. If the inviter mainly has in mind playing the game the way U.S. consultants typically play it, I turn it down.

By paying attention to this criterion, I find that workshop participants frequently seek me out for other kinds of support while I'm working with them as a trainer. My listening ear and distance from their immediate struggle gives them a sounding board they can use as they think out their dilemmas. If they feel isolated, or like small fishes in a big pond, my being there is experienced as affirmation and is empowering

Am I aware of my rank?

I can offer appreciative presence because I'm aware of my rank as a U.S.er, Westerner, expert/writer-of-books, white person, older man. Rank cannot be wished away; it is in the eyes of the beholders. Since rank cannot be ignored without becoming the elephant in the living room, a sensible way to handle rank is to acknowledge it and to use it to support others. I show my awareness of rank when I affirm the intelligence in others and, rather than give answers to their questions (which my ego loves me to do), explore the issues with them in such a way that they discover the answer that's right for their situation.

Am I committed to capacity-building?

As soon as I've worked with new inviters a couple of times and seen that they are pleased with the results of direct education, I ask if they would like to build their own capacity to do that kind of training. I offer to do whatever we can to teach their people to do direct education. For me this is essential because dependency is the opposite of empowerment—if the inviter remains dependent on us to come in and do trainings, an important opportunity is lost.

Characteristically, the training of trainers is an add-on: we continue to do workshops on strategy or team-building in that country and add to our schedule pedagogical training for those from the workshops who are especially talented and interested, and selected by the inviter. This is not a quick process, since the value of direct education is its ability to address the real complexity of adult learning. In Thailand and Russia, at some point we dropped almost completely the other training we were doing and focused completely on capacity building.

Is this the "American model of education" that I'm spreading abroad?

The essentials of direct education go back to Brazilian Paolo Freire and his liberation pedagogy and the popular education movement it spawned. An Asian Buddhist scholar, however, sees connections to an inspiration much further back. After several years of leading workshops in Thailand, which nearly always included Buddhist monks and nuns, a controversy began to arise about "whether Karen Ridd and George Lakey were foisting upon traditional Thais an exotic, foreign-born technology."

At the next workshop one of the new participants was a leading monk who was a Buddhist scholar and had, in his student days, been a Marxist revolutionary steeped in Western modes of thought. His goal, we learned, was to examine firsthand our pedagogy and come to his own conclusions. Periodically in the workshop, which was a training of trainers, Karen and I would stop, and the monk would reflect to the whole group his thinking and observations.

We were surprised and reassured to hear, as our interpreter quickly shared the remarks, that there was in his view such ample basis in the Buddha's own teachings for this kind of pedagogy, as well as experiments along these lines at various points along the way, that direct education could be seen as fully in alignment with ancient Buddhist teaching and practice. He further raised the question, Why did Thais and other Buddhists become enamored of the European university tradition (only a thousand years old, after all), forsaking the Buddhist principle of the here-and-now as the seat of wisdom? Rather than following the European and American mainstream educational practice of valuing head over heart, abstraction over experience, and alienation of the life of the mind, wouldn't it have been far more Buddhist to invent a consistent practice such as that which Karen and George were applying?

Handling Ourselves When Working Cross-Culturally

I sweltered in an abandoned movie theater with two hundred punk rockers and horrible sanitation for three days. After one night on the concrete floor, I fled to a motel on the outskirts of town, feeling like a coward, but my bones were telling me that I was 49 years old! Besides, the many bands were scheduled to start playing at 9:00 each night, and there was no place to sleep except on the dance floor itself, so heaven only knew *when* I could bed down!

Betsy Raasch-Gilman, a veteran activist trainer who has a mainstream appearance, thus describes facilitating trainings in the culture of young activist anarchists who had gathered in Louisville, Kentucky, in 2001. Many of these young anarchists had participated in the global justice movement in Seattle and Washington, D.C. Thrilled with the sense of power that they felt in creating temporary autonomous zones during these demonstrations, they now yearned to create alternative structures that might incorporate the values of a more free society in their everyday lives.

Betsy had previously led trainings for the global justice movement in Seattle and elsewhere. For this Permanent Autonomous Zones (PAZ) conference, she planned to lead four workshops on group process and oppression issues, especially classism.

Those three days were excruciating in terms of cultural mismatch. The groups attending my workshops, however, got larger and larger. In spite of the obvious differences in our ages and appearances, participants responded enthusiastically to both content and method. In a classism workshop I suggested that people form discussion groups according to class background, and a small caucus of working-class people shared with one another. Their excitement and relief was palpable. The middle-class caucus groups came up with some good insights into themselves. "It's all very well for us to go hopping freight trains," one person said, "but we know that if we hurt ourselves, we can go to a hospital and our parents' health insurance will cover us. We're not really hobos."

I returned home to St. Paul cautiously hoping that I'd been useful despite the culture gap between me and them. A week or two later, a co-worker at home left me a note that she had heard, via the grapevine, that "consensus opinion at the PAZ is that *you rock!*" It was the sweetest feedback I've gotten in over twenty years of training.

This story reveals a major method for handling yourself when crossing cultural lines: be aware of what is stressful for you and take care of yourself. Betsy's motel escape kept her going! Most of us also find that it helps enormously to have a training partner who can give us support when the going gets rough.

The Near-Disaster I Learned the Most From: A Workshop with Multiple Cultures

Participants came to the three-week workshop from a dozen countries spread over five continents; I was lead facilitator in a three-person multicultural facilitation team. We were trying out a new curriculum that would have been challenging even if all the participants and facilitators were from the same culture.

A conflict emerged that became highly inflamed. Some members of the mainstream believed they'd witnessed an oppressive, sexist act. Others, especially those on the margin, disagreed vehemently but had difficulty asserting themselves fully. The facilitation team split bitterly over the issue, leaving me in charge.

I diagnosed the conflict as a storm; it was about the time we might expect Stage 2 of the group development model. Believing participants were on their way to becoming a high-performance team, I facilitated following the guidelines of Scott Peck. The organizational sponsor began to panic when, after a couple of days, there was no resolution; a high-status participant left in disgust.

Finally I realized that it wasn't an ordinary storm. What was going on was actually a deep culture conflict that couldn't be resolved on its own terms; the group didn't have the container or the skills to do so. I changed course and facilitated us to new ground that enabled the group to continue to learn.

As in any complex conflict, there were many ingredients to this one. Five stand out, however, with compelling lessons for my future work when there are multiple cultures in the room.

- We made the mistake letting "coverage" of newly researched content reduce time spent on container building. We forgot that multicultural training requires *more* time building the container rather than less. The thin walls of the container could not support a hot conflict, and the resulting anxiety added heat to the fire.

- We did not take into account the mission of the partici- pants. Their plan was to go into a situation of conflict in a country almost none of them had seen before, with hazy objectives, side by side with strangers in whom they felt no trust. They brought to the workshop a high anxiety level to begin with, and we did not design for that.

- We did almost nothing to promote self-responsibility in the learners. Dealing as we were with mature adults who'd had a variety of life and work experiences, we made the assumption that they would know how to take responsibility for their own learning in a stressful situation. We forgot that the cultures they came from do not include self-responsibility as a norm in education. They were in a workshop. Why would they operate differently from the way they'd been socialized in the schools of their youth? The result was that, when the conflict raged in the workshop, most participants' reactions were to blame others rather than consider what they could personally do to (a) learn from it and (b) intervene in a problem-solving way.

- We didn't teach them to value curiosity and suspend judgment. When the conflict heated up, we saw little indication of curiosity about anyone who took a different position from their own, or curiosity about those who were remaining quiet. Since the group didn't initially experience activities that emphasized the value of curiosity as an alternative to judgment, it wasn't possible for that to become a reference point to support the group to move from its stalemate.

- Finally, we did nothing to teach them how to wage conflict in a multicultural setting. The mainstream of the group couldn't see that the conflict might have something to do with culture, and the margins didn't speak out strongly. We facilitators did not share skills initially that would enable mainstream or margins to learn from the conflict and move on. Since then I've learned about Barbara Schaetti's team and its methods of inner work in culture conflict (Schaetti, Watanabe, and Ramsey, 2000).

Since this bruising experience, I've heard similar stories from a number of teachers and trainers: a group moving into hot conflict precipitated by an incident that is regarded by one part of the group as oppressive, and the group proves unable to resolve the issue or see the cultural dimension of it. "Calling out" is often the trigger event. Often those who are alerting the group to the sexism or other oppression that they see have experience in working oppression issues successfully only within their own culture. *Going from monoculture to multiculture takes more support than they have probably been getting.*

I've now learned to take my time in the beginning to build an especially strong container, to underline the guideline "Use everything for your advancement," to take account of the mission of the group and its context, to teach the group to value curiosity and suspend judgment, and to build skills for waging conflict in the likelihood that it will arise.

The good news about this particular case is that the sponsor a year later found that the participants who endured this training were, once in the field, a more cohesive and high-stamina group than other project members who had not gotten the training. Painful as it was, including for me, the experience once again supports the principle of sociologist Lewis Coser (1956) that conflict is often a builder of group cohesion.

The Uses of Being an Outsider

In Russia in the early '90s, would-be participants would arrive very late for a workshop, sometimes as late as Sunday afternoon for a weekend workshop. These new arrivals would see no reason why they shouldn't join the workshop at that point if they had friends who were already in the group. For them, the event must be something like a conference where people can arrive any time, and the value of friendship meant that it was a plus to join the group whenever one could.

My Golubka colleagues and I discussed this problem of late arrivals, and agreed that they needed to upset a cultural norm and expectation in order to make this thing called "experiential training" work. Golubka wanted to create new cultural space in Russia for a new social invention. But who would be "the bad guy" who would take the actual heat?

I was given the job.

Each time a latecomer arrived, I went to the door with a colleague to interpret, while another member of Golubka continued the facilitation. I explained to the latecomers that they were not allowed to join the workshop. The dialogue, sometimes quite heated, was faithfully interpreted by the colleague whose body language would suggest that this crazy practice was not *his* or *her* idea!

I was once asked to facilitate a strategy workshop for a Buddhist monk who led his fellow monks and nearby villagers in a movement to save Thailand's rain forest. In addition to the usual means of protest, they were also ordaining trees, solemnly wrapping the huge tree trunks in monks' robes to warn off the loggers. The movement's impact was growing. Only a week before I got there for the workshop, a key movement ally was murdered, and speculation was growing about how long it would be until the leading monk would himself be assassinated.

I'd prepared a design for the three-day workshop, but from the day of my arrival in Thailand, I was getting information that made the design seem inappropriate. In the car driving from Bangkok to the forest, I continued to learn more about the movement, and I continued to become more confused about how to design the workshop. To me, one of the more alarming bits of news was that the workshop would not simply be the head monk and the movement's secondary leadership, but it would be an open workshop where I could expect villagers who had little if any literacy and had never been drawn into discussions about strategy or direction.

Finally, we got there and I was led into the presence of the leader. He looked at me, and also through me. "I see that you are worried about something," he said.

"Yes," I answered. "My plan for the workshop now seems irrelevant, and I don't know what to do."

"Don't worry about what to do tomorrow," he advised. "You will see in that situation what needs to be done; you will understand how to be present in that moment."

Supper was rice and curry served from the wood fire where it was cooked. We stood around holding our bowls and chatting. I was standing next to two NGO staffers from Bangkok who had come to watch the training. After some conversation, I told them I'd noticed that they weren't talking with the villagers. "Why would we?" responded one. "We're from Bangkok. What could we possibly talk about with villagers?"

I was incredulous. "But at least you're from the same country!" I said. "How do you expect me to connect with them when I'm from the other side of the planet?"

The first morning of the three-day workshop dawned with me still without a plan. The head monk led us in a long morning walk through winding forest paths to a cliff with a view and a resident wolf. The other monks walked ahead of me. I walked along with the villagers, encountering the Buddhist precept of mindfulness: whenever my attention strayed to anxiety about what I was going to do in the workshop, I tripped on a root or my head hit a low-hanging branch.

We sat in a semicircle at the cliff edge, and our leader led us in meditation. As a Quaker, I was grateful for such a beginning and went into a relaxed state. He spoke from the silence, about the forest as a lung of the earth, about our duty to live peaceably as part of nature.

Then it was my turn. My prayers had been answered. The anxiety had transformed into curiosity and then into confidence. I began to tell stories, about Australians blockading ships carrying rain forest logs, Americans blockading ships docking to pick up weapons for killing people in Bangladesh, Burmese protesting on a mass scale for democracy, Gandhians interspersing protest with constructive program.

The workshop became a feast of case studies. The stories worked for everyone. The drama caught the unsophisticated people who didn't quite know what this workshop was, and the strategic lessons were noted by the more knowledgeable. Once the workshop had momentum, we were able to create small groups to develop campaign strategy thinking, report back for general discussion, then return again to small task groups.

At the end of the first day, a Thai NGO worker came to me and said she'd been talking with the nuns and village women who were cooking for us. She'd learned that a number of women had asked permission to attend the workshop and were refused, on the grounds that the women's role was to cook while the men studied.

The next morning I chose as a case study an extended coal miners' strike in the mountains of Appalachia, a strike that was losing until the women of the coal towns joined the picket lines and took direct action. "So you see, women can be a very powerful part of social movements, and I wouldn't be surprised some day, if you invite me back to do another workshop, by finding women also in the workshop." I went on with other strategic issues.

On the morning of the third day, I was surprised to find a sprinkling of women in the workshop, their eyes shining with anticipation. We continued with our strategy work, and as we were harvesting the thinking of the task groups, we came to a group that had nothing to report. The face of the task group leader was covered with embarrassment. He clearly believed he owed me an explanation for their lack. "You see," he stammered, "this is so new for us. Our leader has never asked for our thinking before."

The entire room became still.

What happens now? I asked myself. I gave the monk my most open look of inquiry. He shifted in his robes. "Yes," he said gravely, "but we know that the movement is in a dangerous time. I believe it is appropriate for us all to think together."

I exhaled. The elephant in the living room had at last been named — the extreme vulnerability of the movement to repression by killing or jailing of its leader. Outsider that I was, outside the web of rank and deference which makes some kinds of work forbidden, I seized the moment.

"Your leader welcomes you to think with him about the movement's situation," I say as I nod to him. "For the next round of task group work, I'd like you to consider the plans you need to make if the Venerable is arrested: How will you continue your movement?''

The group dug into its task with newly released energy. I watched the monk, who as before sat quietly in his dignified and composed way. The training space was actually an old wooden shed with a large platform on one side. The participants all sat on that platform, leaving a circle of empty space around their leader, a kind of moat. My interpreter and I stood facing the platform and the participants.

The task groups were ready with their reports, which they gave one at a time, including the task group that had not had a report to give previously. The elements of the plans sounded reasonable to me, but the delivery by the task group leaders sounded hesitant, as if they still didn't give themselves the right to take action without their abbot.

Again trading on my outsiderness, I decided to raise the stakes. "I'm hearing the plans you are making, but not your commitment," I said. "So I want to challenge you. If you are serious about taking a new level of responsibility in this movement, I want you to express that by closing the empty space between you and the Venerable."

The day was sunny, but I would not have been surprised if thunder cracked at that moment and a lightning bolt hit the roof of the shed. The villagers looked stunned at the suggestion. After what seemed like a very long time of stillness, someone moved, then another, then another. Gradually, the entire space was filled in with the bodies of villagers and other monks.

I exhaled again, and again looked expectantly at the monk. "And what is that like for you, may I ask?"

The participants held their breath.

Very slowly the words came out. "I am glad you have taken this action." He looked around. "Now I do not feel so lonely."

20

The Drama of Transformational Work

As participants began to leave after a very long training day, I looked around to see if there was someone I should check in with. The evening session was on diversity and that subject always leaves some participants in more turbulence than others. Kathy, a young Vietnamese American woman, was nearby and I moved over to her. "How's it going?" I asked.

"My stomach's tight and I have a headache, but other than that, all right!" she grinned.

"Be gentle with yourself tonight," I suggested. "It would be fine with me if you wanted to share with the group in the morning, whatever you want to."

Kathy grinned again, and slipped out the door.

The next morning we settled into a format I call Open Sharing, a time based on silence when participants can share whatever is on their hearts. I don't ordinarily allow discussion or dialogue; each participant who wishes simply has the space to share.

Very soon after we started, Kathy spoke up. "Last night I felt invisible," she said. "The session was supposed to be about diversity, but I felt completely ignored ... not even walled off, just un*seen*."

She looked at me for support, and got it nonverbally.

"That's how it is for us Asian Americans in the United States, you know — we're the people who are walked right past, the people not talked about ... and certainly the people not listened to!" She faltered.

"I'm listening," I said, "and probably others are listening too, at this moment, so how about you let us know how strongly you feel about this, if you want to. This time is for you."

Kathy let herself go, sometimes yelling and crying. She told us stories from high school, from college, about the countless times when she'd been a high achiever and still regarded as part of the wallpaper.

I assisted the group to stay alert and listen rather than to shut down: "Maybe some in the group remember times when they were ignored and maybe you can relate to Kathy's experience.... Maybe some of the organizers in the group can relate to how this could happen to some people you are organizing."

When Kathy was finished, I modified the Open Sharing format so participants could express the impact on them of Kathy's work. Everyone who spoke found it inspiring to see Kathy stand up for herself so powerfully. Kathy's breakthrough became a vivid metaphor to anchor the remaining work of the weekend.

Looking for Transformational Moments

Most of us who lead groups are used to looking for the teachable moments, the times when the group is particularly open to a new learning. I find it useful to watch also for transformational moments, the times when a group is open to letting go of a *block* to learning.

Individuals enter a course or workshop with many blocks to learning, including limiting beliefs about themselves. "I wouldn't be a good Vietnamese woman if I insisted on the attention I deserve." "I can't speak before the public." "I'm not worthy to ask a person of wealth for money." "I freeze when protests get chaotic." "I'm not organized enough to be in charge of that annual dinner." "I would get too scared if I were arrested." "I'm not enough of an extrovert to be the volunteer coordinator."

"I forget the statistics about out-of-control corporations and can't make a convincing case." "I can't teach the content of the course and pay close attention to the process in the group at the same time."

We all have limiting beliefs, including me. I've encountered some of mine as I've been writing this book, including the belief that telling so many stories about myself is like bragging, puffing myself up—a very big no-no in my working class family.

Since limiting beliefs discourage us even from trying, if we can loosen up or dissolve a limiting belief, we're powerfully opening the door to learning.

Environmentalist and funder Viki Laura List and I used to give workshops for activists on how to fundraise. We found that we could share knowledge and skills in a short workshop but that there was little changed behavior afterward—many participants had beliefs about money and fundraising that limited their ability to learn deeply and apply the learning. To unlock those beliefs, we would need more time for container building, but people weren't interested in giving that much time—again, because they were being driven by their unconscious beliefs about money and fundraising and themselves!

In my experience, when a group has built a strong enough container and becomes clear that empowerment is their job, not mine, the group generates many transformational moments. Human beings have a deep yearning to grow past their limitations. For me it's a joy in this work that I get to accompany some of them on that journey.

The Irritating Young Man in Moscow: Working for the Group and Himself at the Same Time

"I don't think the communication is going right in this workshop," the young man said. "I'm a little frustrated."

I'd noticed that Alex had seemed particularly distant from the group. Perhaps, I thought, he was now ready to join. I asked him, "May I work with you a little while on that? Could I ask you some questions?"

"Sure...I guess so," he said hesitantly.

"The idea would be to clarify some of the communication going on, so you and all of us can be clearer." I paused, and looked around. "Who is someone you see in the circle now that you wish you were in better communication with?"

"Everyone."

"Please take a minute to look around and see if someone stands out as somebody you'd like to be in better communication with. This is a kind of experiment.... I think it will help. Will you try it?"

"Well, OK.... Sasha."

I turned to Sasha to get his permission to participate in this experiment. Then back to Alex: "How about saying to Sasha, 'I'd like to be in better communication with you.'"

Alex laughed with embarrassment. "I couldn't do that."

"Maybe not," I said, joining him. "But maybe you can. Sometimes when we make a statement of what we want, we get it. Or at least we clarify what's happening. What are you feeling right now?"

Alex laughed. "I don't know." He laughed some more. "I guess I feel embarrassed. Can we stop this now?"

"Certainly. You're in charge here. I'm simply making suggestions, inviting you into a lab to do little experiments about communication, so this workshop will get clearer for you. We can stop now, or we can go on, on the chance we'll learn something out of this experiment."

"Yeah." Alex laughed again. "OK, let's go on. What was that I could say to Sasha?"

We continued step by small step until he was able to sit directly next to Sasha and ask to be closer. As I worked with him, I frequently explained to the group what seemed to be happening: "Now he is taking quite a risk, which is a courageous thing to do. How many of you have ever worried about being rejected, and know what that can feel like?" I put up my hand, and nearly everyone else did, too.

The outcome of the work with Alex was not only that he found his communication channel unplugged but that the whole group, which had found him the most irritating member of the workshop, changed its attitude toward him to one of understanding and respect.

On one level Alex and I were working with something that prevented him from being powerful ("I can't ask for what I want so I'll be irritating to get noticed instead"). The game he was playing made it hard to put his skills to work in a team.

On another level I was working with the material of the learning group—its refusal to see what was really going on for the young man, perhaps because rejection was a live theme for the whole group on several levels. (It was a workshop for gay men in Russia, where gays are cast out of society in extreme ways.) In working with the Irritating Young Man, I was really working with the group as well; I felt in deep solidarity with every man in the room who was wanting to feel safe enough in the group to put his own needs and wants forward. The closing circle that evening was quite moving, and the next day of the workshop was "minimum bullshit, maximum honest learning."

As I reflected on the work Alex did, I was struck by how important it was that it was experiential. If I'd just explained Alex's game to him and the group, it would have been interesting but not transformative. He needed to feel the embarrassment and make the decision to risk, and risk again. The group members needed to watch his process, identify with it, and come to new realizations about themselves and him. I needed to keep me and my guesses about Alex and the group low profile, to allow the *participants* to come to gain the knowledge in the only way that would result in change—experientially.

Isn't This Therapy?

Transformational work certainly has some similarities to group therapy. For one thing, it works with emotions, although comedians also work with emotions and we don't call them therapists. Another similarity is that this work takes training—I certainly would hope that no one tries to do these interventions based only on what they read here.

The differences between transformational work in direct education and therapy are, however, substantial. As shown in the story of the Irritating Young Man, my goal was not his healing, nor was it an exploration into the past to give him insight into the source of his painful choice. My goal was simply to loosen up his limiting belief so he could function more effectively in groups working for change. His belief blocked him as a citizen and got in the way of his learning. He needed to unblock so his learning could proceed. I was functioning very much within my role as a trainer or teacher—helping him, and the group, get on with their learning.

That difference in goal also shows up in who I choose to work with. When the container is strong and participants realize that they *could* get some assistance with something that bothers them, transformational moments are everywhere! I choose only those that assist the individual and group to unblock for learning in relation to the curriculum. My role as an educator is content driven, unlike that of typical therapy. The intervention with Alex in Moscow focused on how his difficulty in giving leadership was related to that of many in the room, in a leadership workshop. Kathy's work got my full support because her limiting belief ("I'm destined to be invisible") stood in the way of her full power and responsibility as a citizen, and the entire group needed to know that invisibility is part of the oppression of Asian Americans.

What Do I Mean by *Transformation?*

Writers and teachers use versions of this word in the discourse about change, learning, and growth. It's no accident that the word became more popular in and after the 1960s, because that decade's social movements boldly envisioned change beyond the ordinary. In the '60s, movements went from goals that would result in a change in degree to a change in kind. The 1960s movements associated change with expansion of possibility. The civil rights activists of the U.S. South wanted not just an incremental increase in civic rights and responsibilities; they wanted *freedom*.

One ripple effect of those movements shows up when organizational trainers and consultants who acknowledge the functionality of competent "transactional leadership" nevertheless offer to teach managers how to become *"transformational* leaders," boldly seeking a new level of excellence by tapping into a deeper source of motivation. Such trainers and consultants are using the distinction made by James MacGregor Burns (1978). The YouthBuild Academy for Transformation, for example, therefore offers seminars to teach youth workers how to assist the disadvantaged youth they work with to learn *to free up more of their human potential than ordinary educational methods do* (http://www.youthbuild.org/).

In 1978 Jack Mezirow published an article in *Adult Education Quarterly* that launched an effort to go beyond teaching skills and knowledge, by daring "to recognize, reassess, and modify the structures of assumptions and expectations that frame our tacit points of view and influence our thinking, beliefs, attitudes, and actions" (see Mezirow, 2009). Many publications and seven international conferences have so far been devoted to what he called "transformative learning." Because the work of Mezirow and his followers extends to the frames of reference that people carry in their heads about everything, its reach is enormous.

Direct education's practice—what we call "transformational work"—is consistent with Mezirow's approach but is far more focused. Our focus is on the learner's own limiting beliefs about herself or himself, and how those beliefs are mirrored in the culture of the group. In our version of the concept of transformation, we also pick up on a repeated criticism of Mezirow as being preoccupied with the cognitive map in people's heads, neglecting imagination, intuition, and emotion. For us, it's the appearance of emotion that alerts us to a limiting frame of reference! There's no way we can ignore emotion because we regard it as the tip-off, so we train ourselves to pay attention.

We make this knowledge operational by working in the emotional channel with the "presenting person"—Alex, in the Moscow workshop—whose work with himself or herself also represents the group's work. In that way we tacitly call upon all the participants who use the emotional learning channel to be our allies in the work.

As this next story shows, the result is a modality that extends well beyond cognitive work and yet has everything to do with the maps in people's heads.

Theory Emerging from the Discomfort Zone

The union local pulled together the officers and shop stewards for a team-building weekend retreat, the first of its kind for the Canadian Union of Postal Workers. The leadership wanted to become more proactive in dealing with the inevitable splits and conflicts in the union, so they wanted the retreat to include skill building and new perspectives on what builds and erodes solidarity.

By the afternoon of the second day, the container was fairly solid, so I decided we were ready to take another risk. I asked the group of twenty to do a mingle, in which they would move around and experience a series of one-on-one interactions. Each time they encountered someone, the person initiating would start a sentence with a formula and then complete it. The formula was "Something I'm proud about in my contribution in the union is...." The other person in the pair would simply respond, "Thanks for telling me that," and the two would move on to others.

As I finished the instructions, I could feel the tension in the air; we were surely out of their comfort zones. They reluctantly rose from their chairs and started slowly into the center. Two went directly to the toilet. I could barely hear the sound of the statements being made; they were more like murmurs. After completing one interaction, most people walked aimlessly around inside the circle, staring at the floor. This was not the discomfort zone; this was the alarm zone! I quickly called a halt to the exercise and asked them to return to their seats.

"That was one of the hardest things I've ever tried to do," one man said. "It was torture!" another broke in and got some laughs. One after another expressed the reluctance, almost dread, she or he felt in trying to do the exercise. "You know, it seems like a simple thing — tell something we're proud of! Hell, we're all proud of something! But to say it to somebody, like we mean it.... I just couldn't do it."

"If it seems like a simple thing," I said, "and yet everyone found it really hard to do, then what do you think makes it so difficult?"

Silence. "I gotta say ... I mean, this is going to sound shitty ... but I mean it. I just don't feel that great about myself. I mean, I actually most of the time feel bad about myself." Heads nodded. Others made statements of agreement.

I waited, because I was hoping someone there would say it instead of me. One of the officers spoke next: "OK, I was thinking it was just an individual thing, you know, like I don't feel good about myself, so what? It's just me. But if that's how most of us feel, then we gotta ask why? How come us elected leaders, people who get things done, who have our lives together — why don't we feel great about ourselves?"

Someone else chimed in immediately. "Well, we don't get much help from the outside, do we? Like how many times do they tell us on TV that common people like us are great? Did we hear it in school?

Did we hear it from our families? I never heard anyone give me a lot of respect, I'll tell you that."

The discussion deepened into the dynamics of oppression and how people internalize low self-esteem and then feel frustrated and focus their aggression on people who remind them of themselves. The energy in the group continued to rise as participants rapidly made connections between phenomena that before had seemed unrelated. They were joking now, and doing a lot of laughing.

What surprised me was the excited discussion that then broke out about "problem people" on the shop floor who are endlessly criticizing the shop stewards, and how much more understandable that is now. They were peeling their onion and seeing another layer of internalized oppression.

"And how about this?" another officer said. "How about that we do the same thing to the national leadership of our union? We criticize and complain and act as if they don't do anything right. We never think of really supporting them. Aren't we doing just the same — taking our bad feelings about ourselves out on our leaders?"

"Right," someone else chimed in. "Solidarity begins at home." He pointed to his chest. "It starts right here! We gotta learn to respect ourselves and each other if we're to get the movement we deserve!"

"OK," I said, "It's about time for break. I'd like to challenge you to walk your talk. We could turn the rest of this weekend into a laboratory where you could practice respecting yourself and respecting each other. You could even sneak in an admission that you're proud of something about yourself."

They laughed.

"Would you be willing to turn this into a practice space, and see how it goes?"

"You got us this far, George. We might as well go the rest of the way!" General laughter accompanied nodding heads as we started our break.

What I especially appreciate about this case is that it shows how naturally a group—once it has moved into transformational work—develops theory, again validating Mezirow's interest in the frame of reference as transformative (2009). The workers peeled their onion from the top layer (we feel bad about ourselves) to the next layer (one reason we get targeted is because our fellow workers feel bad about themselves) to the next layer (and we target our leaders in the national office for the same reason). The workers identified key dynamics of internalized classism. The story demonstrates that workers without a college education can generate good theory, and what they mainly need from the facilitator, as they do their theory work, is active listening, confidence in them, and a few good questions.

A Teenager Accesses His Inner Power

The group of forty activists had come together in Cambridge, Massachusetts, to explore issues of spirituality and social change. Many of them had as a learning goal to become more assertive in pressing for change and at the same time not rely on a self-righteous energy that distances them from those they are confronting. We were two-thirds of the way through the workshop and had built a strong container. I offered a version of an activity I learned from veteran facilitator Nadine Bloch.

In small groups, individuals took turns creating small group sculptures that represented each one's vision of how she or he could be more powerful. Each small group then chose one of the individual's sculptures to be presented to the whole group. I led a debrief after each presentation.

Carlos, a teenager still in high school, was selected by his group to present his sculpture to the whole. As his small group posed in stillness, the other participants walked around, getting different angles on the sculpture, speculating on the layers of meaning in the work.

I noticed Carlos's eyes misting and could see that the rest of his small group was also moved.

"What was that like for you, Carlos?" I asked, to begin the debrief.

"I suddenly wasn't seeing the vision any more ... you know, the sculpture."

"What were you seeing?" I asked.

"My father, refusing to listen to me when I confront him about stuff."

Carlos began to cry. "He just turns his back, or walks away, or gets mad at me."

He cried harder; one of his small group moved to touch him but I caught her eye and shook my head no. "He accuses me of not knowing anything, that ... I'm too young to know what's up or to challenge him."

I turned to the whole group. "Anybody else here who had someone in their life who didn't think they had the right to challenge them?"

My hand went up along with everyone else's. "It's not so easy to hear the voice within when a loud voice outside is putting us down," I commented.

Heads nodded. The participants were with Carlos, doing their work along with him.

"What would you like to say to your dad, Carlos, if he were here right now?"

"Lay off, will ya? I'm your *son*. I'm a good person." Heavy sobbing now. "And I am smart. I make mistakes, but I *do* see what's right and what's wrong."

Carlos suddenly looked up, straightened his back.

"You know what?" He started to grin through the tears. "If I said that to my dad, that way, he'd have to admit it.... Or maybe he wouldn't.... But it wouldn't matter because I'd know it's true." His grin broadened and he noisily blew his nose.

"I'd know it's true," he repeated with a note of wonder.

I turned to the group. "How many of you have seen some hint of Carlos's power this weekend?"

Hands were raised vigorously. "How many of you are seeing it right now?" They began to cheer with rowdy whoops. Carlos laughed, wiped his eyes, laughed some more, then doubled over with big belly laughs. The group was tracking him and kept up the cheering, enjoying the sunshine in his face.

"Time for our break," I shouted over the cheering, and I suggested to Carlos that he be sure to check in with his buddy, as his small sculpture group began to give him enthusiastic hugs.

Limiting Beliefs Come from Someplace

In Carlos's transformational work, it's clear that his relationship with his father has something to do with how much he allowed himself to express his power as an activist. Many limiting beliefs are thrust upon us and we accept them: "I'm only a faggot"; "We who come from poor families are dumb." But sometimes we make up limiting beliefs at critical points in our lives in order to survive: "I'll be very, very small, and then maybe they won't notice me and hurt me so much"; "I'll be obnoxious, and then I won't be overlooked"; "I'll be a saint for the family—then they won't know how I really feel about them."

It doesn't really matter to me as a facilitator where or when the limiting belief got started. That's one of the ways transformational work is different from traditional therapy. Maybe Carlos will experience a new degree of freedom from the workshop and decide to work with a therapist to heal the old wounds and restructure his relationship with his dad. I would rejoice in that. My intervention with Carlos was quite modest: *to assist him to peel a layer or two of his onion, in a way that assists the whole group to move forward.*

I don't want to claim that this kind of intervention guarantees transformation in the sense of fundamental behavioral change. It might or might not have that result, often depending on how much support is outside the workshop for new behaviors. What I know I'm doing is transformational work—peeling the onion, loosening the hold of a limiting belief, opening a door to learning knowledge or skills that earlier could not be internalized. I want to be about the business of transformation, even though I can't know in most educational settings how far it will go.

What Actually Takes Place in Transformational Work?

Participants in courses, as in other settings, are protective of their limiting beliefs. They're afraid to act outside their limits, like the union leaders who hesitated to claim proudly a positive contribution they made. There's something familiar about holding back on our power, familiar like that favorite sweatshirt or old pair of sneakers. Participants prefer, therefore, to stay in their comfort zones. Many facilitators and teachers collude with this protectiveness and provide sessions that maintain everyone inside their comfort zone, including the trainer. (Yawn!)

On the other hand, in their heart of hearts, people also know they could make a bigger impact than they do; they know that if they somehow went all out, they'd get a chance at living some of their dreams. They yearn for the support and encouragement to step out of their comfort zones and step into their power.

When they do step out, they confront their limiting beliefs. *That's the doorway to the transformational possibility.* We trainers can tell they are standing at the door because we witness something different: emotion, confused talking, different body language or facial expression. Carlos's eyes begin to tear up. Union leaders perspire, stare at the floor, leave the room.

Limiting beliefs are held in place by repressed painful emotion. A participant is starting to do transformational work when she or he is feeling that emotion and *starting to express it.* Simply feeling the pain is not transformational. On Saturday night Kathy's stomach was tight and her head hurt. Starting to *express* the pain on Sunday morning began the process of transformational work.

Facilitators and teachers who do transformational work assist participants, with permission, to go more fully into that painful emotion and express it, whether the expression takes the form of laughing, crying, sweating, shaking, yawning, raging, or nonrepetitive talking. The union leaders laugh and buzz with connections they're making; Carlos sobs in the middle of his sculpture group; Alex laughs and his face gets red.

By expressing a painful emotion, participants actually reduce the emotion's ability to hold a limiting belief in place. The limiting belief gets jiggled loose, and another view becomes possible. "I don't have to be obnoxious in order to get attention in this group; I could simply ask for what I want." "I can share my thinking and experience in a group and refuse to accept invisibility." "I am a smart young man even if my dad doesn't know it, and I can act on my intelligence." "I am worthy, intelligent, and a proud contributor to this society even if it puts me down as a worker."

The release of painful emotion is not an end in itself. Release is necessary, but it is not sufficient for our gaining a new measure of freedom. To free up our power, we need new frameworks of thought to replace old limiting beliefs. We also need new ways of relating to each other and ourselves. "How many of you have seen a glimpse of Carlos' power this weekend? And are seeing it now?" (Cheers.) "We working class people are internalizing the oppression, and even taking it out on each other!"

We also need some practice of a new behavior to gain confidence that we literally can act outside our old limiting belief. "Could you ask Sasha whether he'd be willing for you to be close with him?" "Let's treat the rest of the weekend as a chance to try out new behaviors reflecting self-respect and respect for each other."

Kolb's model of experiential education (1984) works yet again:

1. *The experience:* "I'm out of my comfort zone and scared and remembering how angry I was. I'm remembering how defeated I felt when I couldn't speak up for my friend."

2. *Reflection:* "I actually believe I'm too scared to speak up for anybody, but I forgot that I did it just yesterday in this course and I can do it when I choose to."

3. *Generalization:* "Anyone can have their good days and bad days in showing courage, and I could have plenty of good days when I take a risk to stand up for someone."

4. *Application:* "OK, now I'm doing it right here in the workshop—at this moment—taking a risk, and I'm not dead yet!"

To make actual transformation, rather than simply a sentimental moment to remember at the end of a workshop, participants need assistance in changing their belief about themselves and even a revised cognitive framework, or worldview. Nor is this enough. Consistently changed behavior requires confidence, and confidence comes from practice. Practice is also available when participants go home after the workshop, and repeating the new behavior over and over may be necessary before the confidence comes fully and the participant's friends say, "Hey, you've changed!"

Each moment of applying a new behavior—Step 4—is itself an experience: Step 1 in the experiential learning model. On a good day the participant will allow herself or himself to emote about *that* and continue the learning cycle for transformation.

Considering the empowerment potential of transformational work, it's not surprising that more teachers and facilitators are getting themselves trained to add this to their bag of tools.

21

Conclusion: Bringing It All Together

Direct education harnesses two resources generally left untapped: the unique motivation of each learner and the group container.

In the traditional paradigm, participants are usually assumed to bring sufficient motivation because they signed up for the course, although the reality is that the teacher has no idea what combination of factors really lands a person in her or his seat. In direct education, we believe in the power of intention—the usefulness of each individual clarifying how her or his life could be different if she or he learns specific things available in the course, whether skills, knowledge, capacity, attitude, or wisdom.

As facilitators, we hold the attitude that the primary responsibility for each person's growth is her or his own. We expect each one to "do themselves" in the course, including the possibilities of acting out, dropping out, or flunking; the value we add to their process is to remind them continually of their responsibility for their lives, their conduct, their use of each moment in the course. I've never regretted giving an F while teaching a college or graduate school course, because I know that in an ultimate sense, there is no such thing as failure, only feedback.

We use tools that continually remind participants of their personal responsibility: Maximize/Minimize the Value of a Learning Experience, goal setting, goal review, accountability to a buddy, accountability to a marginal or mainstream identity in the group, simulations in which the debrief includes "How did you do yourself in this exercise?" and transformational work, among others. We promote concepts that make the participant accountable to herself or himself: discomfort zone and authenticity.

Direct education harnesses the resource of the group on behalf of the curriculum goals. Even in individualist cultures like that of the United States, participants unconsciously create a group with its norms, values, and atmosphere. Sometimes the group actively supports individuals learning the curriculum, and sometimes not. Rather than leave that to chance, in direct education we consciously encourage a robust container for accelerated learning. Rather than foster a cozy atmosphere where participants huddle and infantilize, we use tools that support rigor and risk.

We know that container building sometimes inspires a group to fight to become a real community, accepting the diversity of the learners more fully than before. We support the group's storm; "If there is no struggle there is no progress," Frederick Douglass taught ([1857] 1985).

However, individuals can make strides toward their learning goals without a group storm that ushers in a high-performance team. We therefore stay unattached regarding a group's decision on that score. We accept that conflict is as natural as breathing, and overall we facilitate in a conflict-friendly way. In direct education we accept the legacy of Mohandas K. Gandhi, who believed that conflict aversion prevents a larger perception of truth. As educators, we must be about the pursuit of truth.

Perhaps the biggest single difference between traditional and direct education is in the relation of the individual and the group. Traditionally, the curriculum treats a group as simply a collection of individuals; it's not surprising that so many people are choosing to stay home and learn through their computers. Direct education invites synergy. The group becomes more than the sum of its parts: a vibrant and abundant resource that accelerates and deepens learning.

Loving the Content Too Much to Rely on Logic

Direct educators understand the linear logic of a field and at the same time want so much to share it with others that they throw the linearity overboard so learners can learn it.

Linear treatments belong in books—and not textbooks, but books that describe the field itself. The curriculum, and materials supporting the curriculum like textbooks, justify themselves not by how they describe the field, but by how well they support *learning* the field.

We believe that for most people learning proceeds best not through comprehending linear, finished statements as in the field's definitions; learning proceeds best through experiences that introduce successive approximations with the aid of various learning channels. The art of curriculum design in direct education is to find the series of successive approximations that works for any sophisticated concept, to find or invent activities that plug into that series, and to make sure to provide opportunities for the concept to be tested through application.

An advantage of group learning is that a group is usually composed of people with diverse learning styles, including the various primary channels of learning: visual, auditory, kinesthetic, and emotional/relational. This means that as the curriculum guides the group to peel the onion of the content, the activities that tap the various learning channels bring an abundance of intelligence to the fore. Everyone benefits, because reality is indeed highly complex; the perception of complexity brings the group into closer alignment with the truth.

For years I privileged in my teaching my favorite learning channels: visual and auditory. I ignored the other major channels through which people learn: emotional/relational and kinesthetic. I didn't know I was marginalizing, hour after hour, those participants who mainly learn through one of the neglected channels.

Direct education systematically designs courses and work-shops for all four kinds of learners. That shift alone accounts for accelerated learning in the group in two ways: it supports the individuals who mainly learn through the kinesthetic or emotional/relational channel, and those individuals in turn are empowered to contribute more fully to the others in the group.

Direct Education Confronts Common Obstacles to Effective Adult Learning

With a variety of tools, we support the natural rhythm of differen-tiation and integration. Traditional education has little respect for this rhythm, leaving participants gasping for breath and learning less than they can. Happily, it is not rocket science to design courses and workshops that support the natural rhythm that exists in all human groups.

We expect groups to be ambivalent about learning things that they "ought to" know more about, like diversity, or history, or health, or dozens of other things. On our good days, practitioners of direct education don't blame groups; we respect them and ask ourselves "What's right here?" Groups may need the chance to express their ambivalence, to consider "on the one hand" and "on the other," so they can sort it out without the pressure of what they "ought to" learn. They may need exercises that enable them to reframe, like the Russians who needed to celebrate defensiveness instead of disavowing it, and then go ahead and learn from (gasp!) an American.

What's right here? is a question that Process Work associates of Arnold and Amy Mindell often ask themselves, and it might be the most important question a teacher can ask in order to peel the onion when confronting one of the many mysteries of a learning group. Sometimes what's right is a group's resistance to the teacher launching yet another generalization in their direction without giving them a chance to reflect on their own experience. In direct education we put first things first: the activity, so everyone can share a here-and-now experience to learn from, then the reflection time so members of the group can share the meaning they make from the experience. After those two steps are done, group members are equipped to manifest their own considerable intelligence and are delighted to have their teacher add some knowledge and theory to the pot, making a zestful generalization time that has a fair chance of getting integrated into the cognitive map of the learners. It's adult education's way of making stone soup.

But Ella Baker and John Dewey are our American mother and father: humans do, after all, learn by doing and that includes applying. Rather than skip the application step for the sake of "coverage of the material," thereby increasing the chance that our course will shortly be forgotten, in direct education we honor the application of learning and seek ways to make it vivid and uncomfortable. Application then transmutes into "experience," and the cycle of experiential education becomes a model for lifelong learning.

Diversity and Anti-oppression Work: Intrinsic Rather Than a Compartment

Direct education recognizes that all groups have far more differences than they want to acknowledge or explore, and this provides a laboratory for tackling blocks to learning.

Using the theory of mainstream/margin dynamics gives a fresh start to the work on oppression that increasing numbers of people are experiencing as a tired discourse. The old ways of doing anti-oppression work, old ways that some Training for Change facilitators used to practice, often result in participants' *learning more about oppression but little if anything about liberation.*

Direct education draws on humanistic psychology and the grassroots experience of liberation movements such as civil rights, women's, and lesbian/gay/bisexual/transgender to evolve a conflict-friendly approach that puts the emphasis on change rather than on blame.

We find that working successfully on difference accelerates the learning of the curriculum's content, because it brings the learners into the here-and-now, where learning happens. Liberation from cultural hang-ups about difference is, it turns out, profoundly on the side of the learning curve.

This recognition also makes groups endlessly fascinating and offers an anti-burnout salve to the veteran facilitator. Each group is unique. We ask ourselves what is going on within it and how learning is influenced thereby. With each group, facilitators get to dance differently. Direct education is a spicy way to work.

Another way to enhance a group's uniqueness is to go into it without a fully planned design. By planning ahead of time only half of the course or less, we stimulate ourselves to pay closer attention to the special needs and wants of each particular group. We heighten our alertness to teachable moments. While remaining faithful to the overall goals of the course, we let the design emerge from the group's themes and its main challenges.

This is not the same as "negotiated design," although negotiation could be built into emergent design. The inclination of direct education is to let the co-facilitators make the judgment calls, staying alert to discomfort zones and mainstream/margin dynamics so that the emerging design assists the group to go over its edges again and again.

Taking on Limiting Beliefs That Prevent Learning

The curriculum may be elegantly designed. The teacher may be well rested with a full toolbox of facilitative interventions. A participant or group may still be unsuccessful in achieving a learning goal because of self-limiting beliefs. The participants may sense the strength of the container and—knowing this is a safe place to "go for it"—signal the teacher that assistance is needed. A story may clarify further.

The tension was building through the second half of Saturday morning of a weekend course. Forty men were in the leadership development seminar, which was focused on how men can break out of male stereotypes in order to make their leadership count more strongly for liberation.

After lunch the participants had a two-hour period to hike or rest. I had been quite clear that we would resume at 3 p.m., and I anticipated that a fair number of the men would be late — in this case a passive-aggressive way to express their anger. Watching them amble in, I decided this would be one of the rare times when I would pick a fight. Reaching for memories of movie drill sergeants, I tore into them for being late.

One man was quicker than the rest to go into his rage, and he lashed back at me. "Who's paying for this workshop, anyway?" he said with heat. "It's a beautiful day and I need my rest. Who do you think you are?"

"I believe you're not only speaking for yourself," I said to him, "but for a bunch of the men here. How about coming up front here and letting it hang out?"

He came up and reached for his anger, but had a little trouble finding it fully. He said the words, but he was holding back.

In a soft voice, between him and me, I said neutrally, "I can take it."

At that point he began to roar like the lion he was. With sweat dripping off his red face, he hurled hard words and obscenities at me. After a period of this, I asked him in the neutral tone of voice I'd used before, "Who and where are you now?"

He stopped, stunned.

"I'm a little boy," he said. "You're my dad!"

He broke into loud sobs. Nearly all the men in the room began to cry. We stayed at that emotional place for a long time, while I reassured them that we all have something going on about our dads, and it's OK for us to feel it.

As the strength of the crying ebbed, I asked the men to get into their small support groups and share two things: a hard thing that stood between them and their dads and a gift they wished they could give to their dad. I invited them to take an hour for that work, since I knew it was critical to their chance of learning new behaviors as a leader. I then sat in a place with a good view of the men and silently cheered them on.

After their small group work I invited them to use the rest of the workshop to practice the new behaviors that would now occur to them.

As shiny-bright and open as we may have been as small children, by the time we reach adulthood we've adopted beliefs that limit us. Direct education works fine without doing transformational work in front of the group; often participants give each other a hand in the secret life of the group, as happened for me in India regarding my racism. For teachers who acquire the skill-set of transformational work, however, direct education creates a container that maximizes support for dissolving obstacles to learning.

Authority and Limiting Beliefs

In Chapter 6 I promised that we would return to the question of what a group is storming over when it enters Stage 2 in Tuckman's (1965) group development model. In Chapter 6 we explored the importance of the group surrendering to the reality of its own diversity. The second issue the group storms about is its dependency on the facilitator. I imagine every reader has been in situations of authority in which she or he was aware of suppressed resentment in the group; it is entirely natural that adults (and those near-adults we call teenagers) will resent dependency and want a different kind of relationship with the person acting as leader. The storm can be seen as the assertion of counter-dependency, and accusations and insults may be directed toward the facilitator during this stage (as well as toward each other).

M. Scott Peck's advice (1988) on facilitating this stage has been valuable for me. As I sit quietly, watching the storm and loving the participants, I believe I hear limiting beliefs that go something like this: "I hate to follow the leader but I doubt that I can do well without following a leader"; "I resent how sure the leader is of himself and I know I'll never feel that confident"; "I've caught the leader being wrong in this course but I'll bet I could never do better myself"; "All my life I've been waiting to grow up and now that I'm an adult I still feel like a child and I'm afraid I always will."

When I sit quietly and pay attention, I see numerous participants try to act grown-up, offering interventions that ought to work, taking leadership of various kinds, and experiencing the very defeat that they fear. I see a dramatic reenactment of the dreaded outcomes expected by their limiting beliefs. A workshop provides a very different experience from the defeats they suffer at work, however, or at school. This time there's the drama but no injury, and, more important, the group spirit is holding them and supporting them to feel the pain of their dependency—until they let go.

The breakthrough is into the here and now, their present adulthood, in which it is possible for them to experience a new relationship with a leader: *interdependence*.

High-performing groups typically have flexible, shared leadership, with the identified leader (in educational settings the teacher or facilitator) seen as a task coordinator, a useful functionary for an in-charge group, a *resource*.

Rank, Authority, and Cross-Cultural Facilitation

Direct education takes the minefield out of cross-cultural facilitation. The more deeply experienced teachers are with direct education, the less they need to worry about working in cultures that are new to them, because direct education puts the group and its needs first and has a toolbox that implements that priority. By embracing the diversity of learning styles, building a container and stressing the individual's learning goals, and placing its elicitive tools in an experiential sequence, direct education avoids the characteristic pitfalls that so often replicate the imperialist theme of domination.

Nevertheless, there is still the work each teacher using direct education must do in order to become aware of her or his social positioning and the inevitable influence of identity and rank. Acknowledging the politics of the situation, clarifying where the facilitator is coming from, acknowledging her or his rank, and most of all doing active listening make a difference in outcome.

When Western facilitators don't rely for authority on the easy ride given by the glamour and power of mainstream identity, we are bound to ask, Where does my authority actually come from? Feminists and anarchists do well to sensitize teachers to this question. We need authority to support our groups to risk and break through, but where do we get the authority to do that?

One source is accountability. Direct educators are accountable to negotiated goals in plain sight, plus an explicit assumption underlying the technology: the empowerment of the participants at the end of the day.

"At the end of the day" is important because we recognize that the *middle* of the day is occasionally a time of storm and stress, of such discomfort that most learners will be tempted to walk out claiming that "the workshop isn't working." I remember one University of Pennsylvania student acknowledged to me at the end of a semester that, mid-semester, he hated me so much that he only kept coming to class to keep me from "winning" in what he imagined to be my wish to dominate and subdue him!

In direct education we respect the yearning of learners to grow, such that a group might put itself through pain and difficulty to do so. We are not afraid of pain. We are at service to a passionate yearning to grow, and we grin with satisfaction when the group rejoices at having come through to the other side.

We are also guided by a humble metaphor: a tour guide in a museum. We don't need a know-it-all attitude because our authority doesn't rest on knowing more than the participants do about the art on the walls. We don't need a condescending attitude because some individuals in the course may be wiser, more integrated, more spiritually developed than we are. We just need to know the museum—in other words, the design of the course and the facilitation moves that enable a group to make it to the end of the tour.

Resources

Appendix A

The Sustainable Educator: Advocacy, Modesty, and Diversity of Gifts

"So please remember!" the young man was imploring the small crowd on this dark night on a street corner in Trafalgar Square, London. "Please remember that next time it might be your neighbor who needs it, or even a member of your family. Please donate blood!"

"You're right about that!" someone in the crowd responded as the boy got down from his soap box. A young woman immediately took his place.

"I want everyone to listen up now because many people in this country do not know the extent of starvation in Africa," she said. "Nor do they know that Britain has a historic responsibility for that. It was our colonial empire that set things up badly, and imperialism is still alive and well in our banks and overseas investments!"

I turned to Sarah, the workshop organizer. "Wow," I said, "that was certainly a transition with different politics."

Sarah grinned. "It's your fault," she said. "You said we could choose any subject we felt strongly about, and he feels as strongly about giving blood as she does about imperialism."

We chuckled together, briefly surveying the crowd. About fifteen people were standing there listening, in addition to our workshop of twenty. I asked Sarah, "Now do you see why we didn't go to Hyde Park for this?"

> Sarah laughed. "Well there it's all become a routine, hasn't it? Even the hecklers are like professionals. This is the real thing. I'm sure I've never seen anyone street speaking on this corner!"

I tell this story to typify my response to an old debate in education about the role of advocacy in teaching and training. I don't take the position an activist might be expected to take—advocate, advocate, advocate! Nor do I take the other extreme, which I've heard best expressed by a colleague: "By the end of the course no one in the class is sure whether I'm for or against the death penalty. We've discussed it thoroughly and I've challenged all sides. My job isn't to tell them what I think, only to make sure that they think it through for themselves."

I suppose I take a middle course. The street speaking activity, which I've facilitated in Asia, Africa, and New Zealand as well as in the United States and Europe, reflects my thinking. I set up an edgy activity, one that takes participants out of their comfort zone. The activity itself has a political tradition behind it, although not exclusively left wing; I think of it as heavily populist in tone—going to the people, projecting confidence in their ability to weigh opinions and take action. Then I ask participants to speak on any subject they care passionately about and that it need not be "political" or take a certain line—I've had participants in the same workshop who took antagonistic positions on abortion, for example. Street speaking reflects my activist values but on the other hand doesn't urge a particular content and in that way is neutral.

I participate as one of the series of speakers, and I speak passionately on some political issue or other—they witness my taking a stand. It's deeply satisfying to the activist inside me to advocate passionately in front of them. However, I'm not protecting myself with privilege—I'm as likely to get heckled as they are, if not more so because I project more confidence. (I admit I'm still nervous inside no matter how many times I do it.)

One of the reasons I object to using my teacher's spot in the training room as a bully pulpit is that I have so much privilege there—it seems unfair for me to press my view when I have so much more rank than the workshop participants. I also think that my activist teacher friends who do press their views—and I realize that they feel it's their integrity that's at stake—overlook the fact that they are the ones who have designed the course; *the design itself has political implications* no matter what activities are chosen. It's the teacher or trainer who assembles or chooses the curriculum, and asks, for example, the women if they would like to hold a speak-out—hardly a politically neutral activity! The teacher already has the major political input through the organization of the course or workshop—why should we feel as though we're letting someone down if we don't launch into our side of a debate on, say, the nature of racism?

I agree with my colleague that the main thing is for the participants to think for themselves and learn rather than for me to get an audience for my views. I also agree that controversy is healthy, and if a margin is not present in the room to present an unpopular side, I might well express it although not claim it as my own. I disagree with my colleague that we shouldn't state what our views are, because I believe it is part of my accountability to be as transparent as possible when asked about my choices.

What works for me, when someone asks me or there's an obvious gap because I haven't yet spoken to an issue, is to say something like "I know there's a lot of interesting thinking on all sides of this question, and here's where I happen to come out at this time." In other words, I contextualize it to take away some of its authoritative impact. I'm fine with people considering it on the merits. When I'm in other people's workshops as a participant, I appreciate having the same space; I experience it as respectful. On the other hand, if a substantial part of the group is African American, I might choose to let my passion show because otherwise they won't believe I have conviction on the subject.

And if I feel frustrated because I haven't been passionate about something that came up in the learning group? That, then, is a reminder that I haven't been to a demonstration lately! In my view, passionate advocacy is for the streets. Supporting the learning group to achieve its goals is for the course and the workshop.

Going with Our Strengths

Consultant Jonathan Snipes and I have in common a Celtic heritage, so we were both excited when he brought to me an ancient, pre-Christian Celtic perspective on diversity, the Wheel of Being. It seems the Celts were trying to understand the mystery of human difference, and came up with a scheme consistent with their view that the universe is fundamentally about energy.

Jonathan found that this ancient Celtic perspective on diversity matches up with the Medicine Wheel of the Lakotas and the view of many indigenous peoples in Africa, Asia, and the Americas. I find that it helps me to understand some of the natural differences among teachers and trainers. It helps me to better understand my own style and to think about possible partners for co-facilitation.

As you might expect, the model is organized by the four directions. Each direction, or energy as the Celts would have it, is associated with a cluster of characteristics. The direction that is strongest in me is the east. People like me are visionaries. We love innovation, to the point that we often prefer to create something new even when the old way of doing it works fine. The fascination with invention can mean that we would rather come up with new ideas today than implement that good idea we came up with yesterday! We're often quick and make intuitive leaps to the big picture. The icon the Celts attached to the east is the blacksmith's forge—a fiery place of shaping and creating.

Another direction that draws me is the south. People of the south are sensitive to feelings, in themselves and in others. They often play a nurturing role in groups, developing conflict resolution skill and awareness about those who are left out. On a team, people with south energy often know before anyone else does when there's turbulence in the field. The Celts' icon for the south is the shepherd's staff; when someone from the south provides leadership, they try to gather the sheep in one place.

The west is the direction of the analysts. People with this energy love data. You cannot overwhelm them with too many bits of empirical reality, because they can always come up with another classification scheme! In a group the people from the west realize what else needs to be known to make a sound decision or a complete model; they're good at pondering and reflecting and coming up with additional considerations.

The Celts gave the icon of the cauldron or stewpot to the west, because this is the energy of simmering and adding more ingredients. West people often serve a group as historians, remembering the by-laws at crucial times. Like the visionaries of the east, the analysts strongly want a big picture. However, the analysts get their big picture in their own way. Often scorning the intuitive leaps of the visionaries, the analysts patiently put the puzzle together piece by piece.

The north is the direction of the in-charge implementer, the one who puts the rubber to the road. In some cultures this is the direction of the stereotyped leader, although leadership in groups can come from any and all of the four directions. The north is often thought of as warrior energy, because people from this direction especially like challenge; it is more stimulating to implement a plan if there are obstacles to overcome, people to persuade or move aside, pressures to withstand.

People from the north are clear about boundaries; they know where they end and you begin, and in this way they can be different from the shepherds of the south who can identify so much with their sheep that they get fuzzy about where the boundary is. A characteristic conflict in a group is between the plea of the south person for inclusion of all and the demand from the north person for clarity on who's in and who's out so the team can set about its task.

Some people are mixtures of these directions, and others are strongly one. In either case, we can make the most of some of our strengths and handle our challenges by asking ourselves where we are on the Wheel. Since my south energy leaves me a bit fuzzy on boundaries, for example, I find it useful to configure seats in the training room in a U shape, with me and my co-facilitator sitting in the open space at the top of the U. In contrast to an O shape, the U leaves space between me and the participants, space that supports me to maintain a boundary and not get sucked into whatever dynamic may be seizing the participants at the moment.

I sometimes encounter educators familiar with this scheme who urge participants to embody all four directions, in the name of holism. I don't agree with them. The individualistic bias of modern Western middle class culture regards holism as a goal for the *individual* to attain, but it strikes me as far more sensible for it to be a goal for the *group* to attain.

I agree with the Lakotas, who as I understand it believe the Wheel needs to be expressed strongly on the *collective* level. As long as the people as a whole incorporate the four directions, why not have individuals be strongly north, or strongly south—encourage them to be their authentic selves as fully as they like? In fact, it might serve the team better if its members are strongly in one energy or another, to increase the group's total reach and resource. Does a baseball team or a symphony orchestra really do better if everyone's trying to learn everyone else's part?

To me this way of looking at diversity among facilitators and teachers gives us more chances to respect each other, and more incentive to work together. As someone from the east I now have much more appreciation for the ability of someone from the west to revisit the group process, peeling the onion another layer by noticing additional information, moving toward more complex generalizations than I might make.

The west's excitement about filling in the cognitive map of the group is not mine, and yet I can see how valuable it is. My very preference for the Celtic Wheel of Being over the Myers-Briggs typology (Keirsey and Bates, 1984) or the Enneagram (Riso and Hudson, 1999), which I use only occasionally, is a tip-off. A trainer from the west is more likely to see where the Myers-Briggs inventory with its sixteen types is going to be more valuable for the group.

As someone also from the south, I now have much more appreciation for the ability of someone with north energy to confront a participant, an intervention I use rarely and even then with considerable anxiety. When I watch a trainer from the north do tough loving, standing firm while the participant moves from head anger to heart anger and then to healing, I'm deeply moved. I know that the warrior facilitator will see those opportunities more often than I, and use them with more confidence. In the experiential model of learning, also, I recognize that I can dally too long in the first two steps—experience and reflection—and cut short the west's favorite (generalizing) and the north's favorite (applying).

And, on the other hand, I am good at what I do, and I want to become even better because it's the work of the east and south that lights me up. The workshop is probably better if I'm loving what I'm doing, while also (when I'm facilitating alone) doing at least a decent job of filling in for the absent north and west. What is most satisfying of all? Co-facilitating in a team that expresses all four directions—a satisfaction that comes surprisingly often.

Appendix B

The Sustainable Educator: Resilience and Revolution

Richard Dorman from the U.S. Civil Rights Office came to the center of the stage to make the announcement. He looked upset.

In the auditorium were four hundred students and also staff from the Student Nonviolent Coordinating Committee; we were on the campus of Miami University in Oxford, Ohio, to train for 1964 Freedom Summer in Mississippi. This was the second week of training; the four hundred in the first week were already distributed around Mississippi, opening Freedom Schools, doing voter registration among black people who had been disenfranchised. I was sitting in the second row of the auditorium along with others on the training staff.

Dorman looked around, then stared at the paper he had placed on the rostrum. "We've just received word that three of the Freedom Summer workers were killed together in Mississippi — James Chaney, Andrew Goodman, and Michael Schwerner. Chaney was a SNCC field worker. Goodman and Schwerner were student volunteers."

I was stunned. Chaney, along with the other SNCC staff members, had been at high risk for months, I knew. But Goodman and Schwerner were new volunteers like the students sitting around me, and they were already dead!

I thought about the students in the auditorium who we would continue training. What are they imagining waits for them in Mississippi?

How many of them will leave, getting on buses bound for the Northern suburban homes many of them come from?

This was one of the turning points in my whole development as a trainer, although it took years for me to integrate the lesson fully into my practice. In the next few days I watched the SNCC workers build an invincible container, strong enough to hold the shock and grief and fear that rocked our training.

Very few students went home rather than head south to Mississippi.

A colleague asked me recently, "George, after leading 1,500 trainings, why aren't you stale?"

The answer goes back to that auditorium. By placing myself on the edge, I learn things that profoundly shape my practice—and my life.

Social Movements as a Stimulus to Learning and Sustainability

I realize that activism has a generally poor reputation in the United States—mainstream media portrayals bear major responsibility for that. When an activist comes along who can't really be discounted, she or he is trivialized, like turning Martin Luther King Jr. into an icon representing social service. (As far as I know, Dr. King didn't do a day of service in his life!)

I know many educators and facilitators who, reflecting media bias, buy the mainstream's view and hesitate to identify themselves as "activists." I hope readers of this book who are in that boat will take another look. I'd like to pitch a different viewpoint: that conscious connection with one or more healthy social movements is likely to enhance our craft, make it more powerful, and assist us to a more sustainable way of being.

The very mission of activists is growth and change. That makes it harder to get set in our ways. With activism, there are constant opportunities to apply outside the training room what we learn. My colleague Daniel Hunter and I went together to the Philadelphia protest the day after the United States invaded Iraq. It was a crowd of upset people, with a range of feelings available. The protest was mainly about expressing outrage and it needed to be.

Without even discussing it, Daniel and I separately walked from cluster to cluster in the crowd, supporting them and facilitating their empowerment process whatever it was — in one cluster crying, in another telling angry jokes, in a third helping to launch the singing of some healing songs. When Daniel and I reconnected in the crowd, we named what we'd been doing, acknowledging the tacit partnership. We then took the time to go more fully into our own feelings, not knowing what might happen next in the demonstration. "Take care of yourself so you can take care of others."

I remember going to jail with a Quaker friend, Ross Flanagan, for engaging in civil disobedience against the refusal of the U.S. Senate to take responsibility for debating a major escalation in the war in Vietnam. Up until then my arrest experiences had rarely been positive for me because I let my fear shut me down. I withdrew into myself and went into "stoical endurance" mode.

On this occasion I watched Ross engaging at every point in the process, even in the holding cell where most of the prisoners were drunk or bloody or both. Leaning forward, eyes wide open, finding common ground, asking questions when appropriate, Ross was an open system, refusing to cooperate with the dreadful surroundings and instead living in the here and now.

I was astounded, and tried it myself, only to find (duh!) that it worked. The present moment *is* where we're alive, no matter how disgusting or scary the surroundings. If that's not a teaching principle, I don't know what is!

Progressive Social Movements Sustain Educators as Well as Societies

Imagine the United States without the movements to end slavery ... to create social security ... to allow women to vote ... to stop lynching ... to create public education ... to preserve the wilderness ... to end child labor ... to force the end of the Vietnam War ... to ban the sale of poisonous food—I could go on and on. Even though U.S. social movements have not achieved the higher living standards enjoyed in many other countries, it boggles the imagination to think what misery most U.S.ers would live in without the movements that have forced change.

Without positive social movements, domination and greed would have dissolved the glue that holds society together and makes community possible. Movements arise from the margins of society and confront the mainstream with the possibility of growth and development. At one historical moment "woman's place is in the home" and then the mainstream is forced to change: women become business executives, college presidents, political leaders, and artists.

Educators who disengage from social movements give up their personal link to a better future and risk being overwhelmed by feelings of isolation and hopelessness. If I had a hundred dollars for every educator who has become a despairing cynic, I'd be a rich man.

Trees don't flourish when their roots are cut.

The opportunity for educators to sustain themselves and nourish their self-respect is to confront whatever gets in the way of staying close to progressive movements. Restore the balance of differentiation and integration. Extend your roots.

Big Changes, Little Changes

I've always loved drama, from when I was a boy. I like to see and be part of the clash of large forces, decisive gains that cannot be reversed, nonnegotiable demands, the win by the underdog in the last seconds of the game. I like big picture, grand strategy, large vision, the prospect of historical discontinuity suggested by the term *revolution*.

The part of activist tradition that I most identify with is the part that swirls with those images. I've been for unilateral disarmament, the end of segregation *now*, immediate withdrawal from both Vietnam and George W. Bush's war on Iraq, the abolition of poverty in the United States as has been done in some other countries, and full apologies from U.S. war criminals who still command fancy fees on the lecture circuit.

I was more than a little upset when I began to pay attention to how I actually change and grow as an individual. I discovered that I, for one, don't learn by leaping tall buildings at a single bound! In fact, I've never leapt a tall building at a single bound, except perhaps when I was born, and then my mother was doing most of the work.

During an advanced facilitator training I once volunteered to work in the front of the room with a therapist. A deep fear had been wriggling itself loose inside me and, given the opportunity, I went for it in a large, dramatic, and showy way. I discovered the source of the fear: a very frightening episode that happened when I was two.

At break time, one of the facilitation staff approached me and asked if I'd like to do follow-up work in our one-on-one session the next day. I readily agreed, and the drama queen in me looked forward to another blockbuster session in the morning.

The facilitator set up a dialogue between me and little two-year-old Georgie who, she invited me to imagine, was still fearfully hiding out inside me. I saw the metaphor and followed her facilitation, first taking the role of grown-up Georgie talking to the two-year-old and explaining in basic words what I could about what happened. I tried to be as gentle as possible, and very reassuring.

I then took the role of myself as little Georgie, and found no words, only frozen fear. I was astonished. What about yesterday's breakthrough session?

It was a breakthrough, she assured me, because I found little Georgie and his trauma after all these years of repression. Now, she said, something different is required. I need to spend time each day trying to establish dialogue with Georgie. I need to reassure him that he's now safe, that I can look after him, that it's OK for him to breathe easy. Eventually he'll probably respond with words, she said, and if I listen, I'll learn from him. Would I be willing to try this approach?

After I nodded, she said, "Here's the catch. You need to spend time with little Georgie every single day for a month. It can be as much or as little as you can manage consistently. The important thing is, you must be completely rigorous in this commitment, or he will decide you are unreliable and keep his distance. How much, Georgie, can you be certain you can keep to for thirty days?"

I wanted to say thirty minutes, or an hour. Stepping into realism, I said five minutes. So much for drama, for my big-time strategy. No problem, the therapist said. It's not the amount of time, it's the consistency that counts.

Thirty days later I had a great relationship with a relaxed, happy two-year-old I hadn't even known existed.

When I look at the variety of things I've learned and changes I've made in my behavior, I have to admit that they are mostly of that sort: choosing a method that is very realistic with a goal that's achievable. I love drama as much as ever and have no trouble finding it whenever I look, but change? Well, change for me seems to come in increments, by attending to the day-by-day commitments.

This has made a huge impact on my teaching and my training, as well as on my activism. I ask participants to set modest, achievable learning goals. I enjoy the drama of a breakthrough and immediately look for ways that the participants can follow through with new behaviors, on a realistic scale. I use positive reinforcement constantly, knowing that every workshop—and movement—is a bowling team and that bowlers do not make strikes every time they're up. The worry lines on my forehead were set too deeply in the olden days to go away now, but my work and my life are far more satisfying—and sustainable.

I'm still an activist with revolutionary goals, but now I borrow a page from Gandhi when it comes to vision. Gandhi worked with three levels of goals in his struggle for a just India, and his method enabled him to be a leader of an independence struggle who stayed radical to the end of his life.

Gandhi's highest vision for India was written on the ship that took him from South Africa back home to India. It was a breathtakingly radical vision—his version of a beloved community. He was so committed to it that, three decades later when he could have taken state power as the British withdrew, he recommended Nehru so he could go back to building another mass movement that would fight for economic justice and social equality. His role in that struggle was tragically cut short by his death.

Gandhi's intermediate level of vision was an India independent of Britain, the achievement of which came about three decades after he started.

His short-range goal was on the level of campaigns. In the Salt Satyagraha of 1930, for example, he operated as any good politician might, weaving together eleven demands for specific changes short of independence, sticking to goals that were achievable through a couple of years of massive nationwide struggle.

For me Gandhi's model works. I continue to hold to my radical vision for the United States and the world, and much of my writing over the years has been to fill in some of the gaps for that vision. On the second level, I've worked with movements that seek structural changes, to take away the power of the patriarchs, and the homophobes, and the racists, and those who have succeeded Britain in the imperial game. And on the third level, I've joined campaigns with specific, achievable goals, such as forcing the United States to stop the wholesale destruction of the Vietnamese people, or getting the U.S. Navy to stop using the Puerto Rican island of Culebra for target practice, or stopping the needless cutting down of trees on the street where I live.

One of the happiest things about this third level is getting to work with people who don't hold an activist identity for themselves but do want a lot of changes and are willing to work for them. Even someone with marginal identities as strong as mine can enjoy the opportunities to work side by side with people from the mainstream.

Peeling the Onion Once More

This book's intention is to invite teachers and facilitators to support themselves by treating their work as a labor of love, reaching for the excellence that love inspires.

And what do we do when we make mistakes in the work, when we read the group wrong, or when we make a clumsy intervention? This, too, is an opportunity. As an anonymous poet wrote:

> *The process of growth is,*
> *it seems,*
> *the art of falling down.*
> *Growth is measured by the gentleness and awareness*
> *with which we once again pick ourselves up,*
> *the lightness with which we dust ourselves off,*
> *the openness with which we continue and then take*
> *the next step,*
> *beyond our edge,*
> *beyond our holding,*
> *into the remarkable mystery of being.*

Appendix C

For Further Reading

Some readers may want to explore further some of the issues raised in this book with other writers and practitioners. Here are some suggestions of authors and films you might like to check out. I may not agree with them on all points, but they bring important experience to the table. Detailed information about these sources appears in the References, which follows Appendix D.

Chapter 1: Introduction: Direct Education for Adult Learning Groups

Jane Vella (2008) presents a coherent account of popular education, some useful suggestions for teachers, and at the same time points to growth edges that are developed in the present book: group dynamics, the importance of safety, the role of emotions, authority, and working with diversity.

Chapter 3: Harnessing the Power of Intention

Unfortunately, Ruth Benedict didn't publish her thinking about synergy between the individual and the group, but she did give her unpublished papers to psychologist Abraham Maslow. Here is her key statement arising from her research on diverse societies:

> From all comparative material the conclusion emerges
> that societies where non-aggression is conspicuous have
> social orders in which the individual by the same act

and at the same time serves his own advantage and that of the group ... not because people are unselfish and put social obligations above personal desires, but when social arrangements make these identical.... Their institutions insure mutual advantage from their undertakings.

Frank Goble's writing (1970) extends the concept further.

Chapter 5: The Secret Life of Groups

M. Scott Peck (1988) strongly influenced how we facilitate a group when it launches a storm (which Peck calls "chaos") in its eagerness to become a high-performance learning group. Other authors have different but compatible ways of describing stages of group formation: Starhawk (1988) and Nadler and Luckner (1992). See also the work of the Tavistock Institute of Human Relations which began in London in 1946 doing pioneering research on small groups (Trist and Murray, 1990, 1993, 1997).

Social psychologist Kurt Lewin (1948) is foundational for the field of group dynamics and for direct education. He integrated his social activism with his ability to see groups as systems that could not be reduced to the level of individual motivations and backgrounds and whose behavior could vary in the moment in complex ways. His immense curiosity about groups pierced the great American individualist myth and made possible a surge of new research and experimentation yielding realistic hope for social change. For a thoughtful overview of Lewin's contribution and further reading, see Mark A. Smith (2009; available online at http://www.infed.org/thinkers/et-lewin.htm).

Chapter 6: Acknowledging Difference to Accelerate Learning

Stephen Brookfield (2000) brings his radical politics to a discussion of the distinction between movement organizing and educating. He agrees with Paolo Freire, the founder of popular education, that the two are distinct roles and approvingly quotes Freire urging teachers to be "critically conscious of the limits of education. That is, to know that education is not the lever, not to expect it to make the great social transformation" (p. 144).

I've used the speak-out in multiple cultures with various generations and classes, and the result is almost always the same: bonding of the group. Participants in the group are generally surprised by this, but it would not be a surprise to Lewis Coser (1956). A sociologist heavily influenced by Georg Simmel, Coser writes that one of the functions of social conflict is to unite the group and bring higher morale.

Mattheus and Marino (2003) created a highly successful adult education approach, "White People Confronting Racism," that integrates the best of traditional anti-racist work into a new no-blame/no-shame approach that emphasizes action.

Chapter 7: Diversity and Conflict Styles

A mainstream film that explores this issue is *Jerry Maguire* (1996). An African American professional football player is played by Cuba Gooding Jr., who won an Oscar for his performance. The athlete is represented by a European American sports agent, played by Tom Cruise. Their communication is challenged by cultural miscues that come to a head in a classic shower room scene, which I sometimes show in seminars.

Chapter 8: Social Class and Diversity

The student speaking in downtown Chicago didn't realize that the "racist worker" knew more about racism than he did. Middle class people are particularly vulnerable to falling into this student's situation, because confusion about the class structure is especially common among middle class people. Owning class people tend to be highly class-aware, and working class people easily recognize that the United States is stratified by class. When I am in a mixed class group and suggest that the United States has less social mobility than the societies of Western Europe, the people in the room who are most surprised are from the middle class. Sociologist-activist Betsy Leondar-Wright wrote *Class Matters* (2005) to assist middle class people to navigate cross-class interactions more skillfully. Another book that assists teachers in this way is by Linda Stout, *Bridging the Class Divide* (1996).

Chapter 9: Authenticity, Emotion, and Learning

Shankman and Allen (2008) offer to college students a guide to emotionally intelligent leadership; they see authenticity as linked to emotional intelligence.

Kochman (1981) reveals different assumptions that many blacks have toward expressing emotion as compared with whites. One is that blacks have, in general, a high level of confidence that they can express emotion strongly and stay in control of their behavior—they don't worry about getting carried away. Many whites believe themselves to be fragile and that if they begin to express strong emotion, they won't be able to stop. Again, each group projects its own beliefs on the other, which gives the teacher or facilitator an important opportunity to assist each group to come to a breakthrough in understanding the other—as long as the teacher doesn't take sides and impose a "right" view of the management of emotional expression.

A ropes course is a series of physical challenges in which individuals and groups need to solve a problem or reach a goal. For example, a rope may hang from the limb of a tree; immediately under the limb may be an "acid pit" which will "injure" someone who falls into it. The group's challenge may be to turn the rope into a swing and assist all the members to swing across the pit to "safety." Not all the challenges involve ropes, but since their invention, these learning tools used ropes often enough to give this approach the name "ropes course." A "high ropes course" includes activities done fairly high off the ground, which invites almost everyone outside their comfort zone. Another name for this way of working is "adventure-based learning," and some people call it "experiential learning." Nadler and Luckner (1992) show how to work with this toolbox.

In a typical River of Life exercise, participants draw on paper their life journey as if it were a river moving over terrain. They might draw white water to represent a turbulent time in their lives, a swamp to represent stuckness, and so on. The metaphor can be specified: the spiritual dimension of their lives characterized as a river, or the social action dimension.

One of the variations on the Object Exercise is to ask participants to wander around the workshop site for twenty minutes and pick up an object that in some way represents a learning they got from the workshop. The objects are placed in the center of the room, and participants each take a minute to share with the group what the object represents. Organizational consultant and facilitator Niela Miller (1988) explains the uses of exercises such as these that invite imagination and creativity.

Variations on the comfort zone diagram and tips on their use are offered in Nadler and Luckner (1992).

Katrina Shields (1991) includes a number of facilitation tools that are consistent with direct education and have proved useful in Australia and elsewhere, as well as the United States. Her tools often have the goal of supporting authenticity.

Patricia Cranton (2006) stresses the development of authentic relationships between participants and teachers, and a teacher's emoting can be seen in that context.

Chapter 10: Structures for Organizing the Content

David A. Kolb (1984) formulated the model of a four-step learning cycle—experience, reflect, conceptualize, apply—and said that he drew inspiration from Kurt Lewin, John Dewey, and Jean Piaget. Kolb's work has strongly influenced experiential education, but it has also stimulated a range of critiques.

Some object to his accompanying proposal of learning styles based on the four elements, a style typology I don't use. Some believe he makes the implicit assumption that individuals think sequentially in the four steps, but if he does assume it, I don't; I observe that individuals race back and forth among various spots in the cycle in the usual internal chaos of a diverse learning group.

There's also a critique of Western cultural bias and of patriarchal/rationalistic bias in Kolb's model, but I find the opposite: that grounding a group's learning journey in concrete, "feeling-ful," and often kinesthetic experience is far more compatible with the diversity of world cultures and gender experiences than is the Western academic tradition. In fact, in direct education we emphasize this so much that we almost always begin learning modules with an experience, even though Kolb and Fry (1975) say that the learning cycle can begin at any point.

Moreover, we place Kolb's model—as a crucial design principle—in the larger context of direct education, an approach that pays enormous attention to all kinds of diversity and nonrational dynamics that are the reality of learning in groups.

A writer who is concerned about Kolb's relation both to epistemology and to empirical research is Peter Jarvis (2006). Mark K. Smith (1996) lists a set of problems he has with Kolb's work, especially the learning styles typology. An online source for critique and also for research reports and application of Kolb's theory is at http://www.reviewing.co.uk/research/experiential.learning.htm.

While I'm sharing here some sources of Kolb-critique for the reader to explore more fully, I'll conclude by quoting one critic, Mark Tennant (1997, p. 92), with what for me, in this book, is the bottom line: "the model provides an excellent framework for planning teaching and learning activities."

The content of the UNITAR workshop in Geneva was drawn from my research on nonviolent action. I based one of my Swarthmore College lectures on this work, "Making Nonviolent Struggle More Powerful: Framing Strategies." http://media.swarthmore.edu/faculty_lectures/?p=60

The importance of eliciting the conflict situations from the experience of the indigenous leaders, as I did in the Applications Relay Race, is emphasized by John Paul Lederach (1995), growing out of his own considerable training work in diverse cultures.

Chapter 11: Building on What the Learners Know

Stephen Brookfield and Stephen Preskill (2005) offer a large array of tools and formats for stimulating discussion, most of them elicitive. They include chapters on how to take into account a culturally diverse learning group and to support discussions that reduce male domination.

Reldan Nadler and John Luckner (1992) describe astutely the dynamics of group learning when using Adventure-Based Learning (ABL), or group challenges. They define ABL as "a type of educational and/or therapeutic program in which adventure pursuits that are physically and/or psychologically demanding are used within a framework of safety and skills development to promote interpersonal and intrapersonal growth" (p. 7). Even for educators who don't intend to use the ABL toolbox, the book stimulates awareness of the stakes for learners and how to become more accurate in your interventions for both the individuals and the group. Their thinking about the use of metaphors alone makes the book valuable.

Chapter 14: Accountability in Direct Education

Starhawk (1990), an activist trainer and writer, distinguishes among power-over (domination), power-with (influence in a group), and power-from-within (inspiration, inner strength). When a course enters a turbulent phase, it helps tremendously to maintain clarity about these three kinds of power, especially when the participants get busy projecting on you! See also Starhawk's seminal work *Dreaming the Dark* (1988) for valuable insights on the dynamics of groups and seeing facilitation as work with energy.

Chapter 17: Edgy Interventions to Accelerate Learning

Arnold Mindell (1992) writes powerfully about the dynamics of groups on their edge and what facilitators can do to assist them to "go over their edges" to accelerate their learning. See especially Chapter 4. In the same book, *The Leader as Martial Artist*, he also offers new insights in Chapter 5 on how to make the most of learning group conflicts, especially when attacks are made on the facilitator. See also his 1997 book, *Sitting in the Fire*.

The book of Freud's where I learned the most about projection and learning is *Group Psychology and the Analysis of the Ego* (1989). At first I resisted its conclusions, then realized that identification is one reasonable strategy among many to learn profoundly, and that much good has come of it, including in my own growth. The trick is to bring awareness to the process.

Stephen Brookfield (2006) offers a multitude of specific suggestions to the teacher on how to navigate a classroom situation. He acknowledges that choosing correct interventions depends on awareness of emotional dynamics in the room.

In their chapter on "edgework" Nadler and Luckner (1992) are particularly helpful with interventions, but the rest of the book has abundant useful suggestions.

Chapter 18: The Power of Framing

George Lakoff's work (2004) emphasizes the importance of framing as a skill for planning social change campaigns. Bandler and Grinder (1979) consider reframing a basic communication task for improving effectiveness in leadership.

Chapter 19: Sensitivity in Cross-Cultural Issues

I've published an essay (Lakey, 2009a) that responds to the charge made by some on the political left that adult education for democracy and nonviolent strategy, when done by Western educators in the Global South, is imperialistic. My article points the reader to those who make the accusations and rebuts some of their claims.

"If you have come to help me, you are wasting your time. But if you are coming because your liberation is bound up with mine, then let us work together." This quote is usually attributed to Lilla Watson (1992), but she requests that the collective origin of the quote be honored.

Chapter 20: The Drama of Transformational Work

Sociologist Thomas Scheff (1979) locates this kind of work in the context of Shakespeare and classical Greek drama, as well as Gestalt and other modes of therapy. He redefines *catharsis* in a way that has influenced this book. A peer counseling system that has influenced both Scheff and me is Re-evaluation Counseling; see its website www.rc.org.

Arnold Mindell (1997) recounts illuminating cases of transformational work from his experience, including ones while working with groups as large as three hundred. The way he and his colleagues in Process Work think about transformation has been pivotal in direct education.

Chapter 21: Conclusion: Bringing It All Together

The fuller quote from abolitionist orator Frederick Douglass ([1857] 1985) is "If there is no struggle there is no progress. Those who profess to favor freedom and yet depreciate agitation ... want crops without plowing up the ground, they want rain without thunder and lightning. They want the ocean without the awful roar of its many waters.... Power concedes nothing without a demand. It never did and it never will."

Appendix A: The Sustainable Educator: Advocacy, Modesty, and Diversity of Gifts

Michael Newman (2006) is an adult educator who urges the advocacy role, as indicated by his title, *Teaching Defiance*. He draws stories from a variety of countries. His book offers a contrasting approach to mine in how to empower the learners.

In working with groups on leadership styles, I often drop the cultural reference to the Celtic Wheel of Being, instead calling the framework the Leadership Compass or TeamTypes. Because my ancestral background is Celtic, I sometimes present the framework with the Celtic reference if I want to make the point that the hyping of modernity in popular culture can lead us to forget the enormous wisdom that lies in traditional ways.

Appendix B: The Sustainable Educator: Resilience and Revolution

Parker Palmer (1998) supports the inner life of the educator, sharing his considerable wisdom about how to be fully present both to the learning group and to oneself. His invitation to honesty, compassion, and courage is a path to sustainability.

Joanna Macy (1998) has been inspiring activists and educators for many years with her combination of vision, analysis, and practical methods for sustainability.

Claudia Horwitz (2002) is director of stone circles, a retreat center and network of spiritual activist educators with a specialty in supporting sustainability (http://www.stonecircles.org).

Spirit in Action, a training and action center in Massachusetts, has spawned a series of Circles of Change for activists and educators who need support for the long haul. Their curriculum guide is available at http://www.spiritinaction.net. Linda Stout (1996) is founder-director.

Appendix D

Tools and Resources
for Direct Education

Many of the named tools in this book are easily recognized on the Training for Change (TfC) website (http://www .trainingforchange.org/).

Other tools are embedded in the stories in the book and might not be recognized; those are named here:

Mingle, Chapter 6

Maximize/minimize the value of a learning experience, Chapter 7

Force field analysis, Chapter 8

Comfort zone diagram, Chapter 9

River of Life, Chapter 9 (see Appendix C for description)

Open sharing, Chapter 9

Relay race/applications relay race/strategy relay race, Chapter 10

Harvesting work from small groups, Chapter 10

Parallel lines role play, Chapter 10

Understatement, Chapter 18

The descriptions of the tools on the website are sufficiently detailed so a reader of this book could try them out. The website also includes direct education tools not mentioned in this book but which have been tested for their reliability and usefulness across cultural lines.

Training for Change (TfC based in Philadelphia) offers frequent trainings in the United States and Canada for facilitating direct education. TfC trainers have worked in twenty countries since its founding in 1971. Each year TfC holds a Super-T, a seventeen-day intensive in direct education for facilitators and teachers. TfC also offers an advanced seminar on how to do transformational training. In addition to its schedule of upcoming trainings, the TfC website offers training-related articles, training reports, and even some handouts.

Opening Space for Democracy, Hunter and Lakey's (2004) curriculum and trainer's manual, has over one hundred facilitation tools, which are indexed for easy reference. The tools are all consistent with direct education and were chosen or invented, then tested, for their usefulness in multicultural contexts. The book also includes a chapter on "how to steal from this book," which gives tips on contextualizing in order to reduce the chance of misapplying a tool. It offers design tips as well: the use of modules and "threads" (two different ways of organizing content). A good part of the book is available for free via the TrainingforChange.org website; the entire book can be ordered through the website in paper or CD-ROM formats.

The Change Agency in Australia is a resource for tools that assist a group to learn analysis of their political situation (for example, "power mapping") and to develop strategy skills. The tools are available on the web: http://www.thechangeagency.org.

The NASA moon survival group dynamics game referenced in Chapter 11 is available at http://www.trainerbubble.com/ PRODUCTS/MOON_SURVIVAL_TRAINING_GAME.ASPX. A source for other survival simulations is http://wilderdom.com/ games/descriptions/SurvivalScenarios.html.

Ilana Shapiro's (2002) booklet *Training for Racial Equality and Inclusion* is based on research into a number of U.S. providers of anti-racist training; she describes their diverse approaches and merits. Training for Change was included in the study.

In *Grassroots and Nonprofit Leadership*, Berit Lakey and colleagues (1995) offer a variety of tools for turning a nonprofit group into a learning organization. That's also the mission of Kim Bobo and associates (2001) in *Organizing for Social Change*, whose tools focus on strategy development and the learning curve of community organizing.

The Process Work Institute, based in Portland, Oregon, offers occasional Worldwork seminars, where facilitators can learn that methodology, as well as a general program of workshops inspired by the pioneering work of Arnold Mindell (1997): http://www.processwork.org.

Alternatives to Violence Project has, since its start in 1975 in New York State, been a pioneer in using experiential adult education in work with prison inmates. Their approach has grown to include countries on five continents, and now includes work with community people as well: http://www.avpinternational.org and http://www.avpusa.org.

How I Design a Workshop: A Summary of the Steps—George Lakey

Designing workshops is a creative activity, which means that different trainers have their own ways of doing it. Here is one way, which works for me.

1. *Learn about the group.* I ask the leaders/sponsors about the group, its history, problems, conflicts, expectations, hopes, experience with workshops. I often ask a contact person, "Who else should I interview? Anyone with a different or unusual perspective?" I do this work by telephone or face-to-face or in a committee meeting (or all

three). I may have a questionnaire that participants fill out, to get broader data.

2. *Formulate goals.* I want goals that are realistic, that respond to the needs/wants of the sponsors of the workshop and/or the participants, and that motivate me. I don't want more goals than I can remember, because my goals control many of my judgment calls as I facilitate the workshop. I want goals that are clear, so I can use them to evaluate the workshop mid-term and on completion.

3. *Brainstorm activities/tools.* Goal-setting often requires making hard choices, so I'm ready for some fun. Brainstorming lightens me up. Sometimes I start by brainstorming "my favorite activities and exercises." These are mostly experiential, but I do include relevant mini-lectures/videos, etc.

4. *Sort the list.* I sort for which activities lend themselves especially to the substance of the workshop and its goals and for the kind of group I'm working with. Sometimes I make another phone call at this point, to fine-tune my diagnosis of the group. I also sort for differently abled: Are there too many activities depending on hearing for this group, or seeing, or running around?

5. *Develop sequence and select.* As I develop a sequence, I select the activities likely to move the group forward in its learning process. Which activities are building blocks that prepare for the next step? I let my expectation of energy flow influence the sequence: When to place cognitive work? Are there high-energy activities after meals? Emotional dynamics—do the activities allow for the highs and lows?

6. *Check for variety of formats.* Does the design move the group into pairs, threes, fours, and so on? Does whole-group time come when most needed (for example, at the end of the day)? Is there some individual time for the introvert? Overall, do I respect the group's need for an alternating rhythm of differentiation and integration?

7. *Check for learning styles/channels.* Is there a mix of auditory, visual, and kinesthetic? Is there sufficient safety-building time before people are asked to risk? What does the whole design indicate I need to say during Agenda Review to anticipate individual needs?

References

Alternatives to Violence Project-International. www.avpinternational.org.

Bandler, R., and Grinder, J. (1979). *Frogs into Princes: Neuro Linguistic Programming*. Boulder, CO: Real People Press.

Billy Elliot. (2000). Written by and directed by Stephen Daldry. United Kingdom.

Bobo, K., Kendall, J., and Max, S. (2001). *Organizing for Social Change: Midwest Academy Manual for Activists*. Santa Ana, CA: Seven Locks Press.

Bondurant, J. V. (1971). *Conquest of Violence: The Gandhian Philosophy of Conflict*. Berkeley: University of California Press.

Brookfield, S. D. (2000). "Transformative Learning as Ideology Critique," in Mezirow, J. (ed), *Learning as Transformation: Critical Perspectives on a Theory in Progress*. San Francisco: Jossey-Bass.

Brookfield, S. D. (2006). *The Skillful Teacher: On Technique, Trust, and Responsiveness in the Classroom*, 2nd ed. San Francisco: Jossey-Bass.

Brookfield, S. D., and Preskill, S. (2005). *Discussion as a Way of Teaching: Tools and Techniques for Democratic Classrooms*, 2nd ed. San Francisco: Jossey-Bass.

Bruhn, J. G., and Wolf, S. (1979). *The Roseto Story: An Anatomy of Health*. New York: Harper and Row.

Burns, J. M. (1978). *Leadership*. New York: Harper and Row.

Cooperrider, D. L., Sorensen, Jr., P. F., Yaeger, T. F., and Whitney, D. (eds.). (2001). *Appreciative Inquiry: An Emerging Direction for Organization Development.* Champaign, IL: Stipes.

Coover, V., Deacon, E., Esser, C., and Moore, C. (1977). *Resource Manual for a Living Revolution.* Philadelphia and Gabriola Island, British Columbia: New Society Publishers.

Coser, L. (1956). *The Functions of Social Conflict.* Glencoe, IL: Free Press.

Cranton, P. (2006). "Fostering Authentic Relationships in the Transformative Classroom," in Taylor, E.W. (ed.), *Teaching for Change: Fostering Transformative Learning in the Classroom* 109 (Spring). San Francisco: Jossey-Bass.

Cross, W. E., Jr. (1971). "Discovering the Black Referent: The Psychology of Black Liberation," in Dixon, V. J., and Foster, B. (eds.), *Beyond Black or White.* Boston: Little & Brown.

Cross, W. E., Jr. (1991). *Shades of Black: Diversity in African-American Identity.* Philadelphia: Temple University Press.

Dewey, J. (1966). *Democracy and Education.* New York: Free Press. First published 1916.

Douglass, F. (1985). "The Significance of Emancipation in the West Indies" (speech, Canandaigua, New York, August 3, 1857, collected in pamphlet by author), in Blassingame, J. W. (ed.), *The Frederick Douglass Papers. Series One: Speeches, Debates, and Interviews.* Vol. 3: *1855–63*, p. 204. New Haven, CT: Yale University Press.

Freire, P. (1972). *Pedagogy of the Oppressed.* Harmondsworth, UK: Penguin.

Freire, P. (1994). *Pedagogy of Hope: Reliving Pedagogy of the Oppressed.* New York: Continuum.

Freire, P., and Horton, M. (1991). *We Make the World by Walking: Conversations on Education and Social Change.* Philadelphia: Temple University Press.

Freud, S. (1989). *Group Psychology and the Analysis of the Ego.* New York: Norton.

Gandhi, M. (1940). *An Autobiography: or The Story of My Experiments with Truth.* Ahmedabad, India: Navajivan.

Gardner, H. (1983). *Frames of Mind.* New York: Basic Books.

Goble, F. G. (1970). *The Third Force: The Psychology of Abraham Maslow.* New York: Washington Square Press/Simon & Schuster.

Homans, G. C. (1950). *The Human Group.* New York: Harcourt Brace.

hooks, b. (1994). *Teaching to Transgress: Education as the Practice of Freedom.* New York: Routledge.

hooks, b. (2003). *Teaching Community: A Pedagogy of Hope.* New York: Routledge.

Horton, M. (2003). *The Myles Horton Reader: Education for Social Change.* Dale Jacobs, Ed. Knoxville: University of Tennessee Press.

Horwitz, C. (2002). *The Spiritual Activist: Practices to Transform Your Life.* New York: Penguin.

Hunter, D., and Lakey, G. (2004). *Opening Space for Democracy: Third-Party Nonviolent Intervention Curriculum and Trainer's Manual.* Philadelphia: Training for Change. http://www.TrainingforChange.org.

Ibsen, H. (1963). *An Enemy of the People.* London: R. Hart-Davis.

Jarvis, P. (2006). *Towards a Comprehensive Theory of Adult Learning.* London: Routledge.

Jerry Maguire. (1996). Written and directed by Cameron Crowe. United States.

Keirsey, D., and Bates, M. (1984). *Please Understand Me.* Del Mar, CA: Prometheus Nemesis Books.

Keller, H. (2003). *The Story of My Life*. New York: Norton.

King, M. L., Jr. (1964). *Why We Can't Wait*. New York: New American Library.

King, M. L., Jr. (1967). *Where Do We Go From Here: Chaos or Community?* New York: Harper & Row.

Kochman, T. (1981). *Black and White Styles in Conflict*. Chicago: University of Chicago Press.

Kolb, D. A. (1984). *Experiential Learning: Experience as the Source of Learning and Development*. Englewood Cliffs, NJ: Prentice Hall.

Kolb, D. A., and Fry, R. (1975). "Toward an Applied Theory of Experiential Learning," in C. Cooper (ed.), *Theories of Group Process*. London: John Wiley.

Kuhn, T. S. (1962). *The Structure of Scientific Revolutions*. Chicago: University of Chicago Press.

Lakey, B., Lakey, G., Napier, R., and Robinson, J. (1995). *Grassroots and Nonprofit Leadership: A Guide for Organizations in Changing Times*. Gabriola Island, British Columbia: New Society Publishers.

Lakey, G. (2009a). "Nonviolence Training and Charges of Western Imperialism: A Guide for Worried Activists," in Clark, H. (ed.), *People Power: Unarmed Resistance and Global Solidarity*. London: Pluto.

Lakey, G. (2009b). "Nonviolent Responses to Terrorism," in McElwee, T.A., et al. (eds.), *Peace, Justice, and Security Studies: A Curriculum Guide*, 7th ed. Boulder, CO: Lynne Rienner.

Lakoff, G. (2004). *Don't Think of an Elephant: Know Your Values and Frame the Debate*. White River Junction, VT: Chelsea Green.

Lederach, J. P. (1995). *Preparing for Peace: Conflict Transformation across Cultures*. Syracuse, NY: Syracuse University Press.

Leondar-Wright, B. (2005). *Class Matters: Cross-class Alliance Building for Middle-class Activists*. Gabriola Island, British Columbia: New Society Publishers.

Lewin, K. (1948). *Resolving social conflicts; selected papers on group dynamics*, in Lewin G. W. (ed.). New York: Harper & Row.

Macy, J. (1998). *Coming Back to Life: Practices to Reconnect Our Lives, Our World*. Gabriola Island, British Columbia: New Society Publishers.

Mattheus, A., and Marino, L. (2003). *White People Confronting Racism: A Manual for a Three-Part Workshop*. Philadelphia: Training for Change. http://www.TrainingforChange.org.

Mezirow, J. (2009) "Transformative Learning Theory," in Mezirow, J., and Taylor, E. (eds.), *Transformative Learning in Practice*. San Francisco: Jossey-Bass.

Miller, N. (1988). *Workshop Design: A Concise Manual*. People*Systems Potential (P.O. Box 132, Nagog Woods, MA 01718).

Mindell, A. (1992). *The Leader as Martial Artist: An Introduction to Deep Democracy*. San Francisco: HarperSanFrancisco.

Mindell, A. (1997). *Sitting in the Fire: Large Group Transformation through Diversity and Conflict*. Portland, OR: Lao Tze Press.

Moore, C. W. (1986). *The Mediation Process: Practical Strategies for Resolving Conflict*. San Francisco: Jossey-Bass.

Nadler, R. S., and Luckner, J. L. (1992). *Processing the Adventure Experience: Theory and Practice*. Dubuque, IA: Kendall/Hunt.

Newman, M. (2006). *Teaching Defiance: Stories and Strategies for Activist Educators*. San Francisco: Jossey-Bass.

Oppenheimer, M., and Lakey, G. (1965). *A Manual for Direct Action*. Chicago: Quadrangle.

Palmer, P. (1998). *The Courage to Teach*. San Francisco: Jossey-Bass.

Peck, M. S. (1988). *The Different Drum: Community-Making and Peace*. New York: Simon & Schuster.

Ransby, B. (2005). *Ella Baker and the Black Freedom Movement: A Radical Democratic Vision*. Chapel Hill: University of North Carolina Press.

Remember the Titans. (2000). Written by Gregory Allen Howard and directed by Boaz Yakin. United States.

Riso, D. R., and Hudson, R. (1999). *The Wisdom of the Enneagram*. New York: Bantam.

Schaetti, B. F., Watanabe, G., and Ramsey, S. (2000). *The Practice of Personal Leadership*. Portland, OR: Intercultural Communication Institute (8835 SW Canyon Lane, Suite 238, Portland, OR 97225; e-mail: ici@intercultural.org).

Scheff, T. J. (1979). *Catharsis in Healing, Ritual, and Drama*. Berkeley: University of California Press.

Shankman, M. L., and Allen, S. J. (2008). *Emotionally Intelligent Leadership: A Guide for College Students*. San Francisco: Jossey-Bass.

Shapiro, I. (2002). *Training for Racial Equality and Inclusion: A Guide to Selected Programs*. Washington, DC: The Aspen Institute.

Sharp, G. (1973). *The Politics of Nonviolent Action*. Boston: Porter Sargent.

Shields, K. (1991). *In the Tiger's Mouth: An Empowerment Guide for Social Action*. Newtown, NSW, Australia: Millennium Books.

Smith, M. K. (1996). "David A. Kolb on Experiential Learning," *Infed (Encyclopedia of Information Education)*. http://www.infed.org/biblio/b-explrn.htm.

Smith, M. K. (2009). "Kurt Lewin: Groups, Experiential Learning and Action Research," *Infed (Encyclopedia of Information Education)*. http://www.infed.org/thinkers/et-lewin.htm.

Starhawk. (1988). *Dreaming the Dark*. Boston: Beacon Press.

Starhawk. (1990). *Truth or Dare: Encounters with Power, Authority, and Mystery*. San Francisco: HarperSanFrancisco.

Stout, L. (1996). *Bridging the Class Divide*. Boston: Beacon.

Tennant, M. (1997). *Psychology and Adult Learning*, 2nd ed. London: Routledge.

Training for Change (http://www.TrainingforChange.org). Training tools, articles, and reports are available at this site.

Trist, E., and Murray, H. (1990, 1993, 1997). *The Social Engagement of Social Science: A Tavistock Anthology*. 3 volumes. Philadelphia: University of Pennsylvania Press.

Tuckman, B. (1965). "Developmental sequence in small groups," *Psychological Bulletin*, 63: 384–399.

Tyler, J. (2009). "Charting the Course: How Storytelling Can Foster Communicative Learning in the Workplace," in Mezirow, J., and Taylor, E. (eds.), *Transformative Learning in Practice*. San Francisco: Jossey-Bass.

Vella, J. (2008). *On Teaching and Learning: Putting the Principles and Practices of Dialogue Education into Action*. San Francisco: Jossey-Bass.

Watson, L. (1992). "Untitled," *Health for Women*, 3: 1. Brisbane, Australia: Department of Health.

Index